A FURTHER SLICE OF
JOHNNERS

A FURTHER SLICE
OF JOHNNERS

Brian Johnston
Edited by Barry Johnston

For all the Johnstons and Oldridges

This edition published in Great Britain in 2003 by
Virgin Books Ltd
Thames Wharf Studios
Rainville Road
London W6 9HA

First published in Great Britain in 2002

Introduction © Barry Johnston 2002
Part I © The Estate of Brian Johnston 2002
Part II © The Estate of Brian Johnston & Complete Editions
Ltd 2002
Part III © The Estate of Brian Johnston & Peter Baxter 2002

A catalogue record for the book is available
from the British Library.

ISBN 978 0 7535 40710 1

Phototypeset by Intype London Ltd

The Random House Group Ltd supports The Forest Stewardship
Council (FSC), the leading international forest certification organisation.
Our books carrying the FSC label are printed on FSC® certified paper.
FSC is the only forest certification schema endorsed by the leading
environmental organisations, including Greenpeace. Our
paper procurement policy can be found at
www.randomhouse.co.uk/environment

www.randomhouse.co.uk
Printed and bound in Great Britain by Clays Ltd, St Ives PLC

Eton I suddenly discovered I could run fast, something I had never done at my private school. Speed was a very important factor in this particular game, so I quickly earned my shorts in my second year, and my house colours in my third.

Each day when there was no football against one of the other houses, a boy had to do a 'time' – take some exercise such as a run, fives, squash, racquets, boxing or beagling. In the Easter half there was a choice of athletics, rugger and soccer to add to this list. I opted for rugger, and in the end got into the school XV. But we were always very bad and used to get thrashed by astronomical margins by schools like Rugby, St Paul's and Beaumont. Once again my running stood me in good stead. I was never a great tackler but prided myself on my skill at selling the dummy. Our house became great experts at seven-a-side and won the House Competition in my last year.

I was severely reprimanded after one match when the XV were playing the Welsh Guards from Windsor. They were a tough lot, and in great trepidation I once actually fell on the ball in defence. The loose scrum, or ruck as it is called these days, formed round me and I was kicked and trodden on amid shouts of 'Get off the ball!' From deep down I shouted, 'Get off mine first!' which was considered very rude. Not half as rude in a physical sense as a rather fat boy called Burke who used to play in the second row of the scrum and let go of wind in a series of tremendous detonations. Eventually he had to be dropped from the side as they could get no volunteers to play in the back row of the scrum.

Looking back, the whole system may seem to have placed far too much emphasis on the ability to play games. However, this did ensure that everyone, even those who were no good, did take some sort of regular exercise under supervision. Nowadays boys are left very much to their own devices, which at that age, though more pleasant for them, is not necessarily a 'good thing'.

My one and only disappointment at Eton was my failure to get into the cricket XI. I was still a wicket-keeper and each summer progressed up the scale, getting my Lower Sixpenny, Upper Sixpenny, Lower Club and Twenty-two – the various colours awarded to the twelve best players in each age group. But in Upper Sixpenny I blotted my copy book and so only just got my colours.

As usual, I was too frivolous and could not resist the chance of a laugh. I was batting with a boy called Hope-toun at the other end who was rather fat and not too quick over the ground. By some fluke I hit the ball quite a long way and called to him to run. I was pretty fast between the wickets and by the time he was turning to start his second run I had completed two so that we were both then running level towards the bowler's end. I soon passed him again so that I had run four as he was halfway through his third. As you can imagine, the whole field collapsed with laughter, and when the inevitable happened and the ball was returned to the bowler's end no one could work out which batsman was out. All would have been well had the captain of the XI not been watching from a distance and come over to see what all the uproar was about. To put it mildly, he was not too pleased. A similar thing was said to have happened in a house match, and they all turned to the square leg umpire for a decision, only to find that it had been his turn to bat and that he was now one of the batsmen concerned!

In my last year a boy called Baerlein who had kept wicket for the school for the last two years decided to stay on for another summer, although he was over nineteen years old before the half started. Naturally for a time I felt miserable about the whole thing, though everyone was very kind and sympathetic, especially our school coach George Hirst, the famous old Yorkshire and England all-rounder. He had a sweet disposition and was loved by all the boys. I used to keep wicket to his bowling and once got a stumping on the leg-side off him, much to our mutual satisfaction. Even in those days, aged sixty, he bowled a lively medium-pace left arm round the wicket, and swung the ball prodigiously. He took me under his wing, and at the Eton and Harrow match took me around with him to the dressing-rooms and even up to the scorer's box at the top of the grandstand. I had one slight compensation for not keeping wicket in the match. Eton had two very fast bowlers, one of whom was particularly wild and inaccurate. Poor Baerlein had a terrible time and actually let 35 byes. I would not have been human had I not had a quiet laugh. But I expect I would have let many more. Anyway, I captained the second eleven, or Twenty-two as it was called, and had far more fun than I would have had in the more austere atmosphere of the first.

The Eton and Harrow match was a great occasion and, all the time I was at Eton and for many years afterwards, we all used to congregate on Block G – the open stand to the right of the sightscreen at the Nursery End. We barracked unmercifully, shouted ruderies and cracked jokes, and it became like a club with everyone returning year after year. So far as we Etonians were concerned the stock jokes were usually about the age of the Harrow players or the number of foreigners or foreign-sounding names in their team. In these days of race relations I am sure we would be imprisoned for some of the things we used to shout out. But it was all good fun and some of my best friends have been those same Harrovians about whom we had been so rude.

In fact, until a few years ago we ran an annual match at Hurlingham between Old Etonian and Old Harrovian Block G teams. The only man who ever took the slightest offence was an unsuspecting Harrow father sitting with his son watching the match. As he did so we fastened the end of his immaculate tailcoat to the seat with drawing pins, so that when he rose to leave he found himself attached to the seat. Childish, I admit, but we had to laugh, and so did he in the end.

3 Best of the Beaks

THE GREAT STRENGTH OF ETON lay in the quality and character of its masters. I may be falling into the old trap, but they certainly seemed greater characters then than the masters of today.

By far the wittiest was Tuppy Headlam, who ruled over his house with a light rein. He seemed to inspire wit – or an attempt at it – from others. He was called the Master, with a soft 'a', and was the first port of call for many Old Etonians when revisiting the school, for he dispensed drinks or dinner with great generosity. During our time there he was especially friendly with the well-known film actress Anna May Wong. He taught us history and his classroom was in his house, and as he often received telephone calls we all took it in turns to go and answer them for him. One day, just after Anna May had been down to see him, the telephone rang and Martin Gilliat (later the Queen Mother's private secretary) was on telephone duty. As he left the room there was much speculation among us and Tuppy himself as to whether the caller would be Anna May. So there was quite a lot of excitement, then a hush as Gilliat returned.

'Who was it?' asked Tuppy.

'Sorry, sir,' Gilliat replied without a smile on his face, 'Wong number.'

Tuppy's own wit could be mildly malicious. Of the four headmasters under whom he served, he said, 'A was a greater man than me, B a better man than me, C a cleverer man than me, and D [long pause] a deafer man than me.'

Another character was Mr Hope-Jones. He had black curly hair, a very loud voice and was a physical fitness fanatic. A tremendous enthusiast in everything he did, he was a very keen Scoutmaster. One rather cold day he told his scout troop that he would be the hare and they the hounds. He would have a five-minute start, leaving a trail behind him, and they were to see how soon they could find him. He went off and headed straight for a fairly deep pond by one of the playing-fields. He jumped into the water and waited for his scouts to appear. When they did so he disappeared under the surface with just his nose above water so that he could breathe. Although the trail ended rather obviously at the edge of the pond the scouts pretended they could not find him and searched all round the adjoining fields. Poor Hope-Jones had to stay submerged in the cold water.

One summer holiday he had a bit of bad luck. The headline in our morning paper read: ETON MASTER CAUGHT BATHING IN THE NUDE. Poor chap. He had only gone for an early-morning swim on some secluded beach in Cornwall and some nosey parker had sneaked to the police. In those days it was quite something and I believe he was fined for indecent exposure, so you can imagine all the talk when we got back to Eton.

Then there was Sam Slater, a frightening man with a red face and horn-rimmed spectacles. He used to let out the most enormous sneezes during class. This went on for quite a long time until the master in the next room could stand it no longer. This was Lieutenant-Colonel J. D. Hills, later to be headmaster of Bradfield. He commanded the Corps and, thanks to his habit of somewhat immodestly reminiscing about his wartime experiences, was known as 'the man who won the war'. Anyway, he was determined to win this one and instructed everyone in his class to wait for the next sneeze from Slater and then, at a signal from him, all were to sneeze as loudly as they could. The effect was magical. When Sam let out his next sneeze he was amazed to hear a deafening chorus of ah-ti-shoos! from

Hills' classroom. He took the hint and in future sneezed in a more gentlemanly manner.

'Jelly' Churchill was a great rowing coach and spoke with a lisp. He brought the house down one day when he told a boy, 'Stop thucking your pen.'

Mr Crace was a gentle person and looked like Mr Pickwick. We were in his class one day when a messenger brought him a note. He read it and for some reason seemed annoyed. It was from the Treasurer of the Eton Mission who asked him if he would please collect from his class in the usual way. It was these last four words that got under his skin and he promptly announced that for the next week he would be pleased if we would give what we could afford to the Eton Mission, but *not* in the usual way. We were to do it in any way we liked so long as it was not usual. We thought up all sorts of ideas. We balanced piles of pennies on top of the slightly open door so that when Mr Crace came in they all fell on his mortar board. We arranged to throw coins on to his desk as the school clock struck a particular hour or quarter, so that without warning, possibly while talking to us, a shower of coins would descend on him. If we knew he was likely to refer to a certain book we inserted coins between the pages, or if he was going to use the blackboard we filled the duster with pennies. He loved it, and so did we, and at the end of the week the Eton Mission received a record collection but definitely *not* collected 'in the usual way'.

There were quite a few parsons on the staff. One of them, the Reverend C. O. Bevan, was a very pious man, as befitted his station. Once, a friend of mine named Charles Villiers had been annoying him all morning until in the end 'Cob' Bevan really lost his temper. 'Villiers,' he said in his gruff voice, 'just because I'm a parson you think I can't swear. But I can. Damn you, Villiers, and [a long pause while he plucked up courage] damn you again.' I doubt whether he ever forgave himself.

Quite different to Bevan was 'Satan' Ford, a very fierce man who was a terror to be taught by and for some reason had a strong nasal American accent. He prefaced most of his remarks with 'Boy' and one of his favourite expressions was: 'Boy, your breath smells like last week's washing.' Charming! He once wise-cracked to a stupid boy, 'Boy, you have as many brains as a snake has hips.' But he came off second-best when he was reprimanding a friend of mine called Jimmy Ford. After a few explosive comments about Jimmy's work, 'Satan' said, 'Well, boy, what's your beastly name?'

'Ford, sir,' Jimmy replied smartly, with a smile. He knew he had won.

Mr H. K. Marsden, the Master in College, knew *Bradshaw's Railway Guide* backwards and it was impossible to stump him with any train to anywhere from anywhere. Mr Adie, on the other hand, enjoyed motoring and used to boast that he always passed other cars on the corners as they were then going so much slower. The Provost was M. R. James, a friendly, genial man who wrote all those ghost stories. One of the real treats when one was an older boy was to be asked to supper with him and listen to him reading P. G. Wodehouse out loud until tears of laughter ran down his cheeks.

The headmaster was Dr Cyril Alington, a keen writer of detective stories and later Dean of Durham. He was a distinguished grey-haired figure with an imposing presence, greatly respected by the boys. He was perhaps most famous for his Sunday evening chats from the pulpit of College Chapel. All the lights were turned off and there were just two candles lit on the lectern of the pulpit. His talk lasted about ten minutes, often less and there was always complete silence throughout the congregation of five hundred boys, except for the occasional cough. He always finished with a strong punchline, paused, then slowly blew out the candles – puff, puff. Another pause, then up would come the lights and it was all over. Beautifully staged and very effective. One always felt like applauding. I remember that in one of his talks he was trying to show how the story of Jesus' trial and crucifixion would not have been sensational news in those days. For Pontius Pilate it was just another job, similar to hundreds he had to deal with. Dr Alington illustrated this by telling the story of a writer who some years later wanted to find out more about the trial of Jesus, so he obtained an interview with Pontius Pilate. 'Jesus of Nazareth,' said Pilate. 'No, I don't remember the name. Who was he?' Puff, puff.

Although normally so calm and dignified, Dr Alington was slightly taken aback one day when giving communion in College Chapel. He gave the Holy Bread to a boy called Danreuther who for some unknown reason put it into his pocket. The Doctor's hoarse stage whisper echoed round the altar steps: 'Consume it here.' With that, the crisis was over.

An unusual character was A. C. Beasley-Robinson, a highly religious man who ran the Boy Scouts and was always understood to be extremely rich. He drove an open yellow Vauxhall tourer and during the holidays was a keen rider to hounds. He prepared me for my confirmation, and when he took over his house he had one of the rooms converted into a chapel. I doubt if the whole time he was at Eton he ever missed a single service in either upper or lower chapel. When he finally left he treated himself to a full season's hunting in the shires, then gave up everything to become a monk.

Just after I left Eton there was a boy called Trotter in his house who was an expert at all things to do with radio and electricity. In fact, when I joined the 2nd Battalion Grenadier Guards during the war he was the signal officer. Anyway, he put his knowledge to good (?) use by wiring up the house and placing microphones in strategic places, including under Beasley-Robinson's dining-room table in the private part of the house.

I wonder if Beasley ever realised how many of his dinner-party conversations were monitored. Trotter soon became one of the best-informed boys in the school and knew most of the gossip about the masters, boys and even the dames! But even if Beasley had discovered Trotter's secret I am sure he would have forgiven him. He was that sort of man.

One of the doctors at Eton was called Amsler, a tough character who stood no nonsense. It was his job every summer half to issue any 'excused camp' certificates to members of the OTC. Some people disliked the idea of camp, though in fact it was great fun. One summer half there was a bigger queue than usual in his surgery of boys trying to get off. He listened patiently for some time to their feeble excuses, carrying out brief examinations of the more genuine cases. But after an hour or so he lost his temper and his patience. This was bad luck on a boy called Stirling, later to become the Lord Mayor of Westminster. He genuinely had a bad attack of rheumatism, and was bent double as he struggled up to Amsler's desk. Amsler must have thought he was trying to be funny, putting on an act. He interrupted Stirling's 'Please, sir, I've got rheumatism' with a curt 'Next man, please.' Poor Stirling had to go to camp.

Amsler also used to referee at the school boxing. One year there was only one entrant for the heavyweight division, a large boy called Balmain. This meant that he would have a walk-over and automatically win the cup. But according to the regulations, if there was no fight there was no prize money which normally went with the cup. So Balmain found another boy in his house called Congreve to whom he offered a pound just to enter for the heavyweight division. Congreve had never boxed before, but agreed to the proposal when Balmain promised not to hurt him in any way. There was a packed house in the gymnasium when the final bout of the evening was due to start, and a surprised 'Ooooh!' from the spectators when they saw Congreve step into the ring, hardly knowing which corner to go to.

When the bell went the two boxers danced around, bobbing and weaving, but making sure never to get within striking distance of each other. The crowd roared with laughter. But not Dr Amsler. After about a minute he stopped the 'fight' and warned both boxers that if they did not box properly he would stop the contest and declare it null and void. This would, of course, have meant no cup or prize money for either boxer.

What came over Congreve I don't know, but at the words 'Box on' he rushed at Balmain, swung his right arm and with a tremendous hook of which Dempsey would have been proud knocked the astonished Balmain flat out on the canvas. Pandemonium erupted, and the look on Congreve's face when he realised what he had done was worth going miles to see. But it was nothing to the look on Balmain's when he finally came round to find that he had not only lost the cup and the prize money but also the pound he had paid Congreve to enter!

After two years my housemaster Monty retired. Our new man was an old Wykehamist who years before had made a hundred against Eton in the annual match. A red-haired man called A. C. Huson, his face was completely purple (he was said to have one skin less than anyone else). He was a bachelor and a really wonderful person, as near to the perfect housemaster as could be. He had a great sense of humour, was kind and understanding, and I owe him as big a debt as anyone else in my life. He died ten years after I left as a result of a strangulated hernia – brought on, I am sure, by a strange habit he had.

In those days the Eton housemasters used to live very well and entertained each other at super dinner parties with only the best wines and beautifully cooked food. Furthermore, they always changed for dinner. Immediately after the meal the other housemasters used to return to their houses for their nightly rounds of the boys' rooms. When these were completed they would return to the party for brandy and cigars. During my last year Huson had been bitten by the keep-fit bug and used to do all sorts of exercises. One of his favourites was to lie on his back and raise his legs up 90 degrees into the air, lower them without touching the ground, up into the air again and so on. Try it, and see how many times you can do it before your stomach muscles pack up. You will be lucky if you do ten. Well, Huson used to come to my room in his dinner-jacket straight from one of these dinners, lie down on the floor and do a hundred of these leg exercises. It was a crazy thing to do following a big meal and it is no wonder that he died in the way he did.

One of his great friends was another red-haired master called Routh. He also had a sense of humour and used to snort through his nose every time he laughed, which was often. His sense of the ridiculous was a great help to William Douglas Home when Mr Routh marked one of the history papers we had to do in 'trials' at the end of the half. One question was: 'Write as briefly as you can on one of the following subjects: (1) The Future of Coal; (2) The Decline of the British Empire; (3) Whither Socialism?' William chose the first question and, bearing in mind the instruction to be brief, wrote as his answer the one word 'smoke'. To his eternal credit Mr Routh awarded him seven marks out of ten. After all, the answer was both accurate and brief.

It is an unusual thing to be able to say, but the food in our house both with Monty and Huson was always excellent. It cost a lot to feed and run a house even in those days. I remember Mr Huson saying that when King George V asked for an extra week's holiday for the boys to celebrate a visit to the school, it was as good as giving £100 to the Huson bank account.

Not all houses were so well fed, especially one on the corner of Keats Lane, which had better remain nameless. About six years after I left one of the boys in this house tried to commit suicide. Luckily he failed, but the housemaster was determined to find out why the boy had tried and summoned the whole house into the dining-room. He asked if they knew any reason why this should have happened. Was the boy being bullied, was he in financial difficulties, was he worried about his work? As usual on occasions like this there was a deathly silence. So the housemaster repeated his questions, saying he was determined to get to the bottom of the affair, even if it meant them all staying in and missing their half-holiday. Thus threatened, a boy at the back of the room held up his hand.

'Yes, Ormsby-Gore,' said the relieved housemaster. 'What is your theory?'

And Ormsby-Gore – later Lord Harlech – replied with an innocent air, 'Please, sir, could it have been the food?'

Collapse of housemaster!

There are also splendid stories told about some of the housemasters' wives, one or two of whom were fairly formidable ladies. One was once at a charity concert given by the local Women's Institute. Somewhat rashly, one of the performers struggled through a recitation of a poem in French. When she had finished to enthusiastic applause, the housemaster's wife turned to her neighbour in the front row and in a loud whisper said, 'Beautifully spoken, and how wise not to attempt the French accent!' Another wife found that her servants were pinching cigarettes from the various boxes in the private side of the house, so she put notices in each one which read: PLEASE DON'T HELP YOURSELF. Unfortunately, when the school holiday on the fourth of June came along and they had a lot of parents to lunch and tea, she forgot to remove the notices before the boxes were handed round to the guests.

At the local Eton flower show there was often intense rivalry between the various houses as to who had the best displays of fruit. There were baskets of apples, raspberries, gooseberries and other fruits on show with the usual cautionary notice stuck in front: PLEASE DON'T TOUCH. One housemaster's wife feared that a rival's apples were better than hers, so she waited for an opportune moment when their owner had left the show tent and placed the following notice in front of her rival's apples: PLEASE TAKE ONE.

Something peculiar to Eton was the office of Dame. Each house had one, they were called M'Dame, and they were a sort of super matron, substitute-mother, state-registered nurse and catering expert all rolled into one. Usually they were even more than that. They became the confidante, comforter and friend of all the boys in the house. They acted as a kind of buffer between the boys and the housemaster and library. They were mobbed, mimicked and laughed at, but at the same time in a funny sort of way were respected and loved. Tea with M'Dame was a regular date each half and there was a saying we used to use about people or things: 'Very good but very old – just like M'Dame's cakes.'

Dames were responsible for the health of all the boys and were expected to deal with emergencies like cuts or injuries at games. In the unmarried houses they did the catering and of course ran the household – the maids, cleaning, linen and so on. To be good they had to be saints, and very often they were. We had two while I was there, Miss Sealey and Miss Hancock. They both took a great interest in the house and often stood on the touchline in icy weather watching juniors playing in a house match. Our Dames also had to deal with the real mothers, who varied from the difficult to the impossible with their demands on how 'my boy' should be treated. God bless them both, and my grateful thanks and apologies for the many ways in which I am sure I must have made their lives more difficult.

In this chapter, I have purposely dealt mainly with the lighter side of Eton life. Many others more qualified to do so have written about its ancient traditions and education. All I would humbly like to say is that the system of each boy to his own room, with his own tutor to guide and help him, was invaluable, and that the traditions and customs helped to create a solid base on which to found one's life. So speaks – a bit pompously, I'm afraid – at least one very satisfied Old Etonian.

4 Oxford

BY THE TIME I WAS due to leave Eton at the end of the 1931 summer half I still had no idea what I wanted to do with my life. I had a feeling that I ought to go into the family coffee business, as my elder brother Michael had gone off to farm in Canada and the other, Christopher, was up at Oxford prior to going into the 14/20 Hussars. Mr Huson persuaded me to go to Oxford while I sorted myself out, so I went up to New College where my father had been 31 years before. I doubt whether I really passed the rather cursory entrance examination, but in those days the family connection was all-important and made entry practically certain. Very different to today, when in some colleges – including, I am afraid, New College – it seems to be more of a handicap than a help.

We were very lucky with our dons, who were most delightful characters. The Warden was H. A. L. Fisher, a brilliant historian who for a short time had been Minister of Education in Lloyd George's government of 1922. He had a habit of bringing into the conversation the phrase 'when I was in the Cabinet', which caused a lot of amusement among his French friends (*cabinet* in French means a WC).

The chaplain was called Lightfoot, and he used to tell us how he had once been 'crucified' with croquet hoops on the college lawn by some undergraduates who were celebrating.

My own tutor was a friendly man with a snorting laugh called Wickham Legge, who once got an unintended laugh when talking to us about Henry VIII and the bad fevers from which he suffered. 'Personally,' said Wickham

Legge, 'if I am in bed with a fever I toss off everything within reach.'

The Dean was a charming man called Henderson who spoke with a broken German accent. He was an expert in dealing with rowdy parties and employed sound psychology. One night some visitors from another college were throwing stones in the quadrangle and had broken one or two windows. The Dean appeared on the scene and quickly summed up the situation. 'Let's all break one more window,' he said to the astonished revellers, 'and then all go off to bed.' So saying, he picked up a small stone and threw it through a window. This apparently satisfied the students, who dispersed quietly and returned to their own colleges.

In other ways, the Dean was a bit old-fashioned in his outlook. For example, some of us once went out with a friend to test his new car. We topped 75 mph – very fast in those days – and were stopped by the police and reported for speeding. The Dean got to hear of it and requested that we go to see him. We all agreed to say that we had only been doing 37 mph as we knew that he disapproved of fast cars. So when he asked us how fast we had been going, as one we all answered innocently, 'Thirty-seven miles per hour, sir.' The Dean stepped backwards as if startled, and a low whistle escaped his lips. 'Ach,' he said, 'if you go at such speeds you must expect to get into trouble.' We were gated for a few days, but goodness knows what would have been his reaction, or our punishment, had we been a little more truthful.

Another don who taught me history had the splendid name of Ogg, and there was also an earnest Wykehamist in spectacles whom we saw from time to time. He deserted teaching for politics and didn't do too badly, ending up as a Labour Cabinet minister. His name was Richard Crossman.

During my first term I made great friends with another freshman called Jim St John Harmsworth. He came from

Harrow and had a wonderful sense of humour and a very funny, pompous way of talking. (He became, by the way, a highly respected stipendiary magistrate in central London.) Together, we decided to have a go at the hunting set, who had their headquarters in some digs in the High. They were all famous point-to-point riders, hunted most days of the week and kept their horses and grooms at some stables outside Oxford. Jim and I asked whether we could call on them for some advice, and in some trepidation went round to beard them in their rooms.

They received us royally, offering huge glasses of sherry at eleven o'clock in the morning as they stood warming their bottoms in front of the fire, every now and then slapping their riding boots with their canes. There was Lord Rosebery's son Lord Dalmeny; John Pearson, later Lord Cowdray; and John Lakin, a famous figure in the hunting and point-to-point world. Jim and I pretended that we each had several hunters and wanted to know how many we needed to bring up in order to hunt at least two days a week. We also asked whether they would advise us to bring up our grooms as well. Naturally we had neither hunters nor grooms, but they seemed to believe us and offered us good advice and lots more sherry. We also enquired about the point-to-point racing, saying we were very keen to take part in the Grinds next term. This set John Lakin off and he proceeded to tell us about some hair-raising incidents in races in which he had taken part. To this day I remember well one of his remarks: 'I had Geoff Fitzhornby racing on one side, Harry Kennard on the other. As we came down the hill I stuck the daggers in and left them standing . . .' We departed firm friends, leaving them with the impression that we would be regular members of the hunting set.

A week later we were asked to attend a party for all the horsey men up at Oxford. Eventually they found out that we had been pulling their legs when no horses or grooms arrived. But they seemed to bear no malice and went on happily slapping their boots whenever we met them.

Jim and I did in fact ride in one point-to-point race in our last year. So did William Douglas Home, which was extremely brave of him as he had never really ridden before, whereas Jim and I had at least done some hunting – as boys. William and I took some practice at a riding school at Headington where it was decided that William should have a large, docile black horse called Nero and that I should ride Tiptop. He was more lively, a nice-looking bay who was said to be a half brother of Tom Walls' Derby winner April the Fifth – though which half they never told me. Jim, by this time, had bought a horse of his own, so was better mounted than either of us.

For some reason we were never allowed to jump either of our horses in practice beforehand, so we had no idea whether we would even get over the first fence. As the day of the race approached I was terrified at the prospect and wished I had never entered. I had tried to pick up some tips by reading various books on riding, was impressed by the arguments in favour of the forward seat and was determined to try it. As it turned out, I was very lucky to have been allotted Tiptop, whom I rode in a racing snaffle. Though of course he did not know it, he could have stopped whenever he wished.

When the starter's flag went down we were left at the post, but Tiptop set off in pursuit of the others and flew over the fences as if he imagined he was that year's Grand National winner Golden Miller. My forward-seat theory went for a burton and I found myself leaning so far backwards that my head nearly hit his quarters each time we went over a jump. We somehow got round without me 'leaving the plate', though once or twice I nearly 'went through the front door'. We finished fifth, one ahead of Jim Harmsworth on his chestnut gelding.

Poor William was not so lucky. Nero refused at the first

fence but scrambled over at the second attempt, encouraged by shouts of 'Nero my God to thee' from some irreverent undergraduates. But he was a long way behind the other horses and did not fancy jumping the second fence on his own. So William reluctantly had to call it a day.

When I returned to the unsaddling enclosure I was given a few cheers by one or two friends, but was surprised to receive a somewhat hostile reception from the other race-goers. It turned out that before the race my friends had gone round the bookies backing Tiptop, saying in loud stage whispers what a good chance he had. As a result, Tiptop had started third favourite. He had also been tipped by an old tipster friend of mine called Captain Dean, who had some wonderful patter such as, 'There's a horse here today that could jump the first fence, lie down, smoke a cigarette and then get up and win.' Or, 'They've sent a horse all the way from Leicester. It's so thin that it reminds me of Napoleon in exile. They couldn't have St Helena horse.' And, 'I've got as many pound notes as Sir Thomas Lipton had tea leaves. I tell you what I'm going to do. I'm going right through the card and at the end of the day when you've backed all my winners I want you to come up to me and say, "Good old Captain Dean. You and I have got a lot in common. Common have a drink!"' But I think he summed up our performances in the saddle perfectly when he said, 'There are jockeys here today who couldn't ride in a railway carriage unless the door was locked.'

Inspired by our attempts at equestrianism we organised a race meeting in the summer on Port Meadow, a large open space by the river. We hired some old hacks and had enough runners for a card of four races. A local bookie shouted the odds and I took over Captain Dean's role as tipster. Everything went fine until the start of the third race when the favourite, rightly deciding that his jockey was no great expert, bolted straight for the river. Unfortunately he failed to stop at the bank and jumped straight in, jockey and all. So the races had to be abandoned, while horse and jockey were salvaged.

At Oxford I read for my degree in history. I averaged around one lecture a day and read books suggested by my tutor, for whom I had to write one essay a week. Looking back, I feel ashamed at the small amount of work I did, devoting most of my time to games and getting up to stupid pranks with friends.

Together we formed a club called the All Sorts, playing rugger against neighbouring schools or soccer against various sides in the town, including a side of waiters from all the hotels. We had numbers on our backs and before every match lined up to be presented to some 'dignitary' with bowler hat and rolled umbrella who was, needless to say, one of us disguised with a false moustache and other paraphernalia. The matches used to be reported in the *Oxford Mail*, an excellent evening paper that, however, once made an awful bloomer. It happened during the gold crisis, which occurred while I was up at Oxford and resulted in the formation of the National Government. Everyone was asked to economise, so quite a few of the colleges decided to cancel their commemoration balls, which normally took place at the end of the summer term. This news was headlined by the *Oxford Mail* as follows: UNPRECEDENTED EVENT: UNDERGRADUATES SCRATCH BALLS! I hasten to add it was only in one edition – which was, of course, a sell-out.

On some summer evenings we would go up to the Trout Inn and after a good supper get into a couple of eights and have a boat race back. It was usually Eton v. Harrow with Eton the winners, as befitted a rowing school, though all of us were dry bobs. In those days there was always something going on.

One Sunday night there was a concert in New College

Chapel, so I disguised myself as a tramp and sat down outside the gate with some old hunting pictures that I had taken down off the wall of my room. I had a cap on the pavement and when the concert was over and people began coming out I started to beg in a whining voice, saying I had a wife and six children to keep, and so on. Some friends mingled with the crowd and tossed coins into the cap, murmuring 'Poor fellow' and 'What a shame'. This encouraged the others to throw in a few pennies. Eventually the proctor was seen approaching with his two bulldogs, so we quickly gathered up the pictures and fled. But I had collected about five shillings, the first money I had ever 'earned'.

New College was a fairly tough place to live in at the time. The rooms were comfortable enough, but if one wanted a bath one had to go across the quadrangle in a dressing-gown in all weathers. Why we did not die of pneumonia I have no idea. Each staircase had a scout who used to clean the rooms, serve breakfast or lunch if required and generally act as a sort of super Jeeves. I had a marvellous man called Honey – who, needless to say, we nicknamed Bunch. Honey had been my brother's scout and he always called me 'our kid'. He was a part-time fireman and had to work overtime on 5 November when the whole city was ablaze with fireworks. This was the only occasion in the year when there was ever any real trouble between the police and undergraduates.

New College was very cosmopolitan. It had a large number of Rhodes scholars from the Commonwealth as well as a sprinkling of Americans. One of these, Bill Crandall, was in his late twenties and almost totally bald. He was full of charm and always tried to say the nicest things to everybody. Unfortunately, he was not always successful. For example, one Sunday some of us went to lunch at the home of one of the undergraduates and Bill, always ready to help, volunteered to carve the chickens. When it was time for second helpings he went to the sideboard and called out to our hostess, 'Would you like some more breast, Mrs Tollemache?' She happened to be the owner of a very large pair of bosoms, so you can imagine our reaction when Bill noticed she had not yet finished and went on to say, 'Oh, sorry, I see that you've still got plenty in front of you!' On another occasion he was trying to congratulate Elizabeth Alington (daughter of the Eton headmaster, and who later married Sir Alec Douglas-Home) on being a personality in her own right. 'Miss Alington,' he drawled, 'I'd like to congratulate you on being yourself without the help of your father.'

So far as games went, I played rugger and cricket for the college and was captain of cricket for two years. I had two unusual experiences at rugger. In one cupper – or inter-college cup-tie – I found to my horror that I had to mark H. G. Owen Smith at centre three-quarters. He was a Rhodes scholar who had made a hundred for South Africa against England at cricket and had also played full-back for England at rugger. During the match, as I had feared, he frequently penetrated my defence. But once, when in front of the posts, he shaped up to try to drop a goal. Instead of tackling him, as I should have done, I sneaked up behind him and whipped the ball out of his hands. He was obviously amazed – that sort of thing just did not happen in the high-class rugger in which he usually played. My triumph was short-lived. Before I could do anything with the ball he swung round and flung me into the mud.

In another match, my shorts were torn off when I was tackled. I went and stood on the touchline while someone rushed off to the pavilion to get me another pair. A friend who was watching lent me his macintosh to put on to cover my confusion! As I stood there the ball came down the three-quarter line, so I joined in on the wing, took the final pass and amid uproar from spectators and players

41

alike scored a try between the posts in my macintosh. The referee was laughing too much to blow his whistle so he allowed the try to stand, though as I hadn't signalled my return to the field of play, I doubt if it was legal.

I used to play cricket at least four times a week, not only for the college but for teams like the Oxford University Authentics, Eton Ramblers and I Zingari. This was delightful cricket, though naturally my work suffered. In fact, I played just as much in my third and final summer when I had my exams to do for my degree. I was able to do this thanks to a crammer called Mr Young. Several of us went to him and his method was very simple: he taught us the outstanding facts and events in each period of history and told us that we must weave these into our answers, no matter what the questions were. The idea was to impress the examiners with our knowledge and it evidently worked as we all got degrees of sorts. However, I nearly gave the game away in one of the questions about Anglo-Saxon times. They had a piece of land called a fyrd, but when Mr Young talked about this I thought he had said 'third'. In the exam I was in a bit of a hurry so to save time I wrote 'the Anglo-Saxon 1/3rd'. One of the dons pointed this out to me during my oral, and I am glad to say that I had the grace to blush! I must also add that I now feel very guilty about resorting to such tactics to gain a degree, which I did – a third.

In spite of playing so much cricket I was never quite good enough to get a blue, though in my second year Brian Hone, the university captain, did play especially in a match for New College in order to assess my form. He did this because it seemed possible at the time that the old blue P. C. Oldfield would not be available through pressure of work for his degree. Oldfield was one of the best wicket-keepers I have seen, amateur or professional. He was very quiet and unostentatious and played for the Gentlemen at Lord's in 1934. The annoying thing about it to me was that he loathed cricket and gave it up as soon as he went down from Oxford. He much preferred point-to-point racing. Had he really enjoyed cricket and had the time to play it, I feel sure that he would have been near to the England side.

The great Wally Hammond once made Oldfield look rather foolish when Gloucestershire played Oxford in the Parks. The giant Christopher Ford – six feet eight and a half inches, and twin brother to Edward Ford who later was one of the Queen's secretaries – was bowling very fast and bringing the ball down from a great height. To counter this, Hammond stood a yard outside his crease. Ford and Oldfield noticed this and at a prearranged signal Oldfield, who had been standing a long way back, began to creep up to the stumps as Ford started his run. The obvious intention was for Ford to bowl a slower ball and for Oldfield to bring off a surprise stumping. But the great man must have sensed something was up, or possibly heard Oldfield approaching from behind. Anyway, just as Ford was about to deliver the ball, coinciding with Oldfield's arrival at the stumps, Hammond simply stepped aside, signifying he was not going to play the ball. Ford stopped in his tracks and a very sheepish Oldfield turned round and went back to his old position, looking just like a boy who has been spotted moving in a game of grandmother's footsteps.

I am not really entitled to criticise Oxford University education since I was so busy enjoying myself that I failed to take real advantage of it. But I have always been surprised that each term only lasts for eight weeks. It seems to be an absurdly short percentage of the year – less than half. By the time one had settled down in the first week of term and attended all the farewell parties in the last, there was not much time left in between. An undergraduate was, of course, meant to work at his books during the vacation, but even in those days, and much more nowadays, many students took jobs, especially in the summer. If there is any value in having a tutor to direct and explain one's studies, it does seem ridiculous that for 28 weeks of the year he is not available to do so. But it obviously suits the dons, and it suited me as it enabled me to play cricket non-stop throughout the summer holidays!

5 And so to Bude . . .

BEFORE I WENT UP TO Oxford my family had moved to a new home at Bude in north Cornwall, where my father had drowned in 1922. It might seem strange to return to the place where my father had died, but it had always been where we spent our childhood holidays and we loved it.

We had been living for four years at Hellens, an old Jacobean house in the quaintly named village of Much Marcle in Herefordshire. It was a lively village and we used to take part in all the activities. My mother ran the Mother's Union and Women's Institute and my sister and brothers and I used to try to provide entertainment at the 'dos' in the village hall. We formed a rough sort of band and even tried our hand at a spot of drama. We used to put on sketches for the annual village concert. One of these was called *George's Ghost*, and it ended in disaster. Just before the dramatic climax and the appearance of the ghost I had to strike a match to light a cigarette for my brother Michael. He was wearing a large fake moustache and unfortunately my match lit the moustache instead of the cigarette. It went up in smoke and my brother had to try to pull it off, to the accompaniment of gales of laughter from the delighted village audience. So the intended drama turned into a farce, and after that we decided to stick to comedy.

Our groom in those days was called Dean. He had enormous ears which he could tuck in. He taught me how to do it, and I can still tuck in my right ear today. This is a trick very few can achieve – a lot depends on the texture and pliability of the ears. I have only met two people who can do it: Mike du Boulay, an old friend from Winchester, and John Woodcock, the former cricket correspondent of *The Times*.

At Hellens we also had a very sweet parlourmaid called Mrs Jones who had the biggest tummy-rumbles in the business. I don't know if it was because she was always hungry or what. Anyway, when we had guests and her tummy started to rumble, my stepfather used to ostentatiously kick his spaniel Shot, who always lay under the table, and tell him to behave himself. It was rather like the apocryphal story of the day when the Queen was meeting an important Head of State at Victoria station. They were driving back to Buckingham Palace in an open state coach drawn by four well-fed Windsor Greys. When the coachman flicked one of them with his whip the horse let out an ear-splitting fart. The Queen and the Head of State were busy waving to the crowds at the time. The Queen, still smiling, graciously muttered to the Head of State, 'I'm sorry about that,' and went on waving. 'Ah, Madam,' replied he, 'the honesty of you English. Had you not apologised I would have thought that it was one of the horses!'

It was at Hellens that my stepfather bought our first ever radio, a big event in those days. A man came to install it so that he could listen to it and decide whether to buy it. It was a super eight-valve set and the whole family assembled as it was switched on. After a minute or so my stepfather commented with disappointment to the man, 'But that sound is just like a gramophone record.' With a gleam of triumph, the man replied, 'That, sir, is exactly what it is. We are listening to one of Christopher Stone's gramophone programmes.' So the radio was duly purchased.

We made the move from Much Marcle to the much smaller house, Homewell, in Bude in 1929, and there on my holidays from Eton I played cricket and tennis in the summer and continued hunting in the winter. Hunting for some reason I thoroughly enjoyed, possibly because so many funny things happened, although I was pretty scared at times. We hunted with a small hunt called the Tetcott, which covered wet and boggy country with banks instead of hedges to jump. This meant that the horse had to jump on to the top of the bank and then off again – which made it difficult if by any chance you suddenly encountered a fence. The horse was so used to banks that it would usually jump right on top of a hedge instead of clearing it, with disastrous results.

The riding field was made up of farmers with a few retired colonels and majors and even one general, plus a few like me at home for the holidays. We used to pull the legs of the retired military by pretending we had suddenly seen the fox. We would gallop madly off shouting 'Gone away!' and hoping the field would follow us. Sometimes they did, and then our day was made.

Once when it was very wet my stepfather, who always wore full hunting pink complete with top hat, was talking to the general outside a cover which was being drawn by the hounds. He was riding a brand-new chestnut hunter which he had just bought in his home country, Ireland. As he was swapping some wartime experience with the general, the chestnut began to sink slowly into the ground as if going down in a lift. They were standing in a bog. Luckily it was not too deep, but it was a marvellous sight with most of the horse under the mud and my stepfather visible only from the waist up. He had to dismount and struggle through the mud in his spotless white breeches and pink coat. The horse was eventually pulled out, but I imagine that if he was watching, even the fox laughed.

Another time the MFH, a retired captain, came to dinner and my stepfather, who was very proud of his port, sought the MFH's opinion.

'What do you think of this port, Dudgeon?' (Note the use of the surname – a military habit.)

A long pause while Dudgeon sipped his port. 'Do you want my candid opinion, Scully?'

'Yes, of course, Dudgeon,' replied my stepfather.

'Well, I'd say it tasted like seaweed!'

As I have said, my stepfather was Irish and after a second's incredulity he exploded. We were all sent out of the room, from which heated voices could be heard for some time.

During one summer holiday something happened which I always try to recall whenever I feel in need of a laugh. We were sitting by the swimming pool at Bude which is full of seawater and built out of the rocks beneath the cliffs. As in most pools one end was very shallow and the other deep enough for people wanting to dive. On this day the water was very murky and a man in a rubber helmet came and stood by us. After taking a good long look at the water, he held his nose, took a terrific leap into the air and jumped into the water. Unfortunately, we were sitting at the shallow end which was only two feet deep. Instead of sinking slowly down as he had intended, his legs crumpled up underneath him as his feet landed on the bottom. As he collapsed spluttering into the water, I am ashamed to say that we roared with laughter.

Based at Bude during the long summer holidays from Oxford, I travelled miles to play cricket anywhere, usually for the Eton Ramblers. I went on tours, staying in private houses for something which has now nearly disappeared – country-house cricket. The host would put up an eleven of his friends and there would be a long weekend or even a week of cricket played on his own private ground against visiting teams. It was the perfect mixture of good, though not too serious, cricket in beautiful surroundings combined with great hospitality and conviviality in the evenings. I'm bound to admit that we got up to some terrible tricks.

Once we were staying in Yorkshire with some great friends called Lane Fox. One of the guests was to be Colonel Cartwright, then secretary of the Eton Ramblers and later their revered president. He was known throughout the sporting world and London clubland as Buns, and was a remarkable character. In 1946, when the Moscow Dynamos were touring England, he and I after a generous lunch at White's stood wedged in the crowd at Stamford Bridge to watch them play Chelsea. The crowd was 81,000 – still, I believe, a record for the ground – and I have seldom been so frightened in my life. We were against a crush barrier and even the massive figure of Buns was nearly crushed and winded every time the crowd pressed forward.

Anyway, back to our cricket tour in Yorkshire. We persuaded our hostess to tell Buns when he arrived that owing to the late departure of the last guests the maids had not had time to do his room out properly. So would he please excuse anything that had not been tidied up or cleared away. We asked her to do this because we had got hold of a chamberpot and filled it with lime juice, sausages and loo paper and placed it under his bed. We made sure that it was just sticking out so that he would be bound to see it. Sure enough he did, though we were not able to see his reaction when he first spotted it. Anyhow, when he discovered its true contents he chased us all round the house and threw it all over us.

But our practical jokes did not always come off. Every summer we used to stay with Edgar Baerlein and his family during the Eton Ramblers tour of Lancashire and Cheshire. He was a former tennis and racquets champion and, even then, at the age of 56, was still a wonderful games player. I remember when we were staying he decided to take up lawn tennis, and engaged a professional from Manchester to come over and teach him the basic techniques. We left them to go and play cricket, which, as it happened, finished a little early. When we returned they were still playing, and there was no doubt who was winning. With his marvellous eye, the cut he got on to the ball and his instinctive placing, Baerlein had the professional chasing all over the court.

In his championship matches he had always been famous for never giving up or admitting defeat, which is why we met our match in him. Before dinner one night we filled some of his favourite chocolates with toothpaste, and after the port had gone round we waited in expectation, hardly able to suppress our laughter. He offered the chocolates around, but we all refused one. Suspecting nothing, he took one himself and popped it into his mouth. He was engaged at the time in a long argument with someone about games – he had a theory that golf was a competition, not a game, as nothing could be done to interfere with one's opponent's play (other than by cheating). We waited breathlessly for him to spit the chocolate out as soon as he bit on the soft centre. But we waited in vain. He carried on with his conversation as if nothing had happened, chewing away at the chocolate apparently quite unconcerned, though froth was oozing out of the corners of his mouth. In the end he swallowed it without turning a hair. He had called our bluff and our joke fell flat.

One trick which I would not recommend was played on a member of our team called Gerald Best. He was so tall that he used to sway in the breeze, and he was nicknamed Percy Pinetree. We bought some kippers and tied them on to the cylinder block of his car engine when he was not looking. At the end of play he got into his car, started up and then had to wait a few minutes in a queue to get out of the ground. Almost immediately smoke and a horrible smell came from under his bonnet, much to his amazement. I am sorry to say that a passing dog sniffed the odour of the kippers, leaped at his car and tried to scratch his way through the bonnet. We were *not* popular.

At the end of one of these tours some of us went to Blackpool to savour the delights of the Golden Mile. We 'did' the funfair, including paying sixpence to look through a hole in a barrel. Sitting inside was the notorious Rector of Stiffkey, who claimed to have 'saved' the souls of many London chorus girls. Poor chap. What a way to earn money, sitting there all day with hundreds of people peering through the bung-hole at you. We also tried one of those talking weighing machines. When I got on the voice said, 'Eleven stone four pounds' – I was a slim young chap in those days. Then it was the turn of Buns. On he got and the voice said, 'One at a time, please'!

Playing cricket for the Eton Ramblers was tremendous fun and we travelled miles to get a game. The Ramblers is a club like the Free Foresters or I Zingari – it has no home ground of its own but plays up to eighty matches every season. A friend of mine named John Hogg was due to play with me in one match against Sandhurst at Camberley. At the last moment he could not play for some reason, so obtained a replacement, another Old Etonian called Scaramanga, who was a very good bat but could only bowl friendly leg breaks. John, on the other hand, was a very good all-rounder and a top-class medium-pace bowler. The manager of the match was a rather irate colonel by the name of Darell who had been relying on Hogg's bowling to get the opposition out. So he was obviously very annoyed when I explained to him what had happened. He turned to Scaramanga and testily asked him his name. 'Scaramanga, sir,' he replied, to which Darell snapped, 'Stop joking, boy. What's your proper name?'

Another family with whom we used to stay a great deal were the Turners. The father, Geoff, was extremely rich and had huge business interests in India. They lived in a fabulous white modern house with a large estate near Hungerford, with wonderful shooting and fishing for those who enjoyed that sort of thing. They were exceedingly hospitable and the comfortable, centrally heated house was always full of guests. The whole family used to enjoy a drink or two and it was funny to see the different ways in which it used to affect them. Geoff, for instance, used to start reminiscing about the time he had spent in Japan, prefacing his remarks with the phrase, 'You boys all know why I went to Japan.' None of us including his family had the slightest idea, though his stories were full of vague hints about the secret service. When he died after the war I remember writing to one of his sons, Nigel, who was my particular friend. After the usual condolences, I added a PS: 'Now we shall never know why he went to Japan.' And we never did.

Mrs Turner after a few drinks used simply to drop off to sleep, even at a dinner party – just like the dormouse at the Mad Hatter's tea party. One of the daughters used to get a bit annoyed and once picked up a Christmas pudding off the dining-room table and hurled it through the serving hatch into the kitchen, where it luckily missed the cook. The effect of alcohol on Nigel's brother John was once nearly disastrous. After rather a good dinner he went to throw a log on to the large open fire. Unfortunately he forgot to let go and went on to the fire with the log, but luckily was quickly pulled off.

All these antics, though, were capped by Pinnock, the butler, who one evening at dinner had obviously been at the port. As he swayed round the table serving the vegetables, Mr Turner shouted to him, 'Pinnock, you're drunk!'

'Well, sir,' replied Pinnock, dropping a few peas into the lap of one of the guests, 'it's about my turn.'

When I was at Bude during the long vacation I used to run the cricket side, which played on the tennis courts on the edge of the cliffs. It was always very windy, which made the judging of high catches very difficult. The old tennis court lines also led to a certain amount of confusion. My stepfather was once going for a short run against the New College Nomads, who were on tour in Cornwall. He flung himself at full length with bat stretched out and was furious when given out. 'But look,' he said to the umpire, 'my bat is over the line.' It was gently pointed out to him that it was the baseline of one of the tennis courts.

I also used to play a lot for a team which was run by Lord Carrington, father of the present peer. The team was called Millaton after his house in the little Devonshire village of Bridestowe. It was a beautiful ground, very small, with a thatched pavilion and very short boundaries. There were always two or three parsons playing, especially an old boy called Arundell. He was mad about cricket and was said to say 'over' instead of amen at the end of a prayer. He kept wicket as he was not mobile enough to field anywhere else. A local rule had to be made that boundary byes counted two not four, otherwise extras would always have been top scorer. Arundell was inevitably nicknamed the Ancient Mariner, as 'he stoppeth one of three'.

I first heard the following story as referring to him, though in later years it was always told about that grand old actor A. E. Matthews. It was said that each morning Mrs Arundell used to take her husband up a cup of tea and a copy of The Times. He would drink the tea, read The Times right through, then finally check on the obituary column. If he wasn't in it, he got up!

Bude was a happy place in those days with lots of young people of my own age. One of them was called Micky Thomas. He had a very attractive sister called Marjorie, with whom I was 'friendly'. Nothing serious of course, but she used to come and see me at Eton during my last year and afterwards at Oxford.

One holiday-time she said she had an actor friend coming down to stay; he was in the Liverpool Repertory but was 'resting' at the moment. He was a bit hard up for cash, so would we be nice and kind to him. So of course we were. We saw a lot of this amusing actor who was very short-sighted and wore a monocle when he wanted to see anything at all clearly. He had a high squeaky voice with a slightly querulous tone and was not much good at table tennis. Shortly after this holiday in Bude he married Marjorie, who promptly changed her name to Collette and became the first of his five wives. He then got a part in Terence Rattigan's *French Without Tears* and, after that, as they say, Rex Harrison never looked back.

6 A Taste of Coffee

IN JUNE 1934 IT WAS time for me to go down from Oxford. I had enjoyed three very happy years, not too productive perhaps in the development of my knowledge, but of great value in helping me to understand and live with my fellow beings. But I was no nearer to deciding how I wanted to earn my living. After a series of family conferences, it was decided that I should go into the old Johnston coffee business.

It was now a public company, the Brazilian Warrant Co. Ltd, its chairman a kindly if occasionally irascible man called Arthur Whitworth. He was a big 'noise' in the City and among other things was a director of the Bank of England. He had also rowed with my father at New College, and his brother had been a famous housemaster at Eton. So he knew something about me, and took great trouble to plan my future for me. I shall always be sorry that in a way I let him down. But more of that later.

The plan was for me to learn the business in the London office for a year and then go to our agent in Hamburg for a few months. After that I was to go out to Brazil for two years to see how the coffee was grown, graded and shipped. Looking back, it all sounds terribly dull. Anyway, after a final cricket fling for the rest of the summer, I reported in October to No. 20 King William Street. I wore a new pin-stripe suit, which was too tight under the armpits, white stiff collar and shirt and the inevitable bowler hat and rolled umbrella.

I went to live with a very rich cousin, Alex Johnston, who was also my godfather. He was a pillar of the City, being chairman of a large insurance company and deputy chairman of one of the 'Big Five' banks. He and his wife lived in a large house in Queen's Gate. They had no children, but made up for it in staff: there was a butler, footman, housemaid, under-housemaid, cook, 'tweeney' and chauffeur. My relatives were kindness itself and I was thoroughly spoiled. Edward the footman was appointed to look after my every want. I had my own latch-key and I am afraid that I treated the house as an hotel or base for my social life. But I paid my rent regularly once a week by staying in to play bridge.

Cousin Alex was a fantastically good-looking man with impeccable manners, a wicked twinkle in his eye and a liking for the opposite sex, to whom he paid outrageous compliments. One elderly lady nearly fainted with joy when he told her, 'Many seasons have passed you by since I last saw you, but spring is the only one that has touched you.'

He also told a good story and was quite a wit himself. One evening we had been playing bridge and his male partner had made a series of terrible calls, and they were going down a large number of points. At the end of a particularly disastrous rubber the friend asked to be excused to go to the lavatory. When he had left the room, cousin Alex commented, 'Well, for the first time this evening I shall know what he has got in his hand!'

His wife Audrey treated me like a son and thoroughly spoiled me, but bullied cousin Alex unmercifully. The main character in the house was the old butler with the splendid name of Targett. I used to go 'below stairs' to watch him play endless games of cribbage with a friend of his, who was a one-legged tailor. (By that I mean that he had a wooden leg which he used to unscrew and park under the table, not that he made one-legged trousers.) Targett was a great betting man and used to give me tips in a hoarse whisper as he handed round the fish or the veg.

So I enjoyed two years or so of luxury living at no cost to myself and learned how the rich live and why they become rich. Cousin Alex used sometimes to take me to the theatre, for which we would normally put on a dinner-jacket. But if it was the chauffeur's night off we always went there and back by tube – never by taxi.

To start with the office was like going back to school and I felt just like a new boy. But the staff were all very friendly and helpful and gave me a warm welcome. I was put into the cable office and learned to type with one finger, or two if I was in a desperate hurry. It was our job to decode all the telegrams which came in on the telex from our agents in Europe. These usually contained orders for so many bags of coffee, and we had to forward these on to Brazil in freshly coded cables. The code was not for secrecy but for economy, 'We accept five thousand bags of coffee at forty shillings – FOB' being represented by two or three letters.

I soon got used to the routine and was even allowed to taste the samples of coffee. This meant sucking it up into one's mouth out of a spoon, swilling it round and then spitting it out into a big spittoon. It was not too good for the digestion, and I must admit that in later years I often tasted coffee in restaurants to which I would have liked to give the same treatment.

The man put in charge of me had been with the firm for many years. His name was Frank Copping, a true blue Conservative and an amateur actor of some repute in Croydon. We had a lot of fun. I used to get on to the telephone in another room and with a phoney foreign accent pretend to be an agent complaining about the quality of our coffee.

In between cables we used to play a betting game with coins. One of us would put a pocketful down on the desk and the other had to call heads or tails. We were doing this one day when we heard footsteps coming down the corridor. We hurriedly covered up the coins with a letter just as Mr Whitworth came into the room. He wanted to see a letter from one of our agents and, as luck would have it, it was the one covering our coins. We had to hand it to him and there on the desk were revealed about a dozen pennies and sixpences. He never said anything, but he must have wondered what was going on.

On another occasion I made myself slightly unpopular by cheeking one of the senior staff who gave me a mild rocket for being late.

'Mr Johnston,' he said, 'you should have been here at 9.30.'

'Why,' I could not resist replying, 'what happened?'

But I was not cut out for the City life and never understood its jargon – draft at ninety days' sight, cash against documents less two and a half per cent, and so on. My friends used to meet me for lunch at clubs or restaurants in the City and occasionally we used to sneak off to the Savoy to have steak and kidney pudding on a Thursday. One of the people with whom I used to lunch was Tuppy Headlam, who had retired as a housemaster from Eton. A rich friend of his had given him a 'job' in his stockbroking office in gratitude for the many occasions on which he had been entertained by Tuppy at Eton. All the job seemed to consist of was sitting at an empty desk doing *The Times*' crossword.

On one occasion Tuppy wanted to write to a friend about some shares, but did not know his address. So he decided to cable at great expense a mutual friend who was big-game hunting out in Kenya. The reply-paid telegram read: 'Do you know John Smith's [or whatever the name was] address?' The next day back came the reply: 'Yes.'

My evenings were spent occasionally at deb dances but more often at the theatre or one of the many music halls like the Palladium, Holborn Empire, Victoria or Chelsea Palace. I had a passion for variety and saw most of the great

artists of that time. Billy Bennett – almost a gentleman –
was one of the funniest stand-up comics ever, with his red
nose and hair smarmed down over his forehead. He was
Queen Mary's favourite and used to crack gags such as:
'My brother has a hair on the end of his nose. It's so long
that every time he sneezes he nearly flogs himself to
death!' The immaculate Randolph Sutton in top-hat, white
tie and tails used to sing *On Mother Kelly's Doorstep* with
tremendous pathos. Nellie Wallace, Layton and Johnstone,
the Western Brothers, the big bands like Jack Hylton and,
of course, the Crazy Gang and Max Miller were all my
favourites.

In those days you could usually catch one or other of
the big names at one of the many London music halls. I
saw Flanagan and Allen before they became famous with
the Crazy Gang. They appeared at the Holborn Empire
and finished their act with an unknown song called *Underneath the Arches*. They were a wonderful double act, with
Bud getting all the place-names wrong. King's Cross
became His Majesty's Annoyed, and so on. They used to
finish each gag with the exclamation 'Oi!'

Max Miller, the Cheeky Chappie, was of course the most
daring comic of the time, with his white hat, outrageous
outfit of gaudy plus-fours and his wicked eyes flashing and
winking at the ladies. But if anyone accused him of being
blue, he blamed it on the dirty minds of his audience. He
made sure that his *double entendres* really could be taken
either way, such as: 'A young girl of 21 married an old
man of 85 and on her first night she prayed, "Oh Lord,
make me as old as my husband." And even as she was
praying she felt old age creeping upon her.'

In the theatre I went to musicals and farces, especially
those by Ben Travers at the Aldwych. I saw all of them
and, no matter how funny the modern farces may be,
there can surely never be two better actors of farce than
Ralph Lynn and Tom Walls.

After a year in the City I went to Hamburg where I worked in our agent's office. He was an ex-U-boat captain from the Great War and his assistant was an enthusiastic member of the Nazi Party. Whenever he mentioned the Führer his eyes would fill with tears. It was he who took me to a large Nazi Party gathering in one of the halls in Hamburg to hear Dr Goebbels speak. I felt very conspicuous in my London suit among all the brown shirts. Goebbels ranted on and on and, of course, I did not understand a word. But suddenly he raised his voice to a high-pitched scream and everyone in the hall sprang to their feet, gave the Nazi salute and shouted out one word. My friend quickly translated as I too scrambled to my feet. It was the famous moment when Goebbels offered the German people the choice of guns or butter. Even I could tell that the one word they were shouting was *not* butter. I felt very much alone and apprehensive of the future.

After Germany it was back to the City with occasional business trips round the ports of Europe before setting off for Brazil in June 1936. I went by liner from Southampton and was very unhappy at having to leave all my friends, my cricket and London life for at least two years. Nevertheless I enjoyed my first-ever trip on a liner and was resigned to fate by the time we reached the hot, steamy port of Santos, through which every year millions of bags of coffee and thousands of bales of cotton were exported. As our liner passed through the estuary to the harbour we passed Johnston Island, where in the mid-nineteenth century sailors were billeted to escape from the yellow fever which raged on the mainland.

When I arrived there was a terrific tropical thunderstorm booming and I remember being taken to a house on the beach where I sat on the verandah feeling miserable and homesick. Some trouble had come up about my work permit so I was rushed up-country to one of the company's fazendas, or coffee plantations, to spend a dreary month looking at miles and miles of coffee trees and piles and piles of coffee beans, and little else.

Incidentally, I had started off literally on the wrong foot on my journey up-country. Before getting into the train which wound its way round the mountain up to São Paulo I had unknowingly stepped into a dog's mess. I did not discover this until we had started on our journey, and it was then too late to do anything about it. You can imagine what it was like, especially in that heat. But at least it ensured that my companion and I had a carriage to ourselves.

When my permit was in order I went down to Santos where I spent the next eighteen months trying to learn all about the coffee business. I was not much use as I could never tell one bean from another (which was important for grading) nor taste any difference between various types (which was essential for assessing the value of the coffee). So it was not surprising that I was never given a job with any authority or responsibility.

I even failed on a PR job I was allotted. An important client from New York was due to stop at Santos for a day in a cruise liner. He was a big buyer of our coffee and it was very important that we should keep on the right side of him, so I was instructed to lay on a day's entertainment for him, his wife and two daughters. Accordingly I ordered a big open car to take them up the mountain road to São Paulo for the day. I was at the docks to greet them early in the morning and they were delighted at the prospect of a drive into the interior.

The buyer was in a white Palm Beach suit and panama hat and was smoking a large cigar. The ladies were wearing gay summer dresses with parasols. What they did not know – nor, unfortunately, did I – was that once the tarmac road had reached the top of the mountain it became a dirt track, and in the dry weather the dust was so thick that it was like driving through a sandstorm in the desert. Every time they got behind another car or one passed them they were showered with dust. Needless to say, theirs was the only open car on the road. The Brazilians knew better.

I was ignorant of all this as I waited by the liner to welcome them back. I could hardly believe my eyes when I saw them approaching. It was like *The Black and White Minstrel Show*: their faces were black with just the whites of their eyes and their teeth showing. All their tropical clothes were ruined. They brushed me aside as I tried to apologise. As they disappeared up the gangplank I feared we had lost our most important client. We had. He never bought another bag from us.

There was quite a big colony of English and Americans in Santos and the social life was centred round the Anglo-American club. Besides playing quite a bit of cricket on matting, including a triangular tournament with Rio de Janeiro and São Paulo, we also tried our hand at baseball. Every Sunday morning our American friends used to play us on the beach. Then came the great day when an American cruiser visited Santos and we challenged them to a baseball game on the cricket ground. What a different game it is to cricket! When it was my turn to be striker the catcher kept up a running commentary: 'Come on, boys, this limey is no good. He's nervous, he'll never hit a thing...' and so on. I missed the first two balls the pitcher sent down but was lucky enough to connect with the third (my last chance). It soared over where mid-off would be at cricket, but for some reason the Americans had no man out there. So I raced round and had the thrill of scoring a home run before anyone could retrieve the ball. How I envied the catcher being allowed to talk like that. If wicket-keepers had been allowed to do the same at cricket I reckon I would have played for England.

There was also a large German colony and, with Hitler behaving as he was in Europe, we were very suspicious of them all. One man whom we definitely suspected of being a spy used to travel on the same train as us to and from work. We discovered his name was Herr Kürl, and with a name like that imagine our joy when one day he took his hat off and we saw he was as bald as a coot!

It was at the club in Santos that I first tried my hand at acting and revue work. I compèred the various shows we put on and did the occasional cross-talk act based on all the gags I had heard in the old Holborn Empire days. I also played my one and only star role – the silly ass in *The Ghost Train*. I did the silly part more or less OK, with a monocle and a highly pitched voice. However, the last scene called for the silly ass to reveal himself as a policeman in disguise and to become deadly serious as he explained to the assembled cast exactly how the gun-runners had worked the Ghost Train. I remember my big speech started something like 'It was really quite simple. What they did was . . .' but there and then on the first night I dried up completely. It may have been simple but my mind went blank. I could not remember a single line. I think the audience thought it was part of the play. At any rate it got about the biggest laugh of the evening.

The play was produced by the British consul in Santos at the time. His name was James Joint and he later became our commercial attaché at Buenos Aires, where, appropriately enough, he had the job of negotiating with the Argentineans over meat prices. It was lucky he never had any children, as otherwise I am sure they would have been known as the 'two veg'.

People used to stay in Santos for years, some of them without ever going home on leave to England. One of these was a coffee man called Jack Edge who had come out from Lancashire as a boy and had been in Santos for 25 years. At last he decided to go home to see his old mother, to whom he had always written regularly. So he sailed home and took the train to Liverpool. He had not warned her he was coming as he wished to give her a surprise. He rang the bell of his old home and after the noise of bolts being shot back the door opened to reveal a sweet old lady. 'Hello, mother, I'm your son Jack from Brazil,' said Jack. His mother peered at him carefully through spectacles for a second or two, then said, 'You're not my Jack!' and slammed the door in his face. I believe he later managed to persuade her that he was the genuine article. But what a welcome home!

One of the high spots of life in Brazil is the annual carnival in February, when everyone goes mad for three days on end. All businesses and shops are closed down and the streets are crowded with singing and dancing people. They never seem to stop in spite of the terrific heat, which at that time of year is in the nineties plus maximum humidity. The revelry goes on all night, with bands playing and long lines of people dancing through the streets like a giant Palais Glide. Most of the dancers carry a scent spray which they squirt over each other – a wise precaution in that heat!

It was after one of these carnivals, when I had been in Santos just over eighteen months, that I was suddenly struck down by a strange sort of paralysis. It was a frightening experience as I gradually began to lose the use of my arms and my legs and, after two days, could hardly drag myself along. It was diagnosed as acute peripheral neuritis and I was rushed down to Santos to the house of a member of our firm whose wife happened to be a doctor. They were Jerry and Dorothy Deighton and for six weeks between them they nursed me like a child.

To start with, I could not do anything for myself. I even had to be fed. It was all very frightening and I began to wonder whether I should ever use my arms and legs again. But once again I was in luck as there was a wonderful Brazilian doctor called D'Utra Vaz who had had experience of this sort of disease before (it was a type of beri-beri). He prescribed for me a diet of raw vegetables, lots of tomatoes (which I hate), daily injections in the bottom (I had nearly a hundred) and lots of massage and sunbathing. Gradually I began to get better, and one day to my delight I was able to wiggle one of my toes. What a relief that was! From then on I slowly began to learn to walk again, though I was very weak and had lost a tremendous amount of weight.

I shall never forget the debt I owe to the Deightons. They gave up everything to nurse me and were always cheerful and comforting. I remember asking Jerry why he was called that when his real Christian name was something quite different. 'Oh,' he said, 'it's because all the women sit on me and the men hold me at arm's length!'

As soon as I was strong enough I was put on a liner back to England, accompanied by my mother who had been rushed out to Brazil to be with me. The cause of the disease was all a bit of a mystery. Some people said it was due to a deficiency of vitamin B, and it is true that I had not eaten many fresh vegetables while I was in Brazil. Dr D'Utra Vaz also added that it was often brought on by excessive drinking or childbirth. Whether he was joking or not I don't know, but I was a bit worried as my average intake of drink was only about one gin and tonic a day!

I was sorry to leave all my new friends in Santos, but I had to admit that I had hated my work in the coffee business and was already trying to work out how to escape from it all into something I could enjoy more. Meanwhile, ahead of me lay the happy prospect of seeing all my old friends, recuperating from my illness and enjoying an English summer once again, especially as the Australians were to be the visiting cricket team.

7 Back Home with Home

ENGLAND IN MAY 1938 WAS not the happiest place to come back to. Hitler was ranting and raving and the headlines in the press were daily more sensational and depressing. But come to think of it, they were nothing compared to what we have to put up with now every day. Still, it was a nerve-racking summer and there was a general feeling of resignation and despair.

However, for me personally there were many compensations, though I had to keep to a rigid programme of rest, exercise, no drink, injections and going early to bed. Nor was I allowed to play games. But I was able to catch up with all my friends and spent most of the summer either visiting them, going to the theatre or watching cricket. I was lucky enough to see the second Test against Australia at Lord's where Wally Hammond played one of the great Test innings of all time – a majestic 240 during which he hammered poor Fleetwood-Smith unmercifully with some of the fiercest driving I have ever seen.

There had been one or two family changes while I was away in Brazil. My eldest brother had married and both my mother and sister had been divorced. Our home in Bude was sold; my stepfather remarried and my mother went to live in a picture-postcard thatched cottage in the village of Chearsley in Buckinghamshire. I visited her as often as I could and she lived there very happily, busying herself with good works and her garden. While on the boat out to Brazil she had made great friends with a Major Black, who by chance lived in the next-door village of Haddenham. He had an equally delightful cottage and was also an enthusiastic gardener. But though they saw a lot of each other, they remained just friends.

I think we all missed Bude a bit, despite its sad associations. My mother told me a splendid story of something that had happened to her there just before she left. She had made her way to the local ironmonger's to buy a garden hoe, gone up to the assistant behind the counter and said, 'I want a hoe, please.'

'Yes,' he replied without a smile, 'china or enamel?'

The circumstances of my sister's divorce were rather unusual. She and her husband had four children, the youngest one, a boy, being only a baby. When her husband told Anne that he had met someone called Margaret whom he wanted to marry, she said something to this effect: 'Right. Ask her to come and stay with us for a week. If I like her and think that she would be a good stepmother to the children, I will divorce you and go off with the baby, leaving the other three children for you and Margaret to look after.' And that is exactly what happened! Margaret came to stay, Anne approved, then left more or less immediately for South Africa, where she remained for the next forty years! I still think it an amazing decision for a mother to make, especially as Anne was very fond of her three eldest children and they of her. Anyway, she married an ex-police officer and game reserve warden out there and lived happily ever after in a fishing village called St Lucia Estuary, about 150 miles north of Durban. I was lucky enough to see Anne on my various trips to South Africa. Her house was in an idyllic spot, with hippos at the bottom of the garden, crocodiles in the river and monkeys swinging from tree to tree across the lawn. There was a small colony of white people and the climate was perfect.

On my return to London in 1938, I went once again to stay with my godfather at Queen's Gate, where I was fussed over by all the servants and treated as a semi-invalid – which I suppose I was in a way. But it was not long before I moved to No. 35 South Eaton Place to join William Douglas Home in rooms kept by a remarkable couple called Mr and Mrs Crisp.

The husband was a retired butler, she a cook, and they had met when serving together in a large house owned by some peer of the realm. Mr Crisp – or Crippen, as I used to call him – was a mixture of Jeeves and that wonderful old comedy actor Robertson Hare, and really was the perfect gentleman's gentleman. He had a marvellous sense of humour and sometimes when we had dinner parties would wait at table complete with powdered wig and knee-breeches. If there were any strangers present we used to ask them if they knew of any good butlers who were free, as we were thinking of making certain changes to our staff. Crippen would then pretend to be overcome with shock and would drop a plate or dish on the floor – even over the unfortunate guest himself on one occasion.

He had some good stories about his early days. He told me how once, when he was a pantry boy in a big London house, he was looking out of the basement window, which had bars in front of it, presumably to keep out burglars. But two passers-by must have thought differently as they looked down and saw him peering through the bars. Crippen heard one say to the other, 'Poor boy – and so young, too.'

He was also a football fan and he and I used to go off to watch the Arsenal, where we saw such great forwards as Hulme, Jack, Drake, James and Bastin, and defenders like Hapgood, Barnes, Male and Copping. On one occasion we even saw wee Alex James, baggy pants below the knees, score three goals, which was a soccer sensation as he normally 'made' the goals for others with his brilliant footwork and dribbling.

Mrs Crisp, or Gert, was an absolute saint and a super cook. She treated us just like children, spoiling us if we were good and scolding us if we did not meet her own high standard of manners and behaviour. They had two rooms vacant at this time, one of which had been occupied by Jo Grimond, who had been at Eton with me and, of course, went on to become leader of the Liberal Party. Jo had recently left to get married, so I took his room and another friend, John Hogg – later a highly respected banker – had the other. In spite of the continuing European crisis we managed to have a thoroughly enjoyable summer.

In August I went up to Yorkshire to stay with James Lane Fox and his family. When I was at Oxford I had had a Sealyham dog with one black eye called Blob, and I had given him to the Foxes on my departure to Brazil. Blob had always gone everywhere with me, especially to all the cricket matches in which I played. He used to sit and watch from the boundary edge, then, when we came off the field, would rush out to meet me and proudly carry in my wicket-keeping gloves. One Saturday, the Lane Foxes lost him and searched everywhere for him. Finally they ran him to earth on the village green, where he was quietly sitting on the boundary edge watching the local village cricket match. Rather touching.

Blob was a dog of great character and, though very pleased to see me again, it was obviously better for him to stay up there in the country rather than live in London. I pinched one of the current music-hall jokes of the time and nicknamed him Larwood – because he had four short legs and his balls swung both ways!

During my stay I remember we went on a picnic and listened in on the radio to Howard Marshall commentating on the fifth Test against Australia at the Oval. His deep burbling voice suited the atmosphere of cricket perfectly and we were able to hear him describing Len Hutton's then record Test score of 364, interspersed with such typical comments as 'Bradman standing there, arms akimbo' or 'the Oval sparrows are pecking away in front of the Pavilion gate'. He was a marvellous commentator and, unlike some past commentators in other sports, would be totally acceptable today, so far advanced was his technique.

In September, the crisis finally caught up with us, and with Neville Chamberlain flying off to see Hitler at Bad Godesburg I began to deliver gas-masks to some of the embassies. Then came Mr Chamberlain's dramatic announcement in the House of Commons that Hitler had agreed to meet him yet again: 'He is coming halfway to meet me at Munich in order to save an old man another such long journey...' At that time William Douglas Home's eldest brother Alec, then Lord Dunglass, was Mr Chamberlain's parliamentary private secretary and was going to Munich with him. But he was caught by the sudden announcement and came rushing round to us to borrow a clean shirt, which I was very proud to lend him. William, Gert and I went to see them off at Heston air-drome and also met them on their return. We saw Mr Chamberlain wave his little piece of paper and say, 'Out of this nettle, danger, we pluck this flower, safety.' He looked a frail, tired old man with his black homburg, stick-up collar and umbrella. And what a tiny plane it was in which they flew. None of the posh VIP VC 10s of more recent years.

Whatever people may now pretend, there is no doubt that at the time the Munich agreement was a tremendous relief to the country as a whole. The crowd in Downing Street reflected the feeling of most of us as they cheered Mr Chamberlain when he looked out from a window of Number 10 and shouted, 'It's peace in our time.' It was at least peace for another twelve months and a breathing space in which to build up our forces.

Shortly after this, Mr Chamberlain and I became joint godfathers to one of Alec's daughters, Meriel. It made my day when I read a report of the christening in *The Times*, which stated that the two godfathers, Mr Neville Chamberlain and Mr Brian Johnston, were unable to be present.

By October I was passed fit again and returned to the office. Since I was now supposed to know something about coffee after my stay in Brazil, I was promoted to assistant manager with a salary of £500 a year and a room of my own with an enormous desk which had belonged to my grandfather. I paid a few visits to our agents in Europe, including one to Hamburg, which I found rather frightening. The Germans, though still outwardly friendly, seemed far more arrogant and intolerant of all those who did not support Hitler. He had given them complete confidence in their ability to take on and crush the rest of the world, if necessary. I was very relieved to get home. But I found myself less and less interested in coffee and the City. All I really wanted to do was to be an actor. But I had not got the guts to get out of the rut, in spite of two things that should have encouraged me.

Firstly, William was now not only writing plays but also acting in the West End. In addition, he even got himself temporarily engaged to Ronald Squire's daughter. So there was plenty of theatrical talk and atmosphere at No. 35.

Secondly, I decided to go to a well-known lady fortune-teller to help me to make up my mind. Everything she told me indicated that I was destined for some sort of career in the entertainment world. She even asked me to sign her two visitors books, one which she kept for all her clients and the other which she said was for people who would eventually become well known or famous. I was highly flattered to be asked, but even this spur could not persuade me to take the plunge.

I went to stay once or twice with William's family at the Hirsel, their home near Coldstream in Berwickshire. They were a large and united family, and the Earl of Home was as near to being a saint as any man I have ever met. He believed the best about everyone. Although a huge landowner, he was kept on a very tight purse-string by his agent. There was a good reason for this: he was so kind that otherwise he would probably have given it all away. He would be driven around in a battered old Wolseley and whenever he went to London he was given £25 in cash by the agent. Once this pocket-money ran out he used to return to Scotland. It was always said that he spent £5 of it in tips by the time he arrived at Brown's Hotel, where he and the family always stayed.

Lady Home, too, was a marvellous character, on the surface the most unemotional and placid of women. She would sit quietly knitting, listening to all the noisy conversation, which was always going on around her. Then promptly at 10 p.m. the 'wee Lordie', as Lord Home was known, would call out, 'Lil, bed!' and she would gather up her knitting and go off without a murmur. She was a wonderful mother to her large family, though they used to pull her leg unmercifully. In true female style, she had no sense of logic. On one occasion at Brown's Hotel she was in bed with a slight cold, so I went up to say goodbye as they were leaving the next day. I knocked on her door and she immediately called out, 'Come in.' So in I went, only to be greeted with, 'What are you doing? You shouldn't come into my room like this.'

'But,' I replied, 'you told me to come in.'

'I know,' she rejoindered, 'but I thought you were only one of the waiters!'

Everyone now knows about William's eldest brother Alec, but at that time, except for his connection with Mr Chamberlain, he was an ordinary MP who had never held any office. What people may not know about Sir Alec, later Lord Home, is that he was one of the best after-dinner speakers in the country, with a good fund of stories, many of them collected by his wife Elizabeth. On one occasion I heard him speak about a man who asked a friend where the Virgin Islands were. 'I don't know for certain,' was the reply, 'but I imagine they must be some considerable distance from the Isle of Man!'

The second brother, Henry, was a retired major and a famous ornithologist known throughout Scotland as the Birdman. He also painted birds with great skill and accuracy, and I am in fact still waiting for one of a pheasant which he promised me as a wedding present over 25 years ago. Henry was a very good broadcaster and one evening he was broadcasting *Birdsong* for the BBC from a Surrey wood. This was a very popular programme which for many years used to go out 'live' at about 11 p.m. in the early summer. The main object was to get the song of the nightingale, but there was also the joy of hearing and trying to pick out all the other birds as well. Before the war the BBC used to place a well-known cellist called Beatrice Harrison in a punt by the side of the wood and hope that the sound of her cello would entice the nightingale to sing, though whether in complaint or competition was never made quite clear.

After the war we went one better and got Percy Edwards to do his famous bird imitations as a challenge to the real birds. More often than not they would sing back in protest at this invasion of their territory by another 'bird'. A control van used to park outside the wood and from this long microphone leads were run out to four or five chosen spots in the wood where the bird expert thought there would be some birds singing. The vital microphone was, of course, the one placed to catch the nightingale, and this would involve several nights of research. But once discovered, the nightingales seldom left their selected territory.

On this occasion there were four microphones placed in strategic positions: one by a bluebell glade, another by a small bridge over a stream, one near some fir trees and the nightingale one over a group of rhododendron bushes. The programme was due to start at eleven o'clock – 'live', remember, not recorded – so with five minutes to go Henry thought he would have a final check to make sure all the microphones were working. The engineer brought up No.

1 mike and they heard a willow warbler; No. 2 produced a wood pigeon and No. 3 a frightened blackbird. No. 4 was, of course, hanging over the rhododendrons and, as the engineer switched it on, to Henry's horror there was no nightingale but the unmistakable sound of a couple making love.

There were now only three minutes to go before the broadcast, so Henry rushed round to the bush from where the sounds were coming. He shouted to those inside to come out and a shamefaced but thoroughly annoyed couple emerged, the man hurriedly doing up his flies. They protested about this intrusion into their privacy but were somewhat mollified when Henry explained that in a few minutes' time he would have said to the waiting listeners all over Great Britain something like: 'Now, let's listen to the dulcet tones of the nightingale . . .' And goodness knows how far the couple would have got by then!

While staying with the Douglas-Homes, William persuaded me to play a practical joke on an uncle and aunt who lived nearby. He also persuaded Lady Home to ask them over to tea to help entertain a strange clergyman who was staying at the house. He was deaf and behaving in a very eccentric way. Needless to say, I was the clergyman – with a thick pair of horn-rimmed spectacles, hair parted down the middle (I had some then) and dressed in a dog collar and dark clerical suit out of the dressing-up chest.

At the time they were expected I began to walk up and down the middle of the drive reading a Bible. When their car approached I pretended not to hear, so that they had to stop and hoot. I then stepped gingerly aside, raising my hat as they drove past. This set the scene ideally as they were now convinced that I was a 'case'.

Later, I joined them at tea, where I was seated next to the aunt to whom I immediately began to make amorous advances, putting my hands on her knee and so on. As I was meant to be deaf William proceeded to shout at me, but I pretended not to hear. The uncle and aunt did their best, but soon gave up. They were soon saying rude things about me. I just sat there, nodding and smiling, and I heard them mutter, 'It's hopeless. He's quite mad. Why on earth did you ask us?' The family, who were in the know, were in hysterics, especially when William deliberately upset a hot cup of tea over me and I let out an unclerical expletive.

When we went into the drawing-room after tea, the aunt sat down on the sofa; pretending that I could not see very well, I sat down on her lap. She let out a scream. I then asked her if she would like to come for a walk with me in the shrubbery. By now she was becoming quite hysterical and her husband was becoming more and more annoyed, saying things like, 'What the hell does the lunatic think he's up to?' I asked to be 'excused' for a minute and left the room. I quickly changed into my sports jacket and flannels, removed my spectacles, parted my hair at the side instead of in the middle, then strolled unconcernedly back into the room. William introduced me as myself, explaining that I had been in Edinburgh. It took quite a few minutes before the aunt and uncle realised what had happened and I am glad to say that they took it very well.

8 My Military Debut

AFTER THE INVASION OF CZECHOSLOVAKIA it became more and more obvious that war was not only inevitable but imminent, and some of my Eton friends and I thought we must do something to prepare ourselves for it. We had all been in the Corps at school and at one of our lunches in the City decided we should try to get on to the reserve of some regiment. We were unanimous in thinking that if we had to fight we might as well be in the best and most efficient regiment, so we went right to the top and applied to the Grenadier Guards, the senior regiment of the Foot Guards.

My first cousin 'Boy' Browning was then commanding the 2nd Battalion. They had just returned from two years in Egypt and were stationed at Wellington Barracks. Boy was later to become the founder and first commander of the Airborne Division, and it must have been due to him that I and five or six others were accepted for training by the Grenadiers and placed on the Officer Cadet Reserve. This involved reporting on one or two evenings a week throughout the summer of 1939 to Wellington Barracks, where we were taught weapon training, basic tactics and regimental history and traditions.

We reported for the first time one evening in May, coming straight from the City in our bowlers, white stiff collars and dark suits. We were welcomed in the officers' mess by Boy Browning, who offered us drinks and gave us a short informal talk. This was fine, we thought, as we sipped our drinks and sat in deep comfortable armchairs. A great institution, the Army! When we had had a second round of drinks Boy smilingly suggested that we might like to meet the regimental sergeant-major who, he said, was waiting for us out on the parade-ground. Innocently we left the comfort of the mess and walked out on to the steps.

As soon as we emerged a roar rent the air as the RSM bellowed out to us to get into a double and fall in in front of him. Before we knew what was happening we found ourselves marching up and down the vast parade-ground in double quick time, being told we were a lazy lot of so and sos. 'About turn, quick march, right turn, mark time, halt!' The orders came out like machine-gun fire and we were soon sweating and panting for breath, wondering why on earth we had ever volunteered. After twenty minutes of utter hell we were dismissed with a 'Goodnight, gentlemen. See you later in the week.'

RSM Tom Garnett was a wonderful man and soldier with whom I was to serve for most of the war. We had experienced Guards discipline at its best – or worst, depending on how you looked at it. We limped back to the mess and sank into our chairs as Boy dispensed some badly needed drinks. We were definitely in a state of shock. He then gave us an enthralling talk about the Brigade of Guards and the reasons for their fanatical emphasis on discipline in all their training of officers and Guardsmen alike. Keith Bryant, in his book *Fighting with the Guards*, put it all very succinctly when he detailed the six basic qualities instilled into every Guardsman: cleanliness, smartness, fitness, efficiency, pride and invincibility.

The acceptance of these six qualities demands a tremendous amount from any man but, if achieved, result in the perfect fighting machine – a man who can obey any order without question, no matter how bloody it may seem. Hence the endless, and to the outsider seemingly pointless, hours of drill. Naturally, this automatic acceptance of an order demands an even higher standard for those in command. It becomes absolutely essential that every order is the right one and practicable, something of which I was very conscious when I became an officer later on.

Meanwhile, we were slowly being put through the mill as the summer advanced and after our first experience always made sure we were suitably dressed. Bowler hats and suits were replaced by grey flannels and cricket shirts, and after each parade we used to retire exhausted for supper to the houses of those who were married.

The political clouds were gathering, so I got in as many games of cricket as possible, mostly for the Eton Ramblers. Also, whenever I was in London for the weekend I used to go round the corner to St Michael's, Chester Square, to hear Canon Elliott preach. What an actor he would have made! He had a deep voice, a fine appearance and used to lean over the front of the pulpit and just talk – no notes, no reference books. He had the rare gift of making each member of the congregation think that he was talking to them personally.

One Sunday he made a plea on behalf of poor families, who due to high unemployment were desperately short of food and clothing. He had a list of deserving cases and suggested that members of his congregation should adopt a family and look after them. I decided to carry out his suggestion and was given a family in Durham, a married couple with four children. The husband was unemployed and not in the best of health and, as a consequence, his family were pretty badly off. I got in touch with them, wrote to them regularly and sent them a little money or groceries from time to time. At least they could feel that someone was interested in their plight.

I also asked Elizabeth Dunglass to visit them when she was staying with her father Dr Alington, who had become the Dean of Durham. This she kindly did, but for various reasons I have never managed to visit them myself, a fact of which I am rather ashamed. But two of the sons once came to see me in my BBC office when they were down in London, and to this day I still write to Mrs Corbett and send her a small present every Christmas.

At this time I was rather keen on a very attractive girl called Cynthia, though I don't flatter myself that she was at all keen on me. However, we used to have a lot of fun and after weeks of trying I at last persuaded her to go out with me to a theatre and supper. In order to impress her I persuaded a friend, Nigel Turner, to dress up as my chauffeur, disguised with fake moustache and spectacles. But I spoiled it all by getting carried away when he nearly had an accident and I sacked him on the spot. Cynthia thought this was unnecessarily harsh and told me in no uncertain terms what she thought of me. So I did myself more harm than good. She did not even think it at all funny when Nigel whipped off his disguise and revealed who he was.

I was due some holiday in August and, after a cricket tour in Yorkshire, James Lane Fox, William and I were crazy enough to go off to Cap Martin in the South of France. We realised the possible danger of being stranded by the outbreak of war but thought we would have one final fling. The Kennedy family were also there. We knew them in London and used to go round to see them in the US Ambassador's house in Prince's Gate. We were particularly fond of Jack, later President John F. Kennedy, who seemed to appreciate even our worst jokes. But we had only been in France for a few days when there was a general panic and everyone was advised to return home at once. The weather was terribly hot and the trains and steamers were packed, so we had a very uncomfortable journey back home, arriving on the last day of August.

We had only just made it, and promptly got down to filling sandbags. We were doing this outside Westminster Hospital on Sunday, 3 September when the frail voice of Mr Chamberlain announced over the radio that we were at war with Germany.

Shattering though the news was, it came in a way as a relief after all the months of tension and we continued shovelling sand into the bags. But we were soon rudely interrupted by the air-raid siren and were all rushed down into the mortuary for shelter. We reluctantly had to hand it to Hitler for being so much on the ball that within a few minutes of war being declared his bombers were approaching London. As it turned out it was, of course, only a false alarm, but it had given everyone quite a fright and we returned somewhat chastened to No. 35 to tuck into Mrs Crisp's roast beef and Yorkshire pudding.

The next few days were full of activity. William, who was an admitted pacifist and conscientious objector, immediately joined the fire service and I tried to do the same. But when they learned that I was in the Officer Cadet Reserve I was told to wait for instructions from the Army. I looked into the office from time to time but there was little business and an air of unreality about everything. I realised, too, that once I had joined up I would never return to the City, no matter what happened to me in the war. It was the break I needed to escape from a business life. Hitler had done for me what I had not had the guts to do for myself, though I had a strong feeling of guilt at letting the family business down. But I was probably flattering myself. I imagine they must have been as relieved as I was.

After a week or so and much badgering of the Grenadier Headquarters, I was ordered to report for a medical inspection. With a lot of other naked men I had to go through some fairly undignified routines and, as a result, have always appreciated the old joke about the recruit who started to run as he thought the doctor had said 'off' instead of 'cough'. Very painful! I passed all right, but there was one awkward moment when I could not read all the letters on the card with my rather short-sighted right eye. But the doctor must have realised how disappointed I would be if

I failed, or perhaps they were short of budding officers. Anyway, he made it easy for me by opening the fingers of his hand which was covering my left eye, so that I could read all the letters with that eye.

My other friends also passed and in October we reported to the Royal Military College at Sandhurst for a four-month course. It was being turned into an OCTU – Officer Cadet Training Unit – and we were its very first victims. There were lots of people like myself, most of them in their middle twenties who had come from jobs in the City or one of the professions. It was just like going back to school, but the great thing was that we did not have to think. Everything was organised for us. We were told exactly what to do and soon automatically did it.

After the first shocks of reveille at 6 a.m. and long doses of PT and drill, we soon settled down and began to enjoy ourselves. The course was a strange mixture of war and peace. Each of us still had a room to himself with a batman and our company sergeant-major, a great character called 'Dusty' Smith, would call us 'sir' with one corner of his mouth and hand out the most terrible rockets with the other. 'Mr Johnston, *sir*, stop being so dozy and get a –– move on!' That sort of thing. It was even funnier with the regimental sergeant-major. We had to call him 'sir' as well. He used to say, 'I call you sir, and you call me sir. The only difference is that you mean it!'

We soon became physically fit and moderately efficient and, unless we were on guard duties, were free from midday Saturday to midnight Sunday, which meant a mass exodus to London as soon as the last parade was finished. This led to complete chaos on the first Saturday. We kept our cars in a garage in Camberley and had asked for them to be brought up to the parade-ground by midday Saturday. We were out on our first route march and were marching back to be dismissed for our first weekend off. We rounded the bend to go on to the parade-ground and it looked like

81

a car park at a football match. All the cars were parked in the middle and we had to be called to a sudden halt and dismissed where we were. Our company commander was naturally very annoyed, and from then on we had to go down to Camberley to collect our cars.

On the occasional weekends when we were not given leave we had to attend church parade and go to chapel. One Sunday the padre accused us of not putting enough in the collection and urged us to be more generous in future. This rather annoyed us. So the next time we went to chapel we all filled our pockets with pennies and half-pennies. A friend called Tom Blackwell, who was richer than most of us, even had several pounds' worth of coppers in those paper bags issued by banks. When the NCOs came round with the gold plates we poured out our coins and the plates were soon full to overflowing. Pennies were spilling out all over the aisle and more plates had to be fetched from the altar. The look on the NCOs' faces was a mixture of anger and disbelief that such a thing could happen in their chapel. But they could do nothing about it. There was even more chaos up at the altar when they tried to transfer the contents of each plate on to a master plate so that the padre could bless the offering. The master plate had to be taken several times into the vestry to be emptied and each time it was filled the padre had to try to bless it. But the weight of the coins made it very difficult for him to raise it above his head to make the sign of the cross and from behind he looked just like a weightlifter straining to beat a world record. I think we got our own back. At least, there were no more slurs on our generosity.

While the 'phoney' war continued in Europe we were gradually being turned into officers. The various regimental colonels came down to vet us and check up on our progress and by February 1940 we had all been accepted. Then came the final passing-out parade when we put on our officers' uniforms for the first time. The NCOs who had been ordering us around and handing out rockets for the last few months now had to salute us, and I shall always remember the twinkle in Dusty Smith's eye when he 'tore me off' a beauty as I drove away.

It was quite a moment – a commissioned officer in the Brigade of Guards. A bit prefabricated, perhaps, but at least there was the one pip on my shoulder to prove it. I must confess that it was highly embarrassing walking about the West End having to acknowledge salutes as well as give them.

We had been granted a few days' leave before joining our regiments, and I spent mine seeing all the theatre shows I could. I especially enjoyed the wartime jokes of Tommy Trinder. Take this one. A man walking down Whitehall stopped a passer-by and asked him if he knew which side the War Office was on. 'On ours, I hope!' was the somewhat unhelpful reply.

But my leave was soon up. I was ordered to report to the Training Battalion of the Grenadier Guards at Windsor.

9 New Boy Johnston

ALTHOUGH WE WERE NOW OFFICERS, life at Windsor was not much different from that at Sandhurst. We were drilled in a special Officers' squad by RSM 'Snapper' Robinson and the adjutant kept an eagle eye on us as we continued training in weapons, tactics and motor transport. Some of these duties took place on the tiny grass square in the middle of the barracks which in peacetime had been used for cricket and had the shortest boundaries of any ground I have ever seen. They were so short that they only counted two runs. The batsman had to hit the ball over the boundary to score four runs. To get a six he had to hit it clean out of the barracks.

We did have certain duties, such as kit inspections, and we also learned what it was like to be put in charge of a platoon of Guardsmen. These inspections were pernickety affairs with the kit laid out on the bed in a set pattern. The greatcoat and blankets had to be folded in a certain way, knives and forks put in a special order, and so on. Everything had to be scrupulously cleaned and scrubbed. The slightest deviation and the Guardsman was 'put in the book'.

We also began to attend the adjutant's 'orders', where discipline was meted out – our first insight into the rough justice that was administered for minor offences such as long hair, idleness on parade or untidy kit. There was a fearful clatter as the accused was marched into the room in double quick time by a drill sergeant shouting at the top of his voice. The charge was read out and if the accused wanted to say anything in his defence he had to wait to be asked to do so by the adjutant. He would then say,

'Thank you, sir, for leave to speak,' and would be told to go ahead. If he spoke before he had done this the drill sergeant would shout at him to 'stop talking'. This also happened if the accused's excuse appeared to be a lame one, or even if it went on for too long. If the adjutant thought he was guilty he would ask one of us if we had anything to say. This was the chance for the platoon commander to put in a good word for his Guardsman if he wanted. ('A good man, sir. Tries hard. This is his first offence.') Alternatively, he could report adversely on the accused – if, for instance, he was a regular troublemaker.

For more serious offences there were all sorts of safeguards and procedures and for these the accused definitely got a fair deal. He could be sent before the commanding officer or ask for a private interview with his company commander when no one else would be present. Finally, as a last resort he could ask for or be sent to a court-martial.

Five years later when I became a company commander I had to take company orders and never enjoyed them. I felt I was called on to give judgement far too quickly in an impossibly noisy atmosphere. I also felt sympathy for the accused who by the way he was treated was made to appear guilty before his case was heard. I often used to postpone my decision to the next day in order to give myself adequate time to sort it out. I am afraid my NCOs sometimes thought I was a bit of a soft case.

After a few weeks at Windsor we were considered sufficiently trained to take our turn as one of the junior officers on the guard at Windsor Castle. This involved 24 hours in the guardroom up at the castle and a nightly patrol of all the sentry posts to see that all was well. Since the Royal Family stayed in the castle a great deal – it was the wartime home of the two princesses – we at last felt we were doing something practical to help the war effort.

However, I am not sure how effective our methods of guarding really were. In these days of small automatic weapons, hand-grenades or bombs, it seems a bit archaic for a sentry, if he heard footsteps approaching, to call out into the darkness, 'Who goes there?' If there was more than one person the answer would then come back, 'Mr Johnston and others.' The sentry in that case would reply, 'Advance one and be recognised.' But it does seem to be inviting trouble to order a possible enemy to approach any nearer, even if the sentry has his finger ready on the trigger.

There was an hilarious occasion at Sandhurst when an officer cadet was on guard late at night and heard footsteps approaching. Of course he did not know it, but they belonged to a new officer instructor with a very long name who had only just arrived.

'Who goes there?' challenged the sentry.

'Blundell-Hollingshead-Blundell,' replied the officer from the darkness.

'Advance one and be recognised,' said the sentry.

We had various training schemes in Windsor Park and also used to guard the polo grounds there against possible parachute landings. I shared one night's vigil with the Duke of Beaufort, who was commanding a troop of the Household Cavalry. I often wonder what would have happened had the parachutists landed.

By the end of April 1940 things were hotting up in France and Belgium and one by one officers from Windsor were being sent out to join fighting battalions out there. In the first week of May Hitler started his offensive and I was among those told to get the necessary injections at once, collect my full fighting kit and report to Wellington Barracks to await orders to join the 2nd Battalion. It turned out to be quite a long wait, which was occupied by guard duties and strengthening various defences in Whitehall.

Then I got my orders to leave and said all my goodbyes.

I even proposed to a girl with whom I was friendly. Goodness knows what would have happened if she had said yes. I was in no position to marry anyone, nor was it a very good time to do so. Luckily for both our sakes she had the sense to say no.

Then came a terrible anti-climax. The BEF were in retreat and our 2nd Battalion with everyone else fell back on Dunkirk, from which they miraculously escaped without too much loss, except for all their kit. All my orders were cancelled and after a few days I was sent to Shaftesbury where the battalion now was. I found everyone exhausted after days of tough fighting and no sleep and sensed a slight state of shock that the Army had been so hopelessly overrun and beaten in its first encounter with the Germans.

The battalion had to be re-equipped, and my first job was to help in the distribution of all the stores as they arrived. We were in Monty's 3rd Division and it was being given priority to be brought up to fighting strength in order to defend the south coast against possible invasion.

It was here for the first time that I came upon a ridiculous custom of the Brigade of Guards, namely that in the officers' mess no one spoke to a newly joined officer except in the course of duty. I gather in peacetime this could go on for quite a time, but in wartime, at least in our battalion, it lasted for a fortnight. Even friends whom one had known before would avoid or cut one dead. Then suddenly at the end of the period everyone began to smile and talk and from then on could not have been friendlier. I suppose it was intended to put the new boy in his place and prevent any possibility of him getting a swollen head. But frankly it made all those who took part look not only ridiculous but boorish and bad-mannered and I cannot believe that it did anyone any good.

I wish I had known then the following story, which I should have enjoyed telling them. A newly joined officer was ordered to report to his commanding officer, who was determined to make him feel welcome and at ease.

'You'll soon settle down with us, I hope,' he said. 'We are a friendly lot and pride ourselves on making everyone feel at home in the mess. For instance, on Mondays we always have a get-together with plenty to drink. We really let our hair down, and if anyone gets a bit drunk we turn a blind eye.'

'Excuse me, sir,' said the officer, 'but I'm afraid I don't drink.'

'Don't worry about that,' said the Colonel, 'there's always Wednesday nights when we invite some of the girls from the WRAC and nurses from the local hospital to a bit of slap and tickle in the mess. Great fun. A bit of sex does no one any harm. You'll enjoy it.'

'Excuse me, sir,' said the new officer again, 'but I don't really approve of that sort of thing.'

The Colonel was taken aback and after a pause said, 'Good gracious. Are you by any chance a queer?'

'Certainly not, sir,' replied the new officer indignantly.

'Pity,' said the Colonel. 'Then you won't enjoy Saturday nights either.'

As soon as we had been re-equipped we left Shaftesbury to take up positions on the beaches near Middleton-on-Sea in Sussex, where I was thrilled to see Charlie Kunz, the pianist with the soft touch, sunbathing in front of his house. But as the danger of invasion receded we moved first to Castle Cary in Somerset, then to Parkstone in Dorset.

To start with I was put in charge of the mortar platoon, though I had never seen one fired nor in fact ever did fire one in practice as we were conserving our ammunition. For equally good reasons I was given command of the motorcycle platoon – I had never ridden one in my life! Still, I soon learned and even used to ride up a ramp and 'jump' the machine over some barrels. But I could never manage to start the wretched thing with the kick-starter, and was sometimes left stranded as I desperately tried to do so.

The platoon consisted of about twenty clapped-out second-hand machines which the Army had bought off the general public. On manoeuvres or in action I was meant to lead my platoon riding in a sidecar – the sort of machine in which you can see father taking his wife and two kids to the seaside on a bank holiday. It was our job, if the invasion came, to proceed down a main road towards the coast until we met the advancing Germans. What was to happen then was not too clear, though I had a pretty shrewd guess! We had no protective armour of any sort and the Guardsmen were only armed with rifles slung uncomfortably across their backs. I was even worse off as all I had was a revolver. We had no radio link of any sort, so if we had not been shot up first, all we could have done was to belt back up the road and warn our battalion. But on our machines we should have been pushed to get there before the Germans.

It's funny now, looking back, but rather frightening when you remember that my platoon was to be the advance guard of the crack 3rd Division on which the defence of southern England relied. In spite of *Dad's Army*, I still cannot understand why Hitler never invaded.

We thought he had on one night in September. We were playing bridge in the officers' mess when the telephone rang. The duty officer, who happened to be dummy, went to answer it and came back after a few minutes looking white and shaken. He told us it had been Brigade Headquarters who had said 'Codeword Cromwell' and then rung off. The duty officer had gone to the orderly room, looked up the files and found that 'Cromwell' meant that we were to mobilise the battalion at once and get ready to move off as invasion was either imminent or had already taken place.

I wish I could say that we did a Sir Francis Drake and finished our rubber. In fact, we all rushed into action. The battalion was scattered over a large area and, as there was no radio contact, the companies had either to be telephoned or warned by dispatch riders, who also had to winkle the Guardsmen out from pubs, cinemas and so on. In spite of apparent chaos it all worked quite well and the battalion was standing by ready to move off in about two hours. I'm still not clear what really happened that night, whether it was a genuine false alarm or a test of our mobility. Anyhow, as the advance guard, I had been sitting all night in my sidecar at the head of the battalion waiting for the 'off' and as you can imagine I was immensely relieved when we were eventually told to stand down.

In the autumn we moved to Parkstone and it was obvious that my superiors felt I would never make a good fighting soldier. From the motorcycle platoon I was sent on an MT (Motor Transport) course at Minehead, with a view to becoming the transport officer, although I was not the least technically minded. But I had a bit of luck. At the end of the course there was to be an exam which I was dreading. The night before, a friend who had been on the course with me was duty officer and, to his surprise, found the next day's questions in the in tray in the adjutant's room. When he came off duty he rushed round to me with a copy and we hurriedly looked up the answers. As a result I passed with flying colours, though ironically my friend only just passed!

On returning to the battalion I was congratulated on my report and became the transport officer. It was a good job to have. We were left very much to ourselves as everyone else knew even less about it than I did. I had a small élite staff of fitters and storemen and was never short of volunteers since we escaped most of the 'bull' and drill parades.

It was about this time that I indulged in my habit of

giving people nicknames. In a most unGuardsmanlike way I gave people on my staff such names as Honest Joe, Burglar Bill, Gandhi, the Admiral, and even extended it to the officers' mess where the mess sergeant became Uncle Tom. Uncle Tom was a lovely person and looked after us superbly. He had been a cook and made the best chocolate pudding I have ever tasted. I even indoctrinated the regular officers so that in no time one could hear the commanding officer saying, 'Another pink gin, please, Uncle Tom.' Scarcely credible, really, when you consider the traditional discipline of the Brigade of Guards. I was especially pleased with my nickname for one of my fellow officers called Neville Berry. He was known as 'The Hatchet'. (Got it?)

Our Headquarter Company was stationed in an evacuated girls' school and some of the Guardsmen slept in one of the old dormitories. We had three visits that I especially remember.

The first was from Harry Hopkins, President Roosevelt's special envoy, who was flying back to America from Hurn airport after a visit to Mr Churchill. He stayed the night in our mess and breakfasted with us on powdered eggs. He was a quiet, friendly man who looked pale and sick. He quizzed us about living conditions in Britain and showed special interest in our families and their reaction to the bombing and blackout, obviously for the benefit of his master.

The next visit was from the press, who descended on us in a public relations exercise organised by the Army. The idea was for them to see how a battalion worked, so when they came to me I decided to give them good value. I gave a lot of pennies to one of my clerks and sent him out to ring my office every few minutes from a call-box. While I was being interviewed by the press my telephone hardly stopped ringing, and as a result I got a jolly good 'press' the next day saying how hard an MT officer had to work.

Our most important visit at Parkstone was from General Montgomery – he came to inspect the battalion. We had good warning and we prepared what we thought would be an interesting display when he visited our workshops. We had an engine in the process of being taken out of a truck and we took a wheel off one vehicle and jacked up another, with a mechanic lying underneath it.

When Monty arrived I saluted and offered to show him round. But he would have none of it and hardly looked at our display. Instead, he walked straight up to one of the trucks parked near by and asked the driver to switch on his sidelights. The driver went to his cab and turned the switch. No lights came on. Monty went to the next truck and asked the driver to do the same thing. Again, no lights. To my horror, this happened twice more, and Monty in triumph asked one of the drivers why none of the lights came on. I was as eager to hear the answer as he was. The driver explained that a lot of bulbs had been pinched out of parked vehicles so that now whenever they left their vehicles they used to put the bulbs in their pockets. Monty had obviously been tipped off about this habit and wanted to put a stop to it. He told me what a bad habit it was; if there was an emergency and the driver was in a cinema or somewhere, his vehicle would have no lights if someone else was ordered to drive it. I thought I had better not make things worse by telling him that the vehicles probably would not start anyway. The reason for this was that the drivers used to immobilise them by removing the rotor arms from the distributors and putting them in their pockets too.

I remember too that at lunch Monty pointedly quizzed our commanding officer, Lieutenant-Colonel Mike Venables-Llewelyn, on how the weekly five-mile run was going. This was Monty's keep-fit campaign in which everyone in the division from the highest-ranking officers to the lowest other ranks was required to go for a five-mile run once a week. Monty must have asked the question with his tongue in his cheek as Mike had what you might politely call an ample figure and could not have run one mile, let alone five. He got away with it, but I must admit that not many of us ever did carry out the order. We used to set out from the mess at a trot looking very businesslike in shorts and gym shoes, but once round the corner and out of sight we used to go for a walk round the block and sneak back to the mess through the back door. There was not much danger of being found out. The only risk was that one might run into Mike doing the same thing!

While at Parkstone I had my first experience of a court-martial when one of my staff was due to be tried for being absent without leave. An accused man was always allowed to pick any officer in the battalion he wanted to defend him. My chap chose me, although he was going to plead guilty on the main charge. But there was a charge of losing some kit, which he denied, and he thought I might put in a good word for him and make an impassioned plea for mercy. I accepted the case, as I was bound to do, and told the court – consisting of a major, captain and second lieutenant – that my 'client' was pleading guilty on the first charge but not guilty on the second.

This brought the prosecuting officer, our own adjutant Neville Wigram, to his feet to read out a list of the kit that was said to be lost, including small items like a mess tin, knife and fork. When he had finished I thought I would try to show how trivial this charge was against the overall cost of the war and ask for it to be dismissed. So I rose from my seat and advanced towards Neville like Perry Mason used to do in the popular television series. I walked up to him, tapped him on the chest and, looking straight into his eyes, said, 'Captain Wigram, I put it to you –' But I got no further, and no one ever knew what it was that I was going to put. I am ashamed to say that Neville winked at me as I was talking and I burst out laughing and couldn't say another word. I tried to turn it into a coughing fit, went very red in the face and retreated hurriedly back to my seat, muttering something about no further questions.

When I had recovered I did get up to plead for my client, saying what a good chap he was and that there had been extenuating circumstances, taking care not to reveal what they were, as I had not the slightest idea myself. But I am afraid he had to pay for his kit. On reflection, it does seem rather rough justice that he had to be defended by an officer who knew nothing of military law, court procedure or the proper conduct of a case.

10 Technical Adjutant

IN MAY 1941 I RECEIVED two bits of news, one bad, one good. The bad news was that No. 35 South Eaton Place had been wrecked by a landmine which had fallen on the corner of Ebury Street. The Crisps, luckily, were only badly shocked and otherwise unhurt. Most of my things were salvaged, including a bottle of champagne, which, however, I never saw again. A great friend from the 1st Battalion, Nigel Baker, who was on leave at the time, went round to see how the Crisps were and, spotting the bottle, quite rightly opened it and drank to their lucky escape. The house was impossible to live in again, and for the rest of the war the Crisps looked after a retired colonel in the village of Long Crendon, near my mother.

From then on, whenever I was on leave in London I used to stay at the Savoy, a suitable base for my twice-daily visits to the theatre. But for the first 24 hours I always used to stay in my room overlooking the river and have all my meals in bed. Not only was this a much-needed rest but it was such a treat to be alone and in complete quiet. One of the worst things in war was the people and the noise. One was seldom alone, not even in the bathrooms or the loos. So you can imagine what a luxury it was to be cut off from the world for 24 hours, even if there was the occasional interruption from the bombers overhead.

The good news was that a Guards Armoured Division was to be formed and that several battalions were to be mechanised and turned into tank battalions. This meant that all that summer we went on a course at Bovington and I found myself being groomed for the job of technical adjutant. This involved learning some highly technical matters – which, of course, I never really came to understand.

The other battalions sent similar people to myself and of about the same age. I think the reason for this was that the job of technical adjutant was a vital one in a tank battalion. He did not have to be highly technical but needed to be a good organiser and administrator and able to stand up to the four company commanders, or squadron leaders as they were to become. So far as the tanks, scout cars and vehicles were concerned, the technical adjutant's word was law. If he said a vehicle was not fit for action then the squadron leader could do nothing about it.

Two of my companions on the course were a distinguished barrister called Gerald Upjohn, who after the war rose to the heights of a Lord of Appeal, and an old Cambridge golf blue by the name of William Whitelaw, of whom you will no doubt have heard. I met him again in 1971 as a minister in Edward Heath's government when the Prime Minister entertained the victorious MCC team at Number 10 Downing Street.

That day Willie reminded me of what had happened during the test we all had to do at the end of the course. We had to carry out various practical repair and maintenance jobs on vehicles and tanks. Upjohn, Whitelaw and I had been detailed to strip down an engine and then put it all together again. The stripping was easy enough, but putting it together again was a different matter. We had tried it before and knew that we would have a few nuts and bolts left over for which we could not find a place on the engine. The inspecting officer knew that this was liable to happen and that when it did people slipped the spare bits into the pockets of their overalls and pretended that the engine was complete.

Before he reached us we saw the officer asking the other teams to turn out their pockets. So Willie Whitelaw and I took out the few nuts which we had in our pockets and slipped them into Gerald Upjohn's without him knowing. When he came to us the officer looked carefully at the newly assembled engine and said, 'Very good, gentlemen. That looks fine. But just as a matter of routine will you please turn out your pockets?' Willie and I did so promptly and, of course, there was nothing there. But as it happened Gerald Upjohn had not had any nuts over. He was older and more distinguished-looking than us with fine silvery hair, and could be a bit tetchy. He resented being treated like a schoolboy and, protesting strongly that he had nothing to hide, turned out his pockets. To his horror, out on to the ground fell our nuts and bolts.

The officer could not help laughing – I suspect he knew what had happened – but 'Daddy' Upjohn, as we used to call him, was not too pleased with us. Had we been in the dock and he on the bench at that moment, I reckon he would willingly have ordered us the cat! But luckily we all passed out, and in August I reported back to our battalion at Warminster.

I was given an old civilian garage as a workshop, had a staff of about forty fitters and was responsible for the care, maintenance and repair of about 75 tanks and over a hundred trucks and scout cars. It was a splendid job as once again no one interfered with us and we were left to our own devices, so long as we kept all the vehicles 'on the road'.

I was to remain technical adjutant for the next four years until the Guards Armoured Division was disbanded in July 1945. This must be something of a record in wartime, when people are usually moved all over the place. But I was happy and I suppose the battalion must have been too. So it suited us both.

When we became armoured we all had to wear berets and I had to adopt some psychological tactics. I knew what a clot I would look in one. So on the day the berets were issued, I paraded all my staff and said, 'I have called you together so that you can see me in my beret. If any of you want to laugh – and I don't blame you if you do – you may laugh now for two minutes. But after that if ever I catch anyone laughing at me he will be put into close arrest for insolence.' It was a bit unorthodox, but they had their laugh and I never actually caught anyone laughing at me afterwards. So I suppose it can be said to have worked.

We took part in a lot of tank exercises on Salisbury Plain and in the course of these I suffered two physical mishaps. First, my scout car pitched into an old shell-hole and I smashed my face against the armour plating and severely damaged my nose. It was too big and too tough to break, but it was an awful mess and had to have a great many stitches put in it. I still bear the marks today. The other injury was more serious. We used to have to change the tank tracks or replace them if they came off and this meant lifting heavy weights. Somehow or other I ruptured myself doing this and had to have a hernia operation in the military hospital at Salisbury. (This recalled the old joke about the man who went on a holiday to Hernia Bay, stayed at a Truss House Hotel and had a rupturous time.) I was in hospital for three weeks and spent another three recuperating at my mother's cottage, where she had been housing two evacuees from London.

There was a well-equipped theatre in Warminster Barracks where Brigade HQ was situated. So, along with Alfred Shaughnessy who later wrote the TV series *Upstairs Downstairs*, I decided to put on a few shows. I did my usual cross-talk act, this time with my storeman as my stooge. We also had a first-class tenor, a young Irishman called Tom O'Brien, who really had a superb voice. But in one show his big scene was completely ruined. He was supposed to be a homesick prisoner of war in a realistic prison exercise yard with a strand of barbed-wire across the front.

This was very difficult to put up as it had to be uncoiled from the side of the stage during a blackout after a sketch.

On the night in question Tom took up his position and the pit band struck up the opening bars of *Shine Through My Dreams*, a song which normally brought tears to the eyes of the audience and received a tremendous ovation at the end. But when the curtain rose it was obvious that any tears that night would be tears of laughter. Pinned to the barbed-wire was the figure of an officer dressed in mess kit – an unlikely sight in a prison camp. It was, in fact, one of our own officers, Hugh Burge, who had been in the audience at the start but had at the last moment volunteered to stand in for an absent stagehand. He had had no time to rehearse and was just told by the stage manager to feed the barbed-wire out on to the stage. Unfortunately he got caught in it and could only stand there looking helpless throughout the song. The audience roared their heads off and there were shouts of 'Good old Hugh!', 'Why are you so stuck up?' and so on. It was more of a nightmare than a dream for poor Tom O'Brien that night.

We spent two years training with our tanks. From Warminster we went to Norfolk and trained in the battle area which was later used on *Dad's Army* for all the action scenes. It was there that we received our first Sherman tanks, with which we were later to fight.

General Paget, the C-in-C Home Forces, came to inspect us, and very smart he looked in breeches and highly polished riding-boots – but definitely not the correct gear to wear if you intend to inspect a tank. With great difficulty he climbed up on to one of the Shermans and inevitably slipped and slid right down the side of the tank. Highly undignified and very painful.

It was here in Norfolk that the first steps towards a BBC career were unknowingly taken. I was sitting in our mess one day when my friend Nigel Baker telephoned to say he had a chap from the BBC staying in his mess. He was a Canadian called Stewart Macpherson, who was attached to them to gain experience as a war reporter ready for when the second front came. Nigel asked whether they could come over to dinner, and also bring another BBC reporter who was attached to the Irish Guards for the same purpose.

Of course, I said yes, and we had an hilarious evening, which was not surprising because the second reporter was that effervescent Welshman Wynford Vaughan-Thomas. I saw a lot of them during the next few weeks and, though I did not know it at the time, this chance meeting with these two famous broadcasters was to change my whole life.

From Norfolk we went to Yorkshire and took part in a number of exercises involving many miles in the tanks and nights out in the open, even though it was still winter. We bought three white hens which we used to take out with us in a tool box on top of the cab of the store truck. They laid quite a few eggs and we had plenty of 'fry-ups' in the back of the truck.

In the spring of 1944 Winston Churchill paid us a visit and insisted on going for a ride in one of our tanks across country. This could be very rough going, but he seemed to revel in it. Wearing his black 'Derby' hat, halfway between a top hat and a bowler, he stuck his head out of the turret and tapped the driver on the head, urging him to go faster. What a man.

My job in 'action' was to travel in my scout car with the Battalion Headquarter tanks. I was in radio communication with all the squadrons and if they had a breakdown it was my task to direct one of three recovery tanks to their assistance or even go there myself if it was only a minor fault. We were kept pretty busy, especially with tanks losing their tracks.

I had a skilled signwriter on my staff and I got him to

paint a small man with two fingers raised in a Harvey Smith 'V' sign on the front of my scout car. He also painted on the name which I had chosen for it: Fujiar. These letters stood for a well-known Army expression: '-- you, Jack, I'm all right'. Fujiar soon became famous throughout the division and was to be my mobile home throughout all the fighting in Europe. It never broke down and was still going strong at the end of the war.

As spring advanced and preparations for D-Day gathered pace, Monty began to tour the country to visit as many of the 21st Army Group as possible. He liked to gather the troops all around him and give them an informal pep talk. In his 8th Army beret and battle dress he was received with tremendous enthusiasm wherever he went and always departed with the cheers of the soldiers ringing in his ears.

Except, unfortunately, when he visited the Guards Armoured Division, where his reception both before and after his talk was noticeably cool. This was not Monty's fault, though he was obviously a bit shaken by the lack of the usual reaction. But his kind of hearty man-to-man approach was foreign to all Guards' training. To them a general was a general and they expected him to behave like their idea of one. In addition, they had been waiting kicking their heels for about three hours at the airdrome where the parade was due to take place at 11 a.m. Due to typical Army panic at the thought of being late on parade most of the division had arrived soon after eight o'clock. Monty's staff had started the ball rolling by announcing that Monty would arrive at eleven; Corps HQ, just to make sure, gave orders for the division to be drawn up ready by 10.30 a.m.; Division told the brigades 10 a.m. and the battalions 9 a.m., and the commanding officers told their squadrons 8.30 a.m. So we ended up having a 5.30 a.m. reveille and a ridiculously early breakfast. No wonder we were all browned off. Even Raquel Welch would have received a cool reception in those circumstances.

Early in May we moved down the length of England to Hove where our first job was to waterproof all our vehicles. This was to protect all their essential parts, including the engine, in case they had to be driven through the sea when landing in France. There was a big build-up of tension and the whole of southern England was one large armed camp, full of troops and vehicles getting ready for D-Day, which was obviously fast approaching.

The people of Hove and Brighton were most friendly and hospitable, in spite of the way our tanks damaged their roads and pavements. We found time to play some cricket on the Hove County Ground and actually won a one-wicket victory against a team from the Royal Navy. We normally worked till late in the evening and then our adjutant, Charles Sheepshanks, and myself used to retire each night to the Norfolk Hotel where a bottle of Perrier Jouet 1928 was always waiting for us in an ice bucket. We all had the feeling that for some of us this would be the last time we should ever see England, so we decided to enjoy ourselves while we could.

11 War and Peace

ON 6 JUNE 1944 CAME John Snagge's announcement on the BBC that the invasion had started. From then on we were on permanent standby. We reluctantly gave away our three white hens but had two buckets of pickled eggs to take with us in case food was short in France.

After the initial landings, bad weather slowed down the build-up of tanks and it was nearly three weeks before we received our orders to move. One morning the people of Hove woke up to find we had gone, though I suspect the roar and rumbling of our tanks must have disturbed their sleep that night. We moved to near Portsmouth where we loaded our tanks and vehicles on to landing-craft and crossed over to Arromanches in a large convoy. After nearly three years of training and learning to be tank men, we were about to be put to the test. At last we were genuinely at war.

Things got off to a bad start. First, some of the Guardsmen on our landing-craft mistook the washbasins sticking out from the wall for something else and used them accordingly, much to the indignation of the sailors (from then on they referred to the Guardsmen as 'those pissing pongos' – so much for inter-service relations!). Then we had a calamity with our pickled eggs. We had hung the buckets from the roof of the store truck thinking the landing-craft would deposit it right up the beach. But the weather was still rough and our vehicles had to be unloaded quite a way out to sea. This meant driving down a deep ramp into the water. Our driver did his best, but when his front wheels hit the bottom the buckets swung about all over the place and the eggs flew in every direction.

We did manage to salvage a few from the bottom of the buckets and were soon eating our first fried eggs on French soil in an orchard near Bayeux. This was enclosed farming country known as bocage and was quite unsuitable for tanks, which operate best in open country. There were a few minor actions and skirmishes but everyone became very frustrated at our apparent immobility. We discovered later that Monty was deliberately using us as a sitting target to draw the fire and attention of as much of the German Army as possible. This was to enable the Americans under Patton to break out from the west right across France and so trap the German 7th Army in the famous Falaise Gap.

It was not much fun just sitting there being shelled every day, but even that was better than the division's first big battle on 18 July. This was a bloody and chaotic affair fought for much of the time in clouds of black dust churned up by our tanks. The first I saw of my very first battle was hordes of bombers going over us at dawn as we lay in the fields waiting to advance. There were two thousand of them and they were meant to soften up the opposition with their blanket bombing. It looked as if they had succeeded because as we advanced slowly through the dust thousands of bedraggled German prisoners passed us marching disconsolately back to our prisoner-of-war cages. But we were soon to meet tough opposition from some strategically placed Tiger tanks, which with their big guns knocked out nine of our tanks. Most of them blew up and we suffered the inevitable casualties, many through burning. This was our first taste of real war, and it was not much fun.

I am not going to attempt to give you a round-by-round commentary on what we did from then on. I was only the technical adjutant and, although from my own point of view I was often too damn close, I was not one of those actually fighting the battles in the tanks. They are the people best qualified to tell the tale. But I am never likely to forget those hot summer days from June to October. The heat and the dust, the flattened corn fields, the 'liberated' villages which were just piles of rubble, the refugees, the stench of dead cows, our first shelling, real fear, the first casualties, friends wounded or killed, men with whom one had laughed and joked the evening before lying burned beside their knocked-out tanks. No, war is *not* fun, though as years go by, one tends to remember only the good things. The changes are so sudden. One moment boredom or laughter, the next, action and death. So it was with us.

From the frustrations of Normandy with the Americans getting all the headlines and glory, we were suddenly given the green light to 'go'. We made a mad dash across France and Belgium and actually advanced 395 miles in seven days, with a final spurt of 93 miles in one day, 3 September, to liberate Brussels. It was exhilarating and thrilling and our good old Sherman tanks performed wonders as they tore up miles and miles of French and Belgian roads with hardly a breakdown.

The scenes of welcome and enthusiasm were unforgettable and the cheering crowds in the towns and the villages often held up our progress as they thrust flowers, fruit and eggs on to the passing vehicles. Better still, the pretty mademoiselles showered kisses on anyone they could reach – even the technical adjutant.

But it was not roses all the way. Parts of the country were still held by the retreating Germans and hard fighting took place here and there. After passing through one cheering village with the pavements lined with women, children, gay flags and bunting, we rounded a corner and came upon one of our tanks knocked out, with two of its crew lying dead beside it. So all along the route as we raced towards Brussels, joy and sorrow went hand in hand.

Brussels really went wild as our tanks roared into the city late in the evening of 3 September. Everyone was delirious; the hospitality was fantastic and there was no sleep for anyone that night. Unfortunately for us it was short-lived as we left the next afternoon, following hard on the heels of the Germans. They had left Brussels by one end as we entered it at the other and so had had no time to blow up bridges or burn important papers.

More important from our point of view was a secret store full of Krug Vintage champagne to which a friendly Belgian led us. It had been left by the Germans and we distributed a bottle apiece to the tanks there and then and put the rest on to one of our petrol lorries, which for the next few weeks went up to the tanks at night with the petrol convoy, but carried bottles instead of jerry cans.

A fortnight later our tanks made another dash, this time across Holland to capture Nijmegen Bridge. The idea was to link up with the airborne forces who had 'dropped' at Arnhem across the River Waal. As we approached the town of Nijmegen we were met by the officer commanding all the airborne troops, some of whom, like himself, had glided in on our side of the Waal. It was my cousin Boy Browning, now a Lieutenant-General. It was a dramatic moment for him as he greeted his old 2nd Battalion which he had commanded in its infantry days just before the war.

After a desperate struggle a troop of our tanks under the present Lord Carrington captured the huge Nijmegen Bridge, but alas, the planned link-up with Arnhem never took place. If this was a history of war I would try to explain why. Luckily, it isn't. But had the plan succeeded the war would probably have been over by Christmas.

As it was, we spent a cold and unpleasant winter digging our tanks out of mud and snow. It was not until the end of March 1945 that we finally crossed the Rhine and fought our way up through Germany. Although it was obvious that the war was nearing its end the Germans on our front, many of them from the navy, put up a fanatical resistance and we suffered many casualties in the last few weeks. It was a terrible time for the men in our tanks. They knew that either victory or death were just around the corner, but which would it be? For some, sadly, as I've said, it was death.

On the lighter side, I actually captured three German prisoners all off my own bat. At about 5 p.m. one evening I was going up in Fujiar to some tanks of ours in a burning village that a squadron had just taken. It was nearly dark and we were travelling very slowly when all of a sudden three grey figures rose up out of a ditch and ran towards my scout car. I had visions of hand-grenades and quickly pulled down my armoured hatch.

There were loud bangings on the side of the car and I peeped out through the visor at the side. To my relief, I saw six arms in the air and heard voices shouting, 'Kamerad.' Quickly I stuck my head out of the hatch and became every inch a true Grenadier! With signs, I ordered the Germans to clamber on to the car and we bore them back in triumph to Battalion Headquarters where I was treated as a bit of a hero until I owned up as to what had really happened.

By the last week in April the division was on the out-skirts of Bremen and Hamburg and they fell to us on 26 April and 2 May. The next day General Sir Brian Horrocks, our corps commander, paid us a visit and seemed far less enthusiastic than usual. He suggested to our commanding officer that we should take things quietly for a day or two and not attempt to advance any further. He said he wanted to review the situation. But, of course, as he told us after-wards, he knew that the armistice was about to be signed any day and he wished to avoid any unnecessary loss of life in the last few hours of the war. Still, at the time, I must admit that we thought he was getting senile and losing his drive.

We actually heard the good news on the radio on 5 May and it was amazing how calmly everyone took it. Peace. We just could not believe it. So far as I remember I went and sat on the loo out of relief. We had a few celebrations in the mess tent that night and I had a few drinks with my own boys. But the greatest treat was not having to 'stand to' at dawn for the first time since arriving in Europe. Reveille was actually put back to 7 a.m. What luxury!

It seemed strange to be at peace again. After several moves we finally settled down at Sieburg near Bad Godesburg, with our officers' mess in a large and luxurious castle, or schloss. As we travelled across Germany and drove through cities like Cologne we realised what a terrible hammering Germany had received from our bombers. The whole Ruhr was a mass of rubble and the population appeared to be in a state of shock, which was hardly surprising considering what they had been through. Whether they were Nazis or not, the death of Hitler in his bunker, the capture or death of prominent Nazi leaders and the total collapse of their country must have been shattering to a people who had been told they were invincible. They were mostly in a poor state physically and would do anything for a cigarette. But it was difficult to feel sorry for them, at any rate the grown-ups, especially after we had liberated one of the smaller concentration camps. I only looked in from the outside, but what I saw was sufficient. Fellow officers who had to go inside were physically sick. I shall never understand how human beings could have descended to such animal depths.

But it was a lovely summer and our schloss, situated high up in beautiful grounds, was very comfortable. We relaxed and enjoyed ourselves and soon began to play cricket again, mostly on matting, though we did teach the Germans to prepare one very good grass pitch.

As soon as the war was over we had been told that we were going to be turned back into infantry. This meant saying goodbye to our tanks, which we did in a giant parade in front of Monty on Rotenberg airfield on 9 June. In true Guards fashion the tank crews cleaned, painted and polished their tanks and burnished their guns. Over three hundred tanks were formed up in one long line and they dipped their guns in salute as Monty stepped out of his aeroplane. He then made an extremely complimentary speech: 'I want to say here and now that in the sphere of armoured warfare you have set a standard it would be difficult for those that come after to reach . . . You have achieved great results . . . You will long be remembered for your prowess in armoured warfare.' Not bad coming from Monty, especially after that cool reception we had given him before D-Day. It made our three years of training all seem worthwhile.

In return, the armour did him proud. As they filed past the saluting base each tank traversed its gun towards him and once again dipped in salute. The tanks then accelerated and disappeared over the top of the hill, out of sight. As they were lost to view and the roar of the engines faded away, the sound of a band could be heard. From over the top of the hill now came several hundred marching Guardsmen as a symbol that the Guards had once again assumed their time-honoured role as infantry.

I ceased to be technical adjutant after what must be a record four years and was promoted to be a major in command of the HQ Company, with special responsibility for welfare. We soon set about preparing a revue, which we called *The Eyes Have It* (the insignia of the Guards Armoured Division had been an ever-open eye). We staged the revue in a well-equipped theatre in Bad Godesburg where it played to packed houses for a week. We then spent much of the remainder of the summer touring with it round all the units of the division. It was quite an ambitious production, with a pit orchestra, professional sets and lighting. We even imported two girls from Brussels.

I am afraid many of the jokes would not pass the BBC censors, even with today's liberated outlook. Two samples. A man and girl riding a tandem bicycle came to the bottom of a hill. Said the man, 'Get off. We are going to push it up here.' Replied the girl, 'Suits me, but what shall we do with the bike?' Or a honeymoon couple were having a very late breakfast in their hotel bedroom. The bride rang the bell and ordered bacon and eggs for two and lettuce for one. 'What's the lettuce for?' asked the groom. 'I want to see if you also eat like a rabbit,' said the bride. (See what I mean?)

In November it was my turn to be demobbed and Hugh Burge (of the barbed-wire) and I gave a big party in the schloss, with band, cabaret and lashings of champagne. Tom O'Brien sang 'We'll Gather Lilacs', which brought tears to the eyes, and to the same tune Hugh and I sang a song which gained a few drunken laughs. We wrote the words ourselves, and here they are with only one (four-letter) word changed.

We'll go to England when our Age Group goes
We'll change our battle dress for civvy clothes
What we'll do then the Lord God only knows
When we come home again.

One thing is certain, there'll be no more drill
We'll hold CO's orders in the Berkeley Grill
We'll stay at Claridge's and blast the bill
When we come home again.

We'll say goodbye to all our bits of frat
Thank God our wives don't know what we've been at

We'll don again that famous bowler hat
When we come home again.

Between the hours of ten and half past three
It's in the City we shall be
With that blonde typist back upon our knee
When we come home again.

We're glad to go, but there must be regrets
For back in England no one ever gets
Four hundred marks for fifty cigarettes
When we come home again.

And when we go to bed and try to doss
We'll get no sleep, but simply turn and toss
Dreaming of nine-course dinners at the schloss
When we come home again.

We'd like to tell you in our last refrain
If our address you can't obtain
There is one place where we will meet again
When we come home once more.

And as the gentle light of dawning pales
There's one address that never fails
It's 'c/o Millie at the "Bag of Nails" '
When we come home again.

And so I returned to England to sort myself out and decide
exactly what I was going to do with my life. It was with
great regret that I said my goodbyes to all my friends in
the Guards – both officers and men. For five years they
had given me their friendship and, in spite of all the
unpleasant things we went through together, it is the fun
and laughter that I always try to remember.

For instance, I nicknamed my scout car driver Hengist.
He always had a smile on his face and was a tremendously
hard worker. His favourite expression was 'way oop' and

every year I get a card without any Christmas greeting on it. It simply reads: 'Way oop – Hengist'. That is the sort of thing which made it all worthwhile.

And about ten years after the war I received another bonus. I was motoring through Leicester, and in the Midlands and the north in those days many of the policemen were old Grenadiers. I accidentally drove up a one-way street and, as they generally do, all the drivers of the oncoming cars started to hoot and wave their arms. I went very red and stopped, and my heart sank when I saw a very tall policeman walking slowly towards my car. I could sense the drivers' feeling of pleasure that this twerp who had driven up the wrong way and was delaying them was about to be dealt with by the law.

I put my head out of my window as the policeman approached and started to say, 'Sorry, officer –' when he suddenly stopped, sprang to attention and gave me a terrific salute. He was one of my old Guardsmen and had recognised me. My long nose is useful in this respect! He then bent down and for a minute or so we discussed Fujiar, Army food and how brave we had both been, completely ignoring the waiting drivers. He then stepped back, saluted again and directed me up the one-way street. I must say I felt a bit smug as I drove past the other drivers champing at the bit in their cars. Up the Guards!

PART II:
DOWN YOUR WAY

12 Scotland

I AM HALF SCOTTISH, THOUGH which half I'm not sure! Our family crest is a pair of spurs. The story is that a Johnston was dining with friends when the butler came round with the beef course, a silver beef cover over the dish. He went straight to Johnston and surreptitiously lifted the cover. Underneath, instead of the beef, was a pair of spurs – a pre-arranged signal for 'Flee at once – the authorities are after you'. In spite of this I am very proud of my Scottish ancestors and on my visits to Scotland I sometimes wear my Johnston tartan tie. But not the kilt. I wouldn't risk that – far too draughty, though in fact my second son Andrew often wears it as he is mad keen on Scottish dancing and an expert at the reels.

I didn't go to Scotland until I was in my early twenties and then went to the Hirsel near Coldstream in Berwickshire and Douglas in Lanarkshire. This was at the invitation of my friend William Douglas Home, whose family homes these were. I always remember my excitement on waking up in a sleeper as we approached Coldstream and having my first sight of Scotland, up until then a land I had only read about, mostly in history books or Sir Walter Scott novels.

During a stay at the Hirsel in 1938 William and I went to a political meeting on Lanark racecourse. William's brother Alec, then Lord Dunglass, was the local MP and had asked Sir John Simon, then Foreign Secretary, to address the meeting. He waffled away about the Czechoslovakian crisis and how serious it was. Stabbing the air with his forefinger, he asked, 'Who knows where it will end?' William and I felt that if he, the Foreign Secretary, did not know the answer, it wasn't much good asking us!

Thanks to *Down Your Way* I have been to Scotland many times since then. At a rough guess, over fifteen years I must have visited about fifty places, large cities like Edinburgh, Glasgow and Aberdeen, and far distant places like Ullapool and the Isle of Skye. I have never ceased to be amazed at the breathless beauty of the rugged scenery. The glens, the lochs, the rivers, mountains and castles – all form part of a pattern that is so different from the rest of Britain. Some of my happiest hours in Scotland have been spent away from the hustle and bustle of the towns, talking to a gillie on an isolated moor or on the banks of a river with a raging current cascading against the rocks. Wherever one goes there is fierce national pride, coupled with a friendly tolerance of the Sassenachs and a warm welcome.

This has often been embarrassing to me, as I dislike the taste of whisky and the welcome has often been accompanied by 'What about a wee dram?' I must admit that on occasions I have managed to smuggle my tot over to my producer Tony Smith in exchange for his empty glass. But to make up for this there have always been some real Scottish delicacies to eat: smokies, bannock, Dundee cake and so on.

I am still not certain why Hogmanay is so called, nor exactly what Scotsmen do or do not wear under their kilts. Perhaps Bud Flanagan got close to the answer in his crosstalk act with Chesney Allen.

'I've just been up to Scotland. All the Scotsmen were wearing kilts.'

'Really? Did you see the Trossachs?'

'No. It wasn't windy!'

Wherever you go in Scotland you are soon made aware of their great love and enthusiasm for fishing and golf. There are golf courses and links everywhere, and children start playing at a very young age. I have been lucky to visit many famous courses like St Andrews, Troon and Turnberry. When interviewing the professional at North Berwick I actually risked driving the ball off the first tee. It didn't go very far, but at least it was straight. Just as well, really, as these delightful links run alongside the sea.

Although my surname is spelt differently from that of the 'cattle-thieving' branch of the family, we do claim part of the same crest as the Hope-Johnstons, which is also used by the town of Moffat in the valley of the river Annan. It has the feathered spur that appears on my signet ring, topped with some castellations.

When I visited Moffat with the *Down Your Way* team I met local author Molly Clavering. She knew all about the magnificent hill country around the town from years of walking and collecting material for her books. She told me about the Devil's Beef Tub, formerly called the Marquis of Annandale's Beef Stand because the Johnstones of Annandale used to drive their stolen cattle into the bottom of this immense depression, surrounded by precipitous grass hills. Another sight she recommended was the Grey Mare's Tail, nine miles to the east of Moffat, a magnificent waterfall, now owned by the National Trust for Scotland, which has a cascade over two hundred feet high. The local hills are also home to a number of birds of prey – buzzards, merlins, peregrines and even the occasional golden eagle – making the hills a favourite destination for bird-watchers.

But, as Molly reminded me, danger is never far away for the unwary. There is a mountain rescue team in Moffat, which is called out far more often than the innocent appearance of the hills might suggest from a distance. A hunting horn mounted in a case above the door of what was the Council Chamber in Moffat and a little memorial stone beside the present road to Edinburgh are reminders of one such tragedy which befell the guard and driver of a mail coach bound for Edinburgh in 1831.

The two of them left Moffat late one afternoon. Snow was falling heavily. They travelled as far as they could by coach, then abandoned it to ride through the drifts on horseback. The driver was all for turning back, by all accounts, but the guard, who had once been 'faulted' for failing to deliver the mail, insisted on pressing on, saying, 'Come ye or bide ye? I gan on.' So on they went together. Eventually the horses couldn't go any further, so they left them behind and struggled on on foot. The last thing they did was tie the mail bags to one of the snow posts alongside the road, where they were found by searchers after the blizzard had subsided. But it was several weeks before the snow melted to reveal the bodies of the two postmen.

About eighty miles north of Moffat, near Loch Earn, is the village of Comrie, which has the unenviable reputation of being Britain's earthquake centre. In days gone by the earth tremors were fairly frequent and the most violent ones could bring down gables and chimneys. Donald McNab, a retired garage proprietor, told me that he remembered an occasion in 1964 as he was chatting to a customer outside his garage when there was a definite boom followed by a thud and he felt quite a distinct movement under his feet. I asked what sort of special conditions gave warning of a quake. 'We call it an earthquake day,' he replied matter-of-factly. 'It's a humid, overpowering atmosphere and there's something between the sun and us – an intervening medium that is peculiar and yellowish.'

The reason for these alarming upheavals is that Comrie lies on a fault that runs from east to west across Scotland and seems to be at the point where the movement is most clearly felt. Comrie even has its own special earthquake house, built to measure the severity of the tremors. It is a stone structure with a slated roof, standing ten or twelve feet square. The floor is an outcrop of rock over which there is a covering of sand. Wooden pegs are driven into the sand and the earthquakes are classified according to the tilting of the pegs caused by the tremors. It may not be terribly technical, but Donald assured me that it is very effective – and who knows, it probably means more to the layman than the elaborate formulae of the Richter scale.

In Drummond Street in Comrie I found the Museum of Scottish Tartans, which had recently received the award for the best small museum in Scotland. Comrie was an old weaving village back in the seventeenth century and, situated almost right in the middle of Scotland where the Highlands meet the Lowlands, it is in an ideal location for a national museum of this sort. The museum records every known tartan – about 1,300 at the last count. There are lots of fascinating things to see and my eye was caught by a full-length portrait of the famous John Brown, which I was amused to hear was the original from Windsor Castle. In 1901 Edward VII, who hated John Brown, kicked the picture out of Windsor Castle after his mother had died; the museum subsequently picked it up for £30 and today it is worth over a thousand times that!

Anyone in search of the unusual in Scotland is inevitably drawn to Loch Ness and the so-called monster lurking in its depths. So on *Down Your Way* I was fascinated to meet Frank Searle, who established the investigation centre which provides information to Nessie seekers. When I visited him, he had already devoted ten years of his life to studying the monster. In 1969 he set up camp (literally: he lived in a tent for six years, winter and summer) and began trying to decide for himself whether 1,400 years of recorded history were right or whether the beast was really an object of entertaining make-believe.

'I found out that these animals certainly do exist,' he told me categorically. 'There's a breeding herd of them and I've seen two small ones together. The animals resemble the prehistoric plesiosaur more than anything I can come up with. They are dark grey in colour, with small heads, long necks, large bulky bodies and flippers,

119

and they are not as big as one might think from their "monster" image – perhaps up to about 25 feet long. They are fish-eaters, purely marine creatures – not air-breathing.' I had always imagined there was only one monster, but it made sense that they had to breed to keep going and, as Frank said, many people have claimed to see two of the creatures together.

The first recorded sighting of the monsters was about 1,400 years ago. 'Around the year 600,' said Frank, 'the ninth Bishop of Iona, a man named Adamnan, wrote a biography of St Columba and in this he makes several references to people of integrity living around Loch Ness seeing the water monsters.' But how did the monsters get into Loch Ness? 'I'm often asked this,' Frank said, smiling, 'and it's a very simple story. About 7,500 years ago, which is a very short time in history if you stop to think about it, Loch Ness was an arm of the North Sea. Then it was closed instantaneously by a local land upheaval in the area where the town of Inverness now stands. So it would seem that these animals were coming to and fro from the sea, using the loch as a feeding or breeding ground, as many sea creatures use the Scandinavian fjords, and some were trapped.' He went on to explain that the monsters would have to be fish-eaters because the plankton content in Loch Ness is low, and maybe that was why we saw them, because 75 per cent of the fish were within ten feet of the surface. Although he added that if you saw a Nessie for eight seconds you would have had a very good sighting.

It is not that easy to catch a glimpse of these elusive creatures. The water in Loch Ness is peat-stained and filled with tiny particles, which makes visibility almost nil. I asked Frank what happened to their dead bodies, but apparently these sink to the bottom and rest in the peat sludge; it is an established fact that no corpses ever come to the surface in the loch. In ten years Frank said he had made 31 definite sightings of Nessies, some from the bank but more from the surface of the loch, because he admitted proudly to having spent more than 32,000 hours out there in an open boat. Now that is what I call devotion to duty!

Thirty-two miles south-west of Loch Ness you reach the west coast at Fort William, at the foot of Britain's highest mountain, Ben Nevis. Looking up at the clouds that covered its 4,406-foot-high summit (4,418 feet if you stand on top of the cairn up there), it seemed incredible to me that a race is run up there every year. But on the first Saturday in September about four hundred runners set out on the gruelling ten-mile course that leads round the mountain, up to the summit and back down again. The record time when we were there stood at 1 hour, 26 minutes and 55 seconds and was set by a runner from the Lake District. The best runners seem to come from there, where they do a lot of fell running.

There is obviously a risk of exposure and other injuries in a race like this and the organisers are careful to have the mountain well manned to cope with any emergencies. There are mountain rescue teams and about forty doctors drawn from large hospitals in the region, and they are needed too. Some of the runners, particularly the tail-enders, reach the top and have to be physically turned round and pointed in the downward direction. They are so worn out and dazed that if they weren't given a little help there would be a serious risk that they would keep on running over the precipice on the other side!

Taking the Road to the Isles, or the A830 as it is other-wise known, I made my way from Fort William to Mallaig and crossed the sea to Skye. At the far end of the island stands Dungevan Castle, the home of the chiefs of the Macleod clan for over seven centuries. I didn't like the look of the sixteen-foot pit in which the Macleods of days gone by used to keep their unfortunate prisoners, but I was very taken with their splendid drinking horn and the legend attached to it.

Charlie Heron showed me around, and he told me that the horn was used by the clan chiefs when they came of age as a sign that they would be man enough to lead the clan when their time came. And to prove themselves they had to drink this horn full of claret and finish it without stopping or falling down. With obvious pride, he went on to say, 'That was carried out as recently as when John Macleod of Macleod, the present chief, came of age. He carried out the old and original custom in 1 minute, 57 seconds.' The horn holds a bottle and a quarter. I wondered what state the chief was in when he finished. 'I can say this too,' Charlie said, beaming. 'He was down at the village hall at the great celebration dance, dancing until four o'clock in the morning!'

13 The North-West

EVERY AUGUST IN THE 1930s the Eton Ramblers used to have a cricket tour in Cheshire, so I got to know the county well. Black and white magpie houses, lots of woods and meres and cattle grazing in lush meadows. It was a peaceful, picturesque county of delightful villages and its masterpiece, the old walled city of Chester, with so much evidence of the Roman occupation.

The left-handed, or anti-clockwise, racecourse is right in the town and racegoers get a marvellous view as the horses race round the oval course. I once owned one-tenth of a horse, as part of a syndicate of cricketers. The sire of the horse was Grey Mirage, so we named our horse W. G. Greys. I saw him race at Chester one day and to my delight he was leading up to the long final bend, but when the horses came out of it into the home straight, W. G. Greys was nowhere to be seen!

For the Old Trafford Tests it has become a tradition for the *Test Match Special* team to stay at the Swan Hotel at Bucklow Hill, not far from Knutsford. If not playing golf at Mere Golf Club, I usually have a picnic lunch in Tatton Park, and walk round its many acres of woodland and gardens.

Knutsford probably derived its name from a visit made by King Canute in 1017, and it provided the setting for Mrs Gaskell's novel *Cranford*. It is the only place in the world where the roads and pavements are ceremonially decorated with coloured sand. I learned this from Ray Veal, who is known locally as the Sandman. By tradition he and all the other holders of this office use very fine-coloured sand fed through a funnel to write and draw traditional messages and patterns around the town. 'It all goes back to King Canute,' he explained. 'Having forded the river he got sand in his sandals, so he sat on a rock on the other side of the river to shake it out and while he was doing this a young married couple walked by. Canute wished them as much happiness and as many children as there were grains of sand in his footwear.' I just hope he didn't have too much sand in his sandal. Now, whenever there is a wedding in Knutsford Ray writes a traditional message in sand outside the bride's house and, like a chimney sweep at a wedding, he reckons that his visit brings good luck. 'In the thirty years that I've been doing it,' he told me proudly, 'I haven't known one split up yet!'

Old Trafford itself has changed remarkably since we televised our first Test from there in 1952. We used to have a commentary box high up on scaffolding and one of the sights of the day for the crowds was Jim Swanton and Roy Webber climbing the rather precarious ladders. We once had to abandon ship temporarily when a gale was rocking the scaffolding; but we felt fairly safe so long as we had Swanton and Webber to act as ballast. It was here in 1955 that Paul Winslow of South Africa hit Tony Lock for six to reach his hundred. It was a steepling drive straight over the bowler's head and went soaring over the top of our commentary position. It was also from this high perch that we witnessed Jim Laker's incredible feat in 1956, when he took 19 wickets for 90 runs against Australia. That's a record which surely will never be broken. The ground itself now looks a picture with its gaily coloured bucket seats. We occupy a brand-new stand at the Stretford End and have a superb view as we look down from the roof of the stand.

Lancashire is wonderfully served by motorways, weaving their way round the network of industrial towns, which all seem to be joined up together. Three special favourites of mine are Rochdale, which conjures up clogs,

Gracie Fields and the giant frame of its former Liberal MP Cyril Smith; Wigan, because I now know that it has a pier; and Liverpool, because it is the home of the Grand National at Aintree. I have been twice and watched once from a box in the rather old grandstand and once down by Becher's Brook. I must say that it is terrifying to watch the horses jumping and galloping at such close quarters. It is only then that one realises how fast they go.

Down in the south of Greater Manchester is Stockport. While I was there with *Down Your Way* I heard a lot about the local ratcatcher, Ken Edwards, but I hadn't reckoned on meeting some of his prey when we called at his home. As far as Ken was concerned, being able to take home some of the rats was one of the perks of his job, though I doubt if many others saw it in that light. He kept about a hundred of them in cages in his garden, all fully checked by veterinary laboratories and treated with antibiotics, and he trained them for various purposes. For example, Ken and his rats made appearances in horror films like *The Black Death* and *1984*, in which they were trained to attack him.

With his assistant Robin (the two worked under the name 'Ratman and Robin'), Ken also took his rats to discos up and down the country, where thirty of them attacked him on stage as the last word in what he referred to as 'bad-taste entertainment'. A description with which I didn't quibble!

Back in the 1930s we used to have a lot of schoolboy fun on those cricket tours with the Ramblers. We would always visit Blackpool and I have loved the place ever since, with its miles of sandy beaches, the numerous seaside shows, the trams on the promenade, the illuminations and that fantastic Golden Mile with some of the best side-shows in the world. Blackpool's industry is to make fun for people. And how well they succeed, with their theme song of 'I Do Like To Be Beside the Seaside' played for so many years on the organ of the Tower Ballroom by Reginald Dixon. A lovely man. I once did a broadcast of a race he and I had down the Grand National Scenic Railway in the amusement park. There was a double track with each car alongside the other and the winner was the one who was least frightened and therefore braked less. Weight also helped a bit. The awful thing is I cannot now remember who won, though I was certainly heavier than Reginald.

Further up the coast, about seven miles north of Lancaster, is the railway town of Carnforth and when I went there it was on a bright October day. At one time there were three railway stations in the town: one for the Furness railway coming in from Barrow; one for the Midland railway coming in from Leeds and ultimately from St Pancras; and the third for the London North-Western railway coming up from Euston. The main railway station in Carnforth was the setting for the film version of *Brief Encounter* with Celia Johnson and Trevor Howard. The refreshment room used in the film is now the railwaymen's signing-on point.

However, my destination was Steamtown Railway Centre, a working steam museum and home to forty privately owned steam engines, including the *Flying Scotsman* and *Lord Nelson*. During the summer months several of the engines were run by British Rail on their secondary lines as tourist attractions. As a sideline, Steamtown had also developed a restoration centre and, between 1979 and 1982, they restored the ten Orient Express Pullman cars for the English leg of that famous run.

Across the A6 towards the sea I came across a very unexpected American connection in the village of Warton. I was told the story by the village policeman, Graham Parkinson, who welcomed me into his house – called, revealingly, Washington House.

It was in about 1382 that a John Washington crossed the country from County Durham, where the family originated, and settled in Warton, where his line of the family remained until the middle of the eighteenth century. George Washington, the first President of the United States, was born at Mount Vernon in Virginia and never came to Britain, but there is a legend that he remembered his English ancestry when the time came to design the American flag. The Washington family had built the tower to the church at Warton in 1460, and when this was finished Robert Washington carved a stone shield about two feet high into the stonework depicting what he claimed to be the family crest. This showed three stars and underneath them a number of stripes. Apparently this was George Washington's inspiration.

In 1976 the Washington House in Warton was presented with a full-sized American flag by a visiting US senator, on condition that it was always flown on Independence Day and on George Washington's birthday. Graham admitted that he didn't actually have a flag pole, but he made do with levering it out of one of the upstairs windows from where, he assured me, it does fly very well.

I'm afraid that my pre-*Down Your Way* knowledge of the Lake District was confined to Wordsworth, Beatrix Potter and, of course, the Lakes. But this was all from reading or hearsay. My only sad connection was the tragedy of Donald Campbell in his attempt to beat the world water-speed record in 1967 on Lake Coniston. He crashed at 328 mph in his famous *Bluebird* and his body was not recovered until more than thirty years later. I had met him at several sporting functions and found him a delightful companion. He was always calm and self-effacing, but underneath was a spirit of determination, guts and a sense of dedication. He was a man of steel and a tremendous patriot. The record he was seeking was not for himself but for England. He was also a superb driver on land and I felt very proud during one Monte Carlo Rally that he trusted me to drive his Bentley. When I went to the Lake District with *Down*

Your Way I was pleased to discover that he was still a folk-hero among the Lake people.

As a lifelong fan of Laurel and Hardy, I was also delighted to learn that Stan Laurel was born at Ulverston in Cumbria and even more delighted to find that there was a little museum in his honour full of cuttings and photographs of the famous pair. There were even a couple of bowler hats hanging up. This collection was the inspiration of Bill Cubin, another devoted Laurel and Hardy fan. Stan Laurel's birth certificate was hanging on one wall, showing that his father was a comedian, and Bill confirmed that there used to be a tented theatre near Argyll Street where Stan had been born and where his father no doubt appeared. Stan made his own stage debut in Glasgow, traditionally held to be the comedian's graveyard. But he survived the ordeal and rose to international fame in partnership with Oliver Hardy, with whom he made 104 films. Lucille Hardy, Ollie's widow, was of enormous help to Bill when he was gathering material for the museum.

William Wordsworth described the village of Grasmere, twenty miles north of Ulverston, as 'the loveliest spot that man hath ever found', and in the ten years during which he made his home there he wrote many of his greatest poems, including 'The Prelude', which he completed in 1805. Dove Cottage was Wordsworth's first house in the village, nowadays a favourite destination for fifty thousand visitors every year. George Kirby, Dove Cottage museum's curator, impressed on me the poet's passion for walking. 'The mileage was enormous,' he said, 'even by today's standards. It was nothing for him to walk to Ambleside and back [a distance of twelve miles] twice in one evening.'

Dove Cottage was originally built as a public house, the Dove and Olive Branch, and like many pubs in the Lake District a spring was diverted through the house to flow right through one of the downstairs rooms in order to provide a means of keeping the beer cool. It is still flowing through today. This is actually the only water in the house – there is no loo or bathroom.

Wordsworth was also keen on gardening – a sort of therapy for him, George reckoned. Wordsworth had a well in the garden of which he was very proud, though his sister Dorothy referred to it as a muddy pond. As George said, 'There's little doubt that William dug the well himself. No local man would have tapped a stream that dries up in the summer time.'

On the way up the stairs you pass the cuckoo clock which was the subject for one of Wordsworth's poems. 'It's a bit of a nuisance when the children block up the stairs,' George admitted, 'but it's really one of the most popular exhibits in the cottage.' Upstairs there is an extraordinary little room with newspapers all round the walls which served as the children's bedroom. It is the only room in the cottage without a fireplace and, in an attempt to keep it warm, Dorothy tried insulating it with old papers. They are all dated 1800 or 1802 and make fascinating reading.

14 The North-East

I HAVE ALWAYS BEEN TOLD that there are more acres in Yorkshire than there are letters in the Bible. Whoever carried out this time-consuming research I don't know. Nor do I know whether it is true. But no matter, Yorkshire is vast and the biggest county in Britain. And so, as you might expect, it has a tremendous variety of scenery and landscapes with the big industries of coal, steel and wool contrasting with the beauties of the wolds, moors and dales. In west and south Yorkshire especially town is joined to town without any obvious boundary. Factory chimneys, mineshafts and old mills are the main features, but always somewhere just around the corner comes a splendid view or picturesque landscape.

A Southerner has to be careful what he writes about Yorkshire. People from Yorkshire are intensely proud of their heritage and, more than those from any other county, have common characteristics: bluntness, obstinacy and toughness. But, unless one criticises any aspect of Yorkshire, they are friendly and outgoing and always give a visitor a warm welcome. I should explain why I can claim to be such an authority. I married a Sheffield girl, whose father was Master Cutler in 1936. We have been happily married for 42 years, which I hope proves my point about the friendliness and welcome.

I first journeyed north to Yorkshire in 1932. We lived in Cornwall at the time and I motored in a second-hand open Austin Seven which had cost me £17. I had several breakdowns on the way and had plenty of time to admire the countryside as I progressed slowly up the A30 and A1. I stayed with my old school friend Jimmy Lane Fox near

Boston Spa and I was soon involved in winter activities such as a Hunt Ball in Harrogate and a terrifying day out with the Bramham Moor Hunt. I remember the Princess Royal was also out hunting and came back to tea afterwards (no more name-dropping, I promise!).

Since 1952, when the opening of the Holme Moss transmitter enabled the Test matches to be broadcast on television, I have been a yearly visitor to Headingley. I have many memories of all the Tests since then, but the outstanding match was undoubtedly that sensational Test against Australia in 1981 when, thanks chiefly to a brilliant hundred by Botham and some superb hostile bowling by Willis, England won by 18 runs.

Another great friend of mine, Charles Sheepshanks, who was in the Grenadier Guards with me during the war, used to live in a large house with beautiful gardens about six miles outside Leeds. I made one of my worst jokes when staying there during one of the Tests. We were having breakfast when one of his daughters came in with her dog, which she said wanted a drink. She looked around for a moment and then said, 'Has anyone seen the dog bowl?'

'No,' I said, 'but I've seen him play some fine innings!'

About twenty miles south-west of Leeds is the town of Holmfirth, known to many people as the setting for the long-running BBC series *The Last of the Summer Wine*, which has brought a growing number of visitors to the town each year. The cast have made many friends throughout Holmfirth during the two decades or so that the series has been on the air, and most of the buildings have been seen on television at one time or another.

Perhaps less well known is the fact that Holmfirth was one of the earliest places in this country where films were made. These developed from lantern-slide shows created and given by the founder of the local firm of Bamforth's. When moving pictures arrived, he quickly cottoned on to them and began making short comedy films. These frequently involved local people as well as professional actors brought in from theatres in Huddersfield. If the scene of a bank raid was needed, for example, the local bank manager and his staff would be drafted in to take part.

The film-making side of Bamforth's business lasted until the First World War, when shortages of film brought an end to it. The end of the Great War also finished off the highly successful run of sentimental postcards which Bamforth's had developed out of their earlier lantern slides. Where sentiment died, however, comedy took over and from song cards of winsome lasses Bamforth's turned their attention to saucy seaside postcards which have been their hallmark ever since. These haven't changed greatly over the years. The ladies are still more than amply proportioned and the jokes always on the risqué side, which I adore. I love sending Bamforth's cards to my rather pompous friends and imagining the expression on their faces when they find these have been delivered by the postman!

If you go north from Holmfirth you will come to Huddersfield and then Halifax, and 'Catseye' Halifax is the telegraphic address of Reflecting Roadstuds Ltd. This gives an immediate clue to the famous product they make, those marvellous reflectors which line the centre of our roads and have saved so many thousands of lives. Percy Shaw, the inventor of the catseye, developed his idea in the early 1930s and went into production in 1935. During the war the catseye really took off when cars had to travel with masked headlights. The company was ordered to produce 40,000 a week and they haven't looked back. Even now production tops one million a year.

Percy Shaw got the idea walking home at night from his favourite hostelry in Queensbury, which was shrouded in mist for three-quarters of the year. While the trams were still running Percy followed their highly polished rails, but when the trams began to disappear, taking the tramlines with them, he decided that the time had come to do something about getting home. According to his nephew, Trevor, who runs the firm, one night Percy saw a cat sitting on a wall and also spotted a tin can shining in the gutter. As an engineer, he took these two features and set about devising a way of placing a reflector in the middle of the road. The design he ended up with is the familiar cast-iron base into which is set the rubber moulding with the little reflectors like torch bulbs, which are wiped clean by two pairs of rubber 'eyelids'. The company only buys in the raw materials and, when I was there in July 1984, there were 130 people working in the factory, making every single component in the catseye.

During the war I spent many months in Yorkshire when our battalion was stationed at West Lutton Camp and the village of Helmsley. We used to go into Scarborough for our 'recreation', and I'm afraid that we drank the cellar of the Pavilion Hotel dry. This was the hotel owned by the Laughton family, and before the war they had accumulated some superb wines. We were not too popular with the wine-drinkers of Scarborough, since the cellar could not be re-stocked during the war.

Our battalion cricket side were also lucky enough to play on the famous Scarborough Club cricket ground, and one of the pleasures of my cricket commentating life has been the festival there at the end of every season. It has a wonderful atmosphere, with the marquees, the town band and the noise of the 'naval battle' fought every afternoon on the lake below the ground. One of my proudest moments was in 1984 when I was honoured to be asked to be President, which involves hosting the lunches and teas at the festival.

Twenty miles up the coast from Scarborough, lying on either side of the estuary of the river Esk, is the picturesque seaside resort of Whitby. High up on the East Cliff its famous thirteenth-century abbey stands stark and proud, a landmark for centuries to sailors out in the North Sea, although winds sometimes reaching 110 mph have severely eroded what remains of the old abbey.

Whitby has rather eerie associations with Dracula and with the novel about him by Bram Stoker. Up on the East Cliff, just to the seaward side of the parish church, there is a stone seat very similar to the one Stoker describes his heroine Lucy sitting on while Dracula hovers round in the background in the form of a large dog. Needless to say, this seat has become known as Dracula's seat. Apparently some of the most exciting and horrific chapters in the book were written after Stoker had eaten a crab supper at Whitby and subsequently had a horrific nightmare!

As anyone interested in railways will know, Stockton-on-Tees, around the coast from Whitby, has a unique position in the history of steam trains because it was here that the world's first steam-hauled passenger train completed its first journey in 1825. That train had set out from Shildon in County Durham. Shildon was the place nearest to the coalfields of southern Durham from which a railway could be built to the sea with no uphill gradients, allowing either horses or steam engines to pull an economic load down to the port. This first train was pulled by the *Locomotion* and consisted of one passenger coach and fourteen coal wagons, which ended up carrying six hundred passengers by the time they reached Stockton. At top speed the train reached 5 mph.

In my ignorance I had always associated George Stephenson with the first locomotives. Standing in Shildon, that was tantamount to sacrilege! Stephenson did indeed build the *Locomotion*, but the first successful locomotive to be more economical than a horse was built in Shildon by Timothy Hackworth. He was the first railway engineer of real standing, and if you go to Shildon you can visit his house, which has been turned into a very attractive museum near the town's station.

Before I started on *Down Your Way* in 1972 I seldom had occasion to visit the north-east of England. But from what I saw on the way to Scotland I particularly enjoyed Northumberland, with the sea and ragged coastline on one side and the moorland and valleys on the other. Back in August 1934 I was invited to stay for a cricket match at Beaufront Castle near the old market town of Hexham, famous for its ancient abbey, and I remember learning that the castle was one of the many which had been built originally as fortresses against the Scots.

Since 1972 I have been to Northumberland many times. The most northerly town I have visited in the county, and the most northerly town in England, is Berwick-upon-Tweed, that tiny English enclave that lies across the river on the Scottish bank. Berwick has changed hands between the English and the Scots at least fourteen times in its history. Richard, Duke of Gloucester, later Richard III, captured it in 1482 for the English, who have retained it ever since – up to a point, as the people of Berwick are quick to remind you! It is the home of the King's Own Scottish Borderers, who have their headquarters in a splendid set of barracks, the oldest in Great Britain, built by Sir John Vanburgh in 1717. Here they have a smashing regimental museum filled with all sorts of uniforms, weapons, drums and regimental flags.

One unexpected item with a nice story attached to it is the Mons tablecloth, which carries the embroidered signatures of at least a hundred officers. They had all just enjoyed a cup of tea in a little coffee shop outside Mons in 1914 when the two elderly ladies who ran it came up and asked if they would autograph the tablecloth, which they duly did. Come the end of the war one of those officers, who had risen from major to brigadier during the four years of fighting (showing just how many had been killed), found himself back in the same coffee shop. The two ladies produced the tablecloth once again and asked him to sign it a second time. They had spent their war carefully embroidering all the signatures, and once the brigadier's had been embroidered they gave him the tablecloth, which is now among the museum's most treasured possessions.

15 Wales

WALES HAS ALWAYS BEEN A bit of a mystery to me. It is a land of fantasy, song, strange customs and unpronounceable place-names. The Welsh are fiercely and passionately proud of their country in a way no Englishman ever shows that he is proud of England. The Welsh relationship with England is not unlike the love–hate feelings which Australians have for Great Britain. Think of Wales and you see in your mind mountains and valleys, mine-shafts, coal tips and innumerable castles. You can hear male-voice choirs, rugby crowds singing and the bards and poets at the eisteddfods. And in spite of the inroads made by mining and industry, Wales has some of the most breathtaking scenery in the United Kingdom. Breconshire is a special favourite of mine.

So it has always been an adventure to step over the border into Wales. There is something different about it. But the welcome is warm and friendly, and I only have happy memories of my visits. The first one was in 1927 when I went to stay with some friends at Llysdinam Hall near Builth Wells for a cricket match. I remember that I had to change trains at a junction with the exotic name of Three Cocks. We played the match in a permanent drizzle, and at the end of the game our host proudly said how lucky we had been that the rain had held off and that we'd had such a nice fine day! I must admit that whenever I go to Wales, it does seem to rain rather a lot.

The following year I went to stay with a school friend, John Scott-Ellis, at Chirk Castle, the first time I had ever slept inside one. It had been, and still is, a family home since the early fourteenth century. It is set on a hill surrounded by parkland and was my first experience of a stately home. I was allowed to try to shoot grouse on the moors. At the end of the day around the dinner table everyone was saying what their bag for the day had been. When it was my turn I had to blushingly confess that my bag was nil.

During the war we took our tanks by train from Warminster for shooting practice at Linney Head on the lovely Pembrokeshire coast. It was 1943 and the weather and scenery were gorgeous. The tanks were actually broader than the railway wagons on which they travelled and we were told that the railway people had to make sure that two trains carrying tanks never passed each other – otherwise there would have been an almighty crash.

When I joined the BBC after the war my Welsh visits became more frequent. There was cricket commentary both at Cardiff and Swansea, where on one occasion we operated with just one camera – nowadays they have six or eight at Test matches. But, sadly, I never went to a Glamorgan match at Ebbw Vale in the heart of the mining area. It is claimed that a batsman was once patting down the pitch there when he heard a tapping in answer coming from underneath his feet.

This reminds me of the only cricket pitch in the world – so far as I know – which has an elephant buried underneath it! I discovered this at Queen Elizabeth's College in Carmarthen. The playing field, known as the Prisoners' Field, was given to the school by the gaol authorities, but at some time in its history it also played host to a visiting circus. Unfortunately one of the circus elephants died during the Carmarthen stop-over and was buried under what is now the square. No one has ever found any trace of it, but I gather that the difficulties they have in creating a decent wicket do seem to confirm its presence!

Laver bread is a delicacy associated with this part of Wales. When *Down Your Way* visited Laugharne, which lies on the estuary of the river Taf to the north-east of Tenby, I met Elliot James, who had made part of his living collecting the seaweed from which laver bread is made. The seaweed itself is much smoother than the sort of coarse weed I am used to seeing and it is quite distinct from any other. It is also quite scarce and you have to travel a long way to find it. To be honest, the laver bread served in my hotel looked more like mince than bread, but Elliot told me that it is a traditional breakfast dish in Wales, served with bacon or a sausage, or anything else that takes your fancy in the frying pan!

For many visitors Laugharne's greatest attraction lies in its connection with Dylan Thomas, who spent the last five years of his short life in the boathouse below the cliffs. Walking to this little whitewashed house, you pass the small work-shed where he spent the most prolific period of his life, writing some of his most famous works, including *Under Milk Wood*. The views from this little hut and from the house are wonderful. Now that both are owned by the local authority, visitors are able to attend poetry readings on the patio on summer evenings, enjoying the scenery which gave Dylan Thomas himself inspiration and reliving his life in Laugharne through his verse.

Dylan Thomas died in America when he was only 39, and his body was brought back to Laugharne to be buried in St John's churchyard, his grave marked by a simple wooden cross that overlooks the estuary, where the herons he used to watch and write about can be seen on most days walking across the sands at low water.

To my way of thinking there is nothing quite as Welsh as the eisteddfod, and the International Musical Eisteddfod has been held in the town of Llangollen since 1947. According to Nowel Bowen, the chairman of this truly international event, the founders' aim was 'to bring about a level of understanding, respect and tolerance among the people of the world, particularly among those who had been fighting one another for five long, dreary years'. Ten countries were represented at that very first event, which was held in an ordinary marquee on the recreation ground. But in 1957 the organisers had the opportunity to purchase the present-day site, a field peacefully grazed by sheep when I saw it in the middle of June 1981. It is a steep field, ramped upwards from the stage area a distance of 75 yards to the top of the auditorium. The marquee that covers this area looks like an enormous aeroplane and, with its two wings measuring a couple of hundred feet from one side to the other, it is able to hold up to nine thousand spectators. Now up to 34 countries take part and the event lasts five days, filled with competitions and forming an endless chain of musical entertainment.

In the town of Llangollen I came across a sign advertising the premises of Charles Day, a goldsmith. I was visiting the area only a few weeks before the wedding of the Prince and Princess of Wales and, knowing that the then Lady Diana Spencer's ring was said to be made of Welsh gold, I was interested to learn exactly what that was. Charles told me that Welsh gold is mined in a little mine near Dolgellau in Gwynedd and the actual quality of the ore is extremely rich. South Africa will mine down to perhaps one-tenth of an ounce per ton, which is almost invisible in the ore, whereas Welsh gold can be as high as five hundred ounces to the ton, which is the richest yield in the world. Because of its scarcity and the fact that it is all hand-processed from beginning to end, Welsh gold commands a premium over worldwide gold of about 25 per cent.

One of my favourite places in Wales is the holiday village of Portmeirion in Gwynedd. It is an architectural feast of colonnades, pavilions, towers, domes and statues set against a steep wooded hillside on a lovely promontory covered with sub-tropical gardens. Portmeirion has become famous internationally as the location for the 1960s television series *The Prisoner* starring Patrick McGoohan, but the village was the creation of the architect Sir Clough Williams-Ellis, who started work on the site in 1925. There are no permanent residents, but at the bottom of the village is the delightful Portmeirion Hotel, where I met Sir Clough's widow, Lady Williams-Ellis.

She explained that her husband had set out to prove that you could develop a beautiful site without spoiling it. He was a conservationist, but not a conservationist who believed that you should freeze everything and never make any changes. The site had belonged to an uncle of his who had leased it to a woman who had lived on the promontory as a complete hermit. During her stay the grounds had become so overgrown that when she died a man with an axe had to walk in front of the hearse clearing a way through the undergrowth to reach the house. In fact, Portmeirion had become so completely cut off by vegetation that in spite of living only six miles away Sir Clough had never explored it. Instead, in his attempt to find the right site for the creation of his architectural dream he searched all over the world, including islands off the coast of New Zealand. When he finally ventured into Portmeirion, of course, he knew immediately that he had found what he had been searching for.

Once it was appreciated what he was doing, other sympathetic people began offering buildings that were being demolished in different parts of the country. Some, like a colonnade originally erected in Bristol and delivered to Portmeirion as numbered stones on the back of a lorry, could be accepted; others, like the Euston Arch, were clearly too large for Sir Clough's scale and had to be politely declined. Portmeirion became affectionately known by its creator as 'a home for fallen buildings'.

Walking around, there is strong evidence of the influence that Italy had on Sir Clough – the village of Portofino in particular. But the outdoor frescoes you see, and the use of ironwork, also suggest the important role Bavarian architecture played in his conception.

I asked Lady Williams-Ellis whether her husband was satisfied when he had finished. For instance, did he want Portmeirion to grow? She told me, 'What he said was, "I don't want it to get any bigger. It's a nice agile little mouse and I don't want it made into a great big cow." ' Well, it certainly isn't a cow. Like most visitors before me, I found it quite enchanting.

One of my most outstanding memories of Wales was the day when the Barbarians beat the All Blacks at the old Cardiff Arms Park. The celebrations went on long and noisily in the clubhouse after the match – so much so that a sporting quiz which we were recording there for a later broadcast was not an outstanding success. The audience, armed with pints, seemed to want to sing rather than listen to the quiz. But in those days a packed Cardiff Arms Park, especially when the home side won, was surely the most typical and inspirational example of the fervour and national spirit of the Welsh.

In the town of Monmouth I came across a rather unexpected museum devoted to Admiral Lord Nelson – unexpected to me at least, because I didn't know that he had any connection with the town. However, Andrew Helme, the museum's curator, explained that Nelson made a couple of visits to Monmouth one year, most probably to see the naval temple built on a hill outside the town – at that time the only naval war memorial in the country. Today the temple belongs to the National Trust and is open to the public. The nearby Forest of Dean was also an important source of ship-building materials and Nelson wanted to see what the stock of timber looked like. He couldn't have thought very much of it because he wrote a scathing report afterwards.

The museum's collection really began to be amassed

after the centenary of the Battle of Trafalgar, in 1905, and dozens of mementoes from Nelson's life are to be seen. There are interesting details about his appearance from the many pictures of him. For instance, he is often thought of as wearing a patch over his right eye, but in fact he never lost this eye. The wood splinter that blinded him at Calvi detached his retina, but the eye was never removed. Nelson was also a small man, somewhere between five feet three and five feet four and a half. His height is marked on one of the museum's cases for children to measure themselves against. After losing his right arm at Tenerife he had difficulty in drawing his sword from its scabbard. In the museum you can see his service sword, the only genuine fighting sword of his that exists, which has had six inches cut off the end to make it easier for him to draw with his left arm.

If you are motoring through Wales and happen to be keen on books, Hay-on-Wye on the Welsh border is a Mecca for book enthusiasts the world over and the only town in the world with second-hand books as its major industry. Richard Booth, who masterminded the book trade in Hay, told me that his shops stock in the region of a million books on a total of fifteen miles of shelves. To my surprise he said that his principal source was the east coast of the USA, which he visited half a dozen times a year to buy stock. By the same token, American visitors form a substantial portion of his trade, so many of the books find their way back to the States from Hay.

Among this vast range of stock there are still real treasures to be found by the canny searcher. Richard cheerfully admitted that his shops frequently sold books for a few pounds which were sold later in auction rooms for several hundred pounds. He quoted the case of a book of old Canadian letters found in a dustbin which was sold in Hay for a pound or two and later made five hundred in a saleroom. Someone else found a James Joyce manuscript in an old grammar which they bought for a pound in Hay and sold for £1,500 at auction. As Richard admitted, 'I'm afraid that in the second-hand book business the customer's much cleverer than we are.'

I asked why he had chosen Hay, miles from anywhere. 'I think it's very important that somewhere in the world there's one town where the bookshops are bigger than the supermarkets,' he answered. 'In a way, Hay's got a bigger market than London: it's got the whole of the south-west and Bristol, and the whole of the Midlands and Birmingham, and buyers have a beautiful drive of an hour and a half over the Welsh hills to come to the book town.' I must say I can't think of a more pleasant way of hunting for second-hand books.

It would be wrong to leave Wales without recalling some of my many Welsh friends who have brought so much laughter, enthusiasm, exuberance and effervescence into my life. People like Cliff Morgan and the much missed Wynford Vaughan-Thomas, Alun Williams, Peter Jones and Harry Secombe. They were all a joy to meet and always brought with them a tremendous feeling of fun, laughter and friendship. What's more, they could all talk more than me – which is saying something.

16 The North Midlands

SHROPSHIRE IS A BEAUTIFUL COUNTY, said to have been the spot which P. G. Wodehouse chose for Blandings Castle. I have personal reasons for liking it. My son Andrew and his family live in the county and they had a delightful country wedding there in July 1986. My youngest daughter Joanna also spent three very happy and productive years at Derwen College for the Disabled just outside Oswestry. I cannot speak too highly of what they did for her and it was always a pleasure to find an excuse to visit her – especially as there is now a motorway to Shrewsbury instead of the narrow, crowded A5.

Shrewsbury is one of the most attractive county towns in Britain, with the river Severn, views of the Wrekin and lovely old black and white timbered buildings. About twenty miles south-east of Shrewsbury is Bridgnorth, where back in the Middle Ages there used to be a castle dating from the eleventh century. But Oliver Cromwell captured this during the Civil War and blew it to pieces. All that is left today is one tower which stands two hundred feet high and leans at a precarious angle of seventeen degrees – considerably more than the Leaning Tower of Pisa!

A visit to Bridgnorth is a real feast day for railway enthusiasts, and on *Down Your Way* we used to find it very difficult to resist anything to do with steam engines. So I was delighted to find the Severn Valley railway alive and well and still running, despite railway nationalisation and the cuts made to the rail services by Dr Beeching. This is a private railway run almost totally by volunteers, who man the locomotives, sell the tickets, clean the carriages, work the signals and carry out most of the maintenance and repairs to the permanent way as well as the rolling stock. In addition there is a small core of full-time staff who perform the essential administration and commercial functions. Together they operate over twelve and a half miles of track between Bridgnorth and Bewdley, where the line is connected to the British Rail network at Kidderminster.

Here we found a fleet of 34 locomotives, nearly half of which are operational at peak times in the season. These cover all types and classes from 4-6-0s down to tiny little shunting engines. Sadly, they don't have any of the old Great Western King class locos, the biggest and the best. I was told they couldn't get a 'King' over the bridge. The pride of the operation is the Severn Valley Limited Wine and Dine Train, which offers a first-class four-course meal in the hour it takes to travel from one end of the line to the other. My eyes lit up at the thought of this very agreeable way of passing a journey through such lovely countryside.

Staffordshire to me means pottery, especially the Toby Jugs and those lovely blue and white mugs with top-hatted cricketers on the side. It is also where our racehorse W. G. Greys was trained by Reg Hollingshead at his stables at Rugely. It actually won once or twice!

My first visit to Stafford was during the war, when as a technical adjutant I was sent up to English Electric, who were then making the Covenanter and Crusader tanks that we were using. I was told a story about their new public relations officer, who shall remain nameless as he has since denied the story. Anyway, he was on a short list for selection as PRO and there was to be a final appearance before the board in which applicants would be required to make a short speech to prove that they could speak well. Much would depend on their clarity and delivery. Just before it was his turn to go into the boardroom he went to spend a penny and thought he would give a final clean to his false teeth. So he took them out, but he was so nervous that he dropped them down the loo. He only had a minute or so before he was due. So what could he do? What would you have done? All I can say is that no one knows exactly what he did do, but he passed the test and got the job!

It was during the last war that the Air Ministry took over one of the old gypsum mines at Tutbury, a few miles from Burton-upon-Trent, to use as an underground bomb store. On 27 November 1944 one small section of this blew up. Estimates put the total of explosives at four million pounds of TNT, making this the largest man-made explosion in history to that time (the atom bomb the following year was to eclipse it, of course). When I visited Tutbury with *Down Your Way* I was told that structural damage was recorded as far away as Burton and there was considerable damage in Tutbury itself. The gypsum workings were completely blown away and in all about ninety people were killed. Today the crater – half a mile wide and a hundred feet deep – lies just behind the new mine.

I always think that Derbyshire offers more variety than any other county. There is the spectacular scenery of the Peak District National Park, the peaceful beauty of the Dales of Darley and Dove, the river valleys, the cliffs of Matlock, the caves and potholes of Castleton, the Blue John stone which makes such fine jewellery, the stately homes, the crooked spire of Chesterfield, Bakewell tarts and the busy industrialism of Derby itself. I have fond memories of one of the best and most beautiful cricket grounds in England – Queen's Park, Chesterfield. I'm not so fond of the old racecourse ground at Derby, though it has been much improved recently, but on a cold day it can be distinctly draughty! We all know the story of the horse which went automatically to the roller when the number eleven batsman went in to bat. But at Derby it is more up to date. The groundsman actually starts up the engine on the roller and sits there waiting – usually not for long.

The spa town of Buxton will always be famous in the cricket world. In the long hot summer of 1975 the county match against Lancashire was stopped by a snowstorm, on 2 June!

I have always had a special liking for the city of Nottingham. It's a vibrant place full of life and contains so much in the way of entertainment, sport, education and industry. Like most boys I first got to hear of it from the Robin Hood legend, where the Sheriff of Nottingham was a particularly nasty 'baddy'. There is still a sheriff. I met him recently and am glad to report that he bears no resemblance in character to his predecessor.

My first real acquaintance with the city came in 1950 when, because the transmitter at Sutton Coldfield had just opened, BBC TV were able for the first time to cover a Test match at Trent Bridge. I remember it well. It was against that great West Indies side, with Ramadhin and Valentine causing so much havoc with their contrasting spin. West Indies had just won their first ever Test match in England at Lord's, where there were the famous scenes of calypso singing and dancing in front of the Pavilion. They won again at Trent Bridge, thanks largely to a magnificent partnership of 283 in 210 minutes by Weekes and Worrell. After Lord's, which is something special, Trent Bridge has always been my favourite Test ground. It is a friendly place with a warm welcome for everyone and, as it is so compact, one has the feeling of being in the game among the players. Its famous landmark, Parr's Tree, is now, alas, no more, being the victim of a gale. It was chopped up and made into little miniature cricket bats, which were sold for charity.

I mustn't forget the rest of the city, with its theatres the Playhouse and the Theatre Royal, the two football league clubs both adjacent to Trent Bridge, the rowing on the Trent and the racecourse. Truly a city of variety.

Along with its cricket and *Down Your Way* connections, Leicestershire brings to my mind magnificent hunting country, Stilton cheese and pork pies. When travelling in a train through Leicestershire I often look out of the window and imagine myself following one of their famous packs of hounds. It's fun to pick the spots where I would try to jump the fences. From the safety of a railway carriage and not in the saddle, I usually choose the most terrifying of jumps. From the eighteenth century onwards Melton Mowbray has been the Mecca of English fox-hunting, attracting in its heyday the crowned heads of Europe together with the leading lights of the British aristocracy.

It wasn't only in the hunting field that they enjoyed their sport. Melton was the birthplace of the expression 'to paint the town red', a turn of phrase which came into being after a former Marquis of Waterford and a group of companions, who must have been feeling at a bit of a loose end one evening, hit on an unusual pastime. Starting at the Tollgate at one end of the town, they worked their way through Melton Mowbray with red paint and brushes, literally painting everything red – including the watchman. This didn't please him greatly, as one might imagine, and the Marquis and his friends spent the rest of the night in Melton gaol for their trouble.

By the time the Marquis of Waterford got up to his antics Melton Mowbray had already established itself as the centre for the making of Stilton cheese, which derived its name from a village on the old North Road just to the south of Peterborough. The story goes that a farmer's wife in Wymondham, a few miles east of Melton Mowbray, used to make this cheese with its distinctive blue veining and strong taste and supply it to her brother who was landlord of the Bell Inn at Stilton. Travellers staying at the inn spread word of the delicious cheese that they had eaten there and the cheese became known thereafter by the place where it was first sold.

Melton Mowbray's famous pork pies developed as a direct result of Stilton cheese-making in the 1830s. Local pigs fed on the whey, which was a waste product of the cheese industry, and gradually acquired a slightly different flavour from the pork products in other parts of the country. The hunting fraternity gained a taste for this pork and the pies made from it and it wasn't long before the demand for Melton Mowbray pork pies had spread to London.

The ingredients of a Melton Mowbray pie are deliciously simple: pork, salt, pepper and pastry. To make a pie the pastry is raised up a block rather like the side of a jam jar and the meat is put into the hole in the middle. A lid is put on top of this and the pie is baked. These are the various stages, but making a Melton Mowbray pork pie is a little more time-consuming than it sounds, because between each stage the pie has to be cooled in a fridge to prevent the pastry losing its shape. The last ingredient to be added is the jelly, which is poured in through a hole in the top of the pie while it is still hot. This serves two purposes, I gather: it keeps the meat moist, but more importantly it keeps air out of the pie and prevents mould forming on the meat – quite the opposite to the process of making Stilton cheese, in fact.

Until my sister Anne went to live in Lincolnshire I thought that it was all flat, but I found her house right on the edge of a high windy escarpment looking down on the city and a wide fertile valley. Of course, most of Lincolnshire is flat, with long straight roads and ditches and canals. Much of it is only just above sea-level and over the years a wonderful job of drainage has been carried out. There are acres and acres of rich dark soil ideal for agriculture and horticulture. Sugar beet, potatoes, peas, vegetables of every kind, flowers (especially tulips) and fruit – I associate them all with Lincolnshire. And I must not forget the many airfields, especially Scampton, once the base for the famous Dambusters and now the headquarters for the Red Arrows – the best aerobatic and formation team in the world.

In contrast to the fens is the wooded spa town of Woodhall Spa, strangely continental in appearance with its tree-lined roads. I used to stay there during the weekends of Trent Bridge Test matches and was particularly struck by the cinema in the woods – the only one I know so situated.

The coastline offers another contrast, with Grimsby in the north and a number of holiday resorts to the south, such as Cleethorpes, Mabelthorpe and Skegness. They certainly live up to their reputation of being 'bracing' and I always pack a sweater whenever I go there.

Lincolnshire is one of the largest counties in England and you will probably see more windmills there than anywhere else. You get the impression of the Dutch influence wherever you go and when you turn right off the A1 it is the beginning of a journey into a very different part of England.

17 The West Midlands

I WAS LUCKY ENOUGH TO GO to New College, Oxford, so I know the city and the surrounding countryside well. I had a wonderful three years at the university, but I'm afraid I played more than I worked. Cricket and rugby were my games and all the colleges had wonderful grounds. In the summer we used to have a minor boat race, supping at the Trout Inn and then racing down to the boat-houses. I always stroked my eight, as I found it easier to keep in time with the others. So I have many happy memories of Oxford and, although I had to cut down my cricket to four days a week, I managed to get a third-class degree in history. Now, alas, about the only date I can remember is 1066.

A few miles north-west of Oxford lies the village of Woodstock and the magnificent Blenheim Palace. It was following John Churchill's historic victory at the Battle of Blenheim in 1704 that Queen Anne made him Duke of Marlborough and presented him with the former royal hunting park and the funds to construct the splendid palace we see today. Work on the palace continued until 1722, which isn't surprising when you consider that there are in the region of 365 rooms. A century and a half later, on 30 November 1874, Sir Winston Churchill was born at Blenheim, in a room which had been formerly occupied by the first duke's private parson. Small as it is, this room is one of the principal attractions for the thousands of visitors that come to the palace every year.

When I visited Blenheim on *Down Your Way* the present Duke of Marlborough told me that his late father wrote to Sir Winston when they were about to open the house, asking if there was any clear indication of how and why he happened to be born there. 'There were two stories going around,' said the Duke. 'One that Lady Randolph was out with a shooting party in the park and, being bumped around in her carriage, felt unwell and came back. Another theory is that there was a ball going on at Blenheim and, again, she felt unwell and was taken into this room.' The old Duke received this reply from Sir Winston: 'Although present on that occasion I cannot recall the facts leading up to it!'

Inside the room there are one or two mementoes of the famous event that took place there. Sir Winston's baby vest is on display, together with some of the curls trimmed from his head when he was five, and over a looking-glass is a letter from his father, Lord Randolph Churchill, to the local doctor, Mr Taylor, thanking him for his 'careful attention to her ladyship during her confinement'.

The grounds and lake surrounding Blenheim Palace were landscaped by Capability Brown, who created the wonderful vista as you enter through the triumphal arch from Woodstock. According to his Grace, it has been described as 'the finest view in England'.

Moving westwards from Woodstock into the lovely valley of the river Windrush, you come to the popular tourist destination of Burford, sometimes called the Gateway to the Cotswolds. It was there that I met Bob Arnold, who for nearly half a century was known and loved by millions of radio listeners as Tom Forrest of *The Archers*. Sadly, Bob died in 1998, at the age of 87. When I met him in Burford, he told me he had been born just over two miles down the valley in the little village of Asthall, where his father ran the local pub. 'It had its advantages and disadvantages,' he said, when I asked what it was like as a boy brought up in a pub. 'One of the disadvantages was that I had to go to bed very early. My bedroom was right above the tap room and these dear old boys, they'd got no entertainment – the gramophone was a luxury; radio didn't exist – so night after night they used to sing the same old songs, droning away. I couldn't go to sleep, so I had to learn those songs as they sang them.' And those were the songs we heard Tom Forrest singing all around Ambridge for so many years.

It seemed to me that whenever I listened to *The Archers* Tom was always on it, but Bob reminded me that for four weeks he was absent from the programme while on remand in prison. 'I shot a poacher,' he explained. 'Terrible accident, but he died and Tom was put in gaol until the case came up. Regrettably, I had to stay longer than I should have done because one of the scriptwriters realised the Easter recess was on and Tom would have to wait until there was another court. Listeners sent postal orders along. They started a fighting fund: "Get this man out, he's innocent." I remember when the wife and I were in Witney shopping one day, a lady in the street stopped in her tracks and said, "What is thee doing? I thought thee was supposed to be in prison."

'I had to think very quick, and said, "And so I am."

' "Well, what's thee doing out here, then?"

' "It's a bit cold up there today," I replied, "they've got no coal, so the sergeant says to go and have a walk round and get myself back in half an hour."

' "Well, wasn't that good on him," she said, and off she went!'

Gloucestershire, Herefordshire and Worcestershire form a triangle in the West Midlands. For four years from 1924 to 1928 my family lived in the middle of this triangle, in the quaintly named village of Much Marcle. It was in the heart of lovely countryside, with the apple orchards for the cider and the hop fields for the beer. We used to take part in all the village activities and even had the audacity to have a family jazz band with my mother 'on the keyboard'. We lived a typical country life, with the village cricket, rat-hunting and even the occasional 'day' with the rather posh Ledbury Hunt.

One of the main attractions at the meets was the Master's wife, a beautiful lady riding side-saddle and dressed in an immaculate blue riding-habit with top hat and veil. She was none other than the famous musical comedy actress Lily Elsie of *The Merry Widow* fame. She had married Major Ian Bullough, the Master, and felt no doubt that she should support him. But she didn't take a very active part in the hunt and often disappeared after trotting down the road to the first covert.

There were some beautiful houses, one of them called Stoke Edith in Herefordshire. It was the only house I knew which had its own fire-engine, but ironically it had a big fire and was burned down.

We used to go to Gloucester to watch rugger and to Cheltenham for cricket. It was there in 1926 that I saw the Australians for the first time in their baggy green caps. I can especially remember Jack Gregory bowling fast, the gnome-like Clarrie Grimmett bowling his round-arm leg-breaks and googlies, and the 'Governor-General' Charles Macartney perfecting delicate late cuts.

In later years, whenever I did cricket commentaries at Bristol I used to stay at the Ship Hotel at Alveston because I could look out of my bedroom window over the cricket ground on which W. G. Grace played. So when *Down Your Way* went to the nearby village of Thornbury I took particular pleasure in revisiting the hallowed spot in the company of Derek Hawkins, who played for Gloucestershire in the 1950s. He told me that Thornbury Cricket Club moved to the ground in 1871 when the two existing cricket clubs in the town amalgamated. Dr E. M. Grace was the first captain of the club. He was also captain of the national side, as well as being secretary, so he had a busy cricketing life. W. G. was his younger brother and he played at the Ship at Alveston as a guest for Thornbury on half a dozen occasions. And since those first two Grace brothers a further 25 members of the family have played for the club, including Dr E. M. Grace's son, who was also initialled E. M. and also a doctor. Derek recalled fielding for him as a youngster. The doctor used to nip off for the evening surgery, which consisted of some fairly swift consultations, as you might expect!

And then, of course, there is Worcester, with its beautiful ground in the shade of the cathedral, dominated by the Foster family. Seven brothers played for the county, four of them together in one match, so that the side became known as Fostershire.

It is said that whereas the Battle of Waterloo was won on the playing fields of Eton, the Battle of Britain was won on the playing fields of Malvern College, where the Royal Signals and Radar Establishment moved to develop radar at the start of the Second World War. Malvern is also famous for its water, about as pure as you can get it. The oldest records of the special properties of Malvern water go back a good nine centuries. The purity of Malvern water is such that it is practically balanced between acid and alkaline; it will not change the colour of litmus paper. To prove the point, I was told a delightful rhyme:

'Malvern water,' said Dr John Wall,
'Is famous for containing just nothing at all.'

Warwickshire represents hunting and cars for me. In the 1950s it was the heart of the Rootes empire, which made Humbers, Hillmans and Sunbeams. At that time I used to report on the Monte Carlo Rally and got to know all the motor-industry people. One year Sheila Van Damm won the ladies' prize in a Sunbeam Talbot and there was much celebration in the English camp, with champagne corks popping freely. Rather unfortunate timing as it turned out.

Rootes were going through a financial crisis and had sent their financial director down to Monte Carlo to see where economies could be made, especially in the hospitality field. We were in the middle of an uproarious party when in walked a gentleman, straight from London in his pin-stripe suit. There was a nervous silence as he entered, as we had been warned he might be coming. Norman Garrad, the chef d'équipe of the Sunbeam Team, said, 'Gentlemen, I would like to introduce to you our financial director, Mr Goat.' I admit that I had had too much champagne; I just couldn't resist shouting out, 'You must be kidding!' There were gales of laughter, but luckily Mr Goat entered into the spirit of the occasion. He was soon toasting Sheila in champagne and I'm sure he felt that the Rootes money was being well spent.

Many years later, when *Down Your Way* visited Coventry, I enjoyed a look around the Museum of British Road Transport. Barry Littlewood, the manager of the museum, told me proudly that Coventry has been home to about 125 car manufacturers, 300 cycle manufacturers and about 90 motor-cycle manufacturers. The museum has examples from most of these, from an 1897 Daimler up to Richard Noble's Thrust 2, which set a land-speed record of 633.468 mph. They have searched far and wide to find exhibits for the museum. In 1957 they discovered a 1907 Standard, which was being used as a chicken run in Australia.

I spotted a car which brought memories flooding back: the Humber Snipe, which Monty used in Normandy and from which I remember seeing him distribute cigarettes to the troops. 'Monty's known for having two Humbers during the war,' said Barry, '"Old Faithful", which he used in the desert campaign, and the Victory car, which he used in the European campaign.' I knew that this had met with a slight accident at Mulberry harbour and Barry confirmed that it had been dropped off the end of the pontoon while being unloaded. However, the engineer in charge of the car had it all stripped down and back together in working order within 24 hours and it was some time before Monty found out that his car had taken an unplanned dip while coming ashore.

About 25 miles north-west along the M6 is the Borough of Walsall, where I found another fascinating place to visit. The Lock Museum at Willenhall records the local history of making locks and keys and Sarah Elsam, the curator, showed me a vast range of them, from a reconstruction of the simple wooden locks made by the ancient Egyptians to the sophisticated locks of the present day. Among the unusual locks on display I noticed something called a 'bottle lock', which was described as having been used in Midlands homes to prevent servants from stealing wine. This was fitted with little claws which grasped the cork when the key was turned, so that no one could pull it out. Another I spotted was a 'seaman's lock', which originally secured a seaman's chest and was fitted with a bell that rang when the key was turned, to warn the owner if anyone was trying to break in. There was also a combination padlock which opened when you turned the letters to spell 'Amen'.

Wolverhampton, like Walsall, has long been famous for its iron and brass foundries as well as its lock-making. Sadly, the foundries have all but disappeared, but lock-making is still an important industry. Chubb and Sons have been in the business since 1818, and John Hunt, their senior research engineer, explained about the exhaustive tests they have to carry out on their locks and safes. I asked him what was the most successful test they had carried out.

'I suppose one of the most successful was a test on fire-resisting equipment,' he told me. 'After we had developed an internal box to fit into a standard drawer, we demonstrated it to some Scottish bankers. In this box we put a bottle of Scotch and a bowl of ice cubes as well as floppy disks and things like that. The cabinet was put into the furnace at 1,100 degrees Centigrade for an hour until everything was red hot. The handles had melted off, of course, but it was fetched out, dropped thirty feet on to rubble, tipped upside down, put back into the furnace for half an hour and then fetched out glowing red to be hosed down. When it was opened, the papers in the standard drawers were still in excellent condition and the box was taken from the special drawer up into the laboratory. When it was opened in full view of the bankers, the ice cubes were still ice.'

And what of the bottle of whisky? They drank that!

18 The South-East Midlands

EVEN THOUGH I CALL MYSELF half Scottish, I suppose I must really be classed as a Home Counties man. I was born in Little Berkhamsted in Hertfordshire, educated at Eton in Buckinghamshire and for all my working life I have lived in London. In the 1930s and 1940s my mother had a delightful thatched cottage in the Buckinghamshire village of Chearsley and I spent many weekends and holidays there. She took in evacuees during the war. They came from the East End and it was a delight to see them enjoying the life of a quiet village.

Laurence Olivier had a house, Notley Abbey, just down the road near Long Crendon, a picturesque village which has been used in several films. Aylesbury has grown and developed enormously, but High Wycombe is now by-passed by the M40 and seems a rather lonely sort of place. Obviously the by-pass brings more peace and quiet, but the thousands of cars which wound their way through the long valley in which the town is situated brought life and vitality.

Marlow is a lovely riverside town in Buckinghamshire. When I was there with *Down Your Way* I was fascinated to meet Captain John Turk, Swankeeper to Her Majesty the Queen, who is responsible for the well-being of the royal swans on the Thames all year round. Captain Turk's father had been a Queen's Swankeeper and suggested his son as a replacement on his retirement in 1963. His area of responsibility stretches from Sunbury in Middlesex to Pangbourne in Berkshire, a stretch of seventy miles containing a couple of hundred swans. Not all of them belong to the sovereign. Some belong to the Worshipful Company of Vintners and others to the Worshipful Company of Dyers, two very old City of London livery companies.

To distinguish which swans belong to which owner, they are all marked with little nicks on their beaks during the annual Swan Upping, which takes place in the third week of July. For this, the three swankeepers are joined by watermen from the Tideway, who row up river in skiffs in search of the swans. 'When you see a brood of swans,' said Captain Turk, 'you know very well that it's a whole family, because they are always together in families. When we approach them we just ease up our speed, try to pick up their speed and get our boats one behind the other. When I think we're in the right position I give a signal to the first and last boats to go in towards the shore, so we make a semi-circle round them until they are between two boats and the shore.' The Queen's swans are not marked; the Vintners swans have two nicks on their upper mandibles and the Dyers one nick only.

Captain Turk made it all sound terribly easy, but I've always regarded swans as terrifying birds, hissing and flapping about with their powerful wings. 'We catch them round the neck initially,' he explained, 'and pull them towards us as quickly as we can without too much danger to the bird's neck. We lower our knees over their wings to stop them flapping, because they are very, very dangerous. Then we just ease the legs up over their tail and back, tie the legs up, tie the wings up and the bird is helpless. We release the female first and she swims a little way away using the most terrible language. Next go the cygnets, who all swim to their mother, and the cob goes last.'

Apart from the hazards posed by thrashing wings and the ever-present risk of an unexpected swim, Swan Upping sounds a most agreeable pastime. It's colourful, too. All three swan-keepers wear naval caps with the badges of the birds' owners. The Queen's Swankeeper, for example, wears a scarlet coat with white trousers and his swan uppers wear scarlet jerseys and white trousers.

Hertfordshire is a surprising county. Much of it is built up and near London, but it is still possible to get lost in its narrow country lanes within half an hour from the centre of London. As I have said, I was born in Little Berkhamsted and on a recent visit there I found my and my brothers' and sister's births in the church registry.

At the start of the Great War we moved to the village of Offley, about halfway between Hitchin and Luton. There we spent an uneventful war, but I remember well the victory torchlight procession through the village and someone setting fire to the bonfire long before the procession reached it. We used to walk two miles to church and two miles back every Sunday, and were rewarded by being given meringues for lunch – brown sticky ones. It was a lovely, unspoiled part of the country and still is.

When *Down Your Way* visited Stevenage I was shown around the Water Research Centre, where they develop processes for purifying our water and treating and purifying sewage. Living in London, I was naturally curious to know where my drinking water came from and what sort of treatments it had passed through. The answer is that it probably goes through people in Oxford and Reading before coming to me. So I was relieved to hear that it is also purified before coming to my tap. By law the requirement for the water authorities is to provide good wholesome water, which means the removal of all bacteria, any toxic substances and any elements that might discolour the water.

Oddly enough, drinking water is not the purest water available – that goes to the Central Electricity Generating Board's power stations. The water we drink can vary between 50 to 400 parts per million of dissolved salts. These are in no way harmful to you or me; they might even give a little flavour to the water. However, if those dissolved salts were present in the water going into high-pressure boilers used in a power station, they could destroy that boiler within a matter of hours. To provide some idea of the difference between these two grades of water, I was told to imagine an oil tanker filled with water destined for the power station. That would probably contain about one teaspoonful of dissolved solids. If it were drinking water, on the other hand, the volume of dissolved solids would amount to several sackfuls, which would be entirely acceptable for drinking purposes.

Bedfordshire is mostly a county I know from motoring through, but Bedford is a pleasant town with its schools and riverside walks. I also once did a broadcast in a balloon from Cardington. For some unknown reason we chose the winter to do it. It was freezing and there was little room to move in the basket as we had an engineer with our broadcasting gear and the pilot. We were cruising along at about a thousand feet but the extra weight made it difficult for the balloon to rise higher. Suddenly we were approaching some hills and the pilot had no option but to pull the quick-release valve to deflate the balloon. We began to sink rapidly to earth, while I did my best to give a commentary. My teeth were chattering both from fear and cold. We finally landed with a tremendous bump and were shot about twenty feet up in the air. Our gear was flung all over the place, cutting off my commentary. The balloon finally came to rest in a hedge and we had to stand around in the snow waiting for a second party to rescue us. I have rarely been more frightened.

Not far from Cardington is the Shuttleworth Collection of Vintage Aircraft at the Old Warden Aerodrome near Biggleswade. When we were recording in the area with *Down Your Way* I just had to go and see it. Out on the runway as I drove in, there was something that looked as though it was made of paper – it was so unbelievably frail. Most of the collection is housed in seven hangars and the all-grass aerodrome is fully operational – except when the sheep are grazing it!

Richard Shuttleworth, the son of local landed gentry and a real engineer at heart, began his collection of machines with bicycles and cars and then turned his attention to aircraft. He bought his first plane in about 1930 and continued collecting until 1939, when he joined the RAF, only to be killed at the outbreak of the war.

Virtually all of the thirty aircraft are capable of flying, manned by an intrepid team of ten experienced pilots who take to the air in them for flying displays given during the summer months. Insurance restrictions prevent passengers being taken up too, but as Chris Morris, the chief inspector, ruefully told me, 'We engineers do fly in them as ballast . . . and flight test observers, I suppose you could say.'

Outside, Chris showed me a Bleriot aircraft that 'hops' around the airfield, as he put it.

'Hops?' I asked.

'Gets daylight under the wheels,' he explained. 'But we don't let it out of the circuit. It's a bit too dangerous to fly it out of the airfield and back again.'

The wings of the Blackburn monoplane I saw looked terribly thin and the steering-wheel inside the cockpit was minuscule, like the sort you would expect to find in a toy car.

'The wings are very flexible,' said Chris, rather more technically. 'They have to warp in order for the pilot to maintain control. They hadn't standardised the control of aircraft in those days and each manufacturer had his own method of controlling the aircraft. Blackburn decided to put a steering-wheel on his very early planes to warp the wings.'

I was also shown an aircraft which was built in the year I was born, 1912 – the oldest English plane still flying, Chris told me, which was cheering!

Biggleswade was also the home of the World Ferret-Legging Champion, Tony Tuthill, who held the record for keeping seven ferrets down his trousers for no fewer than six and a half hours – a feat which he achieved entirely for charity. He had a ferret with him when we met in the Elephant and Castle down Mill Lane, just off the Market Place. During the course of the interview this little creature cheerfully slipped in and out of the trousers he was wearing and on one occasion popped up through the neck of his shirt. He had never been nipped, he assured me – only scratched a little.

For competition work, Tony told me, he wore a special pair of baggy trousers, which he tied just above the knees to stop the ferrets slipping out of the bottom. But what did he do for the six and a half hours during which seven of these ferrets were roaming around his nether regions? 'Oh,' he answered casually, 'I played darts, dominoes, anything you like!'

The only ferrets I had ever known had ponged a little, but this one of Tony's seemed very clean. Did they have fleas? They didn't, apparently. Just as well, I should think. Having them inside your trousers must be uncomfortable enough.

I was amazed that the only person to take Tony on was a young lady who popped a ferret inside her blouse. That must have taken some doing, although it was a lady ferret, so perhaps they had some sort of understanding. Tony Tuthill disclosed that he only worked with male ferrets. 'You can't trust the females!' he said.

Northamptonshire means shoes to me, and I have the brown and white correspondent shoes which I wear at Test matches made specially for me at Earls Barton. But whenever I think of the town of Northampton I remember the sad day when I visited the England cricketer Colin Milburn in hospital there, soon after he had lost an eye in a car accident. It was a devastating blow to him and left his cricketing future in ruins – just as it looked as if he might at last have been recognised by the selectors as a permanent opening batsman for England. And yet it was his visitors who did the crying. However badly he must have felt inside, he kept smiling and joking, just as he always did.

The first recorded pair of boots made in Northampton was bought by King John in 1213, and the trade has grown there ever since. In the Central Museum and Art Gallery there are lots of curious articles of footwear on display. I was shown some huge boots made to fit an elephant taken on the British Alpine Hannibal Expedition in 1959, when an attempt was made to trace Hannibal's route across the Alps. One boot went on each leg and fitting them was quite a performance, taking two hours at a time. In fact, it didn't take long to discover that the elephant got on quite well without the boots, thank you very much, so they were quietly forgotten.

From the Second World War I spotted one particularly ingenious flying boot, nicknamed the 'escape boot'. This was designed in Northampton in 1943 for aircrews flying over enemy territory and was sheepskin-lined for use in unheated aircraft. Inside was a little knife, which enabled you to cut off the boot's leg to make it look like an ordinary shoe. There was a compass in the heel and a map inside, under the sock. The leg could be used as a waistcoat to keep you warm and there was also a saw in the laces in case you were unlucky enough to get locked up!

19 East Anglia

WHEN I WAS A BOY, my grandfather Reginald Johnston lived in the village of Harlow in Essex in a house called Terlings. What a change he would notice today. Harlow is a flourishing new town and his old house is now a medical research centre. Incidentally, we used to call it 'Tarlings', but they now pronounce it as it is spelled. My grandfather had worked in Brazil with our family coffee business and when he came home he brought with him a black manservant called Otta. I remember him well waiting at table with white gloves. One day, the local otter hunt turned up at Terlings because someone had pulled their legs and told them that there was an otter up at the big house. They got quite a surprise when Otta opened the front door and asked them what he could do for them.

When I was working in the City we would make occasional visits to the Essex seaside towns like Clacton and Southend. One very hot night we motored down after work to Southend, walked along the pier, got a breath of fresh air and drove back again. Although the roads were not so good there was far less traffic and the journey took no longer than it does today. After joining the BBC I broadcast many seaside shows from the end of the piers and enjoyed the local joke:

'It's obvious. It sticks out a mile.'

'What does?'

'Southend Pier!'

Actually, this is wrong, as its real length is, or was, a mile and a quarter. Southend was one of the places we visited in the 1950s and 1960s when we used to broadcast county matches on the old Home Service – half an hour in the morning and half an hour in the afternoon. This was a magnificent 'school' for the likes of Rex Alston, John Arlott and myself. There would just be the commentator and a scorer, which meant one had to keep going for half an hour by oneself. Nowadays, alas, there are no such broadcasts, so the poor would-be commentator has nowhere to learn his trade, except possibly on local radio or in that admirable medium, hospital radio.

Essex was always fun to visit. The county side were a cheerful team who enjoyed their cricket and used to play on a mixture of grounds: Clacton, Southend, Westcliff, Brentwood, Romford, Colchester, Ilford, Leyton and Chelmsford – though I bet I have left one out! They had a travelling circus with a mobile scoreboard on wheels and tents and chairs were all carried around and set up at the various grounds. It wasn't very economical, but it enabled the whole county to see their team.

Essex is one of those counties near London that has become urbanised and commercialised, but it still has thousands of acres of profitable farmland and some of the most beautiful villages in England. For me, it is a perfect mix.

Anyone who travels regularly on the Central Line on the London Underground will recognise the name Ongar – it's the last station at the eastern end of that line. Fewer, I suspect, would imagine that one of the country's architectural gems lies barely a couple of miles from the station in the small hamlet of Greensted. There are only a few houses. There are no shops. But Greensted has a church that is unmatched anywhere else. It's the oldest wooden-walled church in the world. Carbon dating has shown that it goes back to 845, when Saxon craftsmen used the split boughs of an oak tree to construct this simple church measuring 30 feet in length by 10 feet wide. Although the thatched roof has been replaced, the oak walls have stood the test of time for more than 1,150 years and are now so hard that it is practically impossible to drive a nail into the timber. When it was first built, Greensted Church had no windows. What little natural light there was filtered in through small holes. Rush torches provided artificial light, as several scorch marks testify. The smell inside from the mutton fat in which the torches were dipped must have been indescribable!

I'm afraid I know little about Cambridge or Cambridge-shire as I went to the 'other' place. My principal recollections are a college ball in the early 1930s, a speech to the University Cricket Society and commentary on cricket at Fenners. In fact, at a Sunday match there in the late 1950s or early 1960s we tried out the action replay for the first time on TV at a cricket match. (That always makes me think of the Irishman who made a brilliant catch at second slip but missed it on the action replay!)

Traditionally, Fen people have been rather isolated and their folklore carries a stamp all of its own, as I discovered when *Down Your Way* went to Littleport, a few miles north of Ely. In days gone by the men of the Fens didn't believe in cutting their hair, probably because they had heard the story of Samson, whose strength was in his hair. They didn't believe in washing much either – that was reckoned to weaken you! In the damp atmosphere in which they lived ague and fever were common complaints and to counter this poppy-head tea was a popular remedy, amounting as it did almost to opium. Eels were put to a number of uses in the Fens, beyond providing something tasty to eat. Every man and woman thereabouts used to wear an eel garter just above their knee to stop them getting rheumatism. Gold wedding rings were almost unheard of, so they used to get a piece of eel skin and twist this into a wedding ring instead. It was also believed that a roast onion placed in your ear would cure any-thing that might be wrong with it. A roasted mouse swallowed whole was also reckoned to cure whooping cough, or even smallpox.

Miss Eileen Gill, a retired schoolteacher, was a marvellous repository of all these traditional remedies. 'They believed you could cure warts,' she informed me, 'by rubbing the white fluffy stuff inside a broad bean over a wart to make it disappear. When I was a child my mother tried that on me and, strange as it may seem, the wart did disappear.' One final word of caution from her was, 'You must never, never cut your nails on Sunday. If you do, you'll have the devil with you all the week!'

My visit to the Jockey Club at Newmarket yielded the origins of a couple of common idioms in English. On the first floor stands the Stewards' Room, which acted as racing's 'supreme court of justice' until the hearing of serious disciplinary cases was transferred to London. During these hearings the stewards sat at a handsome horse-shoe table while those brought before them stood on a strip of carpet inside the door. This led to the frequently used expression 'to be on the mat'.

The Card Room, adorned by its fine Adam fireplace and gilt-framed oval mirror, contains two card tables, which have given rise to another English idiom. At each corner of the tables are recessed silver candle-holders, which in days gone by were used to provide light for evening card games. A player who had a run of bad luck might justly comment that 'the game had not been worth the candle' and the phrase has remained in the language long after the advent of electricity.

Whenever I watch the races at Newmarket my admiration for the skill of the racing commentators increases even more. The horses come head-on at them stretched across the course, or sometimes in two bunches: one on the stand side, one on the other. It must be the most difficult course in the world on which to commentate, especially compared with the circular courses in America and Australia.

I always think that one is entering a different world in East Anglia. 'Very flat, Norfolk,' said Noël Coward in *Private Lives*. And he was dead right. But I have always found Norfolk a dramatic place with its fens, marshes and constant fight against floods and the incursion of the sea. The roads are straight and often narrow, with a canal running alongside. There are vast stretches of farmland, providing the best in sugar beet, vegetables and cereals. The pace of life, especially in the quiet villages, is much slower than elsewhere in England. And when you want beauty you only have to go to Norwich or for a sail on the Norfolk Broads.

It is the same in Suffolk – large open farmlands with little protection from wind and rain, except in the many attractive little villages. The East Anglian people are friendly, but there is still that feeling of being a stranger.

There is a lovely little theatre in Bury St Edmunds, the Theatre Royal, which was designed by William Wilkins, who designed the National Gallery. To add to its architectural charms it used to enjoy something called the King's Licence, which meant that if anyone could persuade an actor to remain on the premises, the bar could stay open!

In north Suffolk the town of Bungay has become famous as a centre for growing cricket bats. I was told that 70 per cent of the willow grown in England comes from East Anglia, which I could believe, judging by the field near the river Waveney where the firm of Edgar Watts grows over five hundred willows in lines that would do credit to the Guards. Edgar Watts came to Bungay in 1912 and set up business in the first instance as a furniture dealer. A friend from Essex, who knew a bit about splitting out willow to make cricket bats, started him growing his first trees and the trade has developed from there.

These are not weeping willows, but ones grown

specially for cricket-bat-making. The wood is very light and has a very long fibre; it is this fibre that provides the strength for hitting a cricket ball. On average the trees take about fifteen years to reach sufficient maturity to make a man's bat. In view of the number that must be needed, they seemed to me to be planted fairly far apart. But Toby Watts, the managing director, pointed out that they can only use the bottom ten feet of each tree and to keep that growing fast the trees need plenty of light and have to be planted with lots of space around them. About thirty 'clefts' are taken from each willow tree and the firm uses trees at the rate of fifty a week. So they are potentially producing 80,000 bats a year, a lot of which are exported to India, Pakistan, Australia and New Zealand.

During the war, our 5th Guards Armoured Brigade was stationed near the battle area of Thetford – in later years the scene of much of the filming of *Dad's Army*. My whole life was changed as a result of our camping in some woods near Thetford. It was there that I first met the two BBC war correspondents Stewart Macpherson and Wynford Vaughan-Thomas, who had been attached to our brigade to brush up on their war-reporting techniques. After the war I was looking for a job and I happened to run into them again. That was pure luck, but because of it they persuaded me to do a microphone test for the BBC Outside Broadcasts Department. I had had no thoughts of joining the BBC up until then, but I thought I might as well have a go. After I had interviewed passers-by in Oxford Street, the BBC said it wasn't very good but at least I kept talking and didn't dry up. So I got the job and I haven't stopped talking since – all thanks to Norfolk!

When I returned to Thetford for *Down Your Way* I visited the nearby Kilverstone Wildlife Park. Here, Lord and Lady Fisher have created a Latin American Zoo, a Miniature Horse Stud and Miniature Donkey Stud, according to the notice at the entrance – and when Lady Fisher showed me round I could see that it was certainly all of those three.

We started with feeding the monkeys, four tiny little ones snugly wrapped in what looked like hot-water-bottle covers. 'They feel the cold very much,' said Lady Fisher, 'especially the spider monkeys who don't have much fur when they're born. So I knit them little cardigans to keep them warm. The hot-water-bottle covers, as you called them, I call their sleeping bags and I wrap them in furry material so that they can cling on to something soft and furry, which is a substitute for their mother.'

Lady Fisher told me that these baby monkeys, one of which was only three weeks old, needed feeding every two hours. Did she have to do this all through the night? 'Yes, all through the night,' she replied. 'I have them beside my bed in a plant propagator which acts as an electric blanket underneath. I have a thermos and I mix up their milk. They squeak and wake me when it's time to be fed. When I had the first one I didn't have an alarm clock and thought I wouldn't wake up to feed it at the right times. So I rang the exchange for a call at twelve o'clock, three o'clock and six o'clock. There was a silence for a while and then the operator said, "You must be mad." I didn't like to say I was going to feed a monkey or I wouldn't have heard another word.' Just like human babies, the little monkeys are all in nappies. 'The washing machine's going flat out,' said Lady Fisher, with the airy resignation of a seasoned mum.

Lady Fisher rears jaguars too. I saw a splendid black one prowling the park, and later caught a glimpse of the more common spotted variety. She hand-rears them in the house until they get to a size and age when they can be moved into the park.

'And how do you know when that point has been reached?' I enquired.

'When they bite my husband,' was her matter-of-fact reply!

20 London

B
UD FLANAGAN USED TO SING 'Maybe It's Because I'm a Londoner', and I suppose that is what I have become. Although born and brought up in Hertfordshire, I have lived in London all my working life.

I first came to live in London in 1934, when I joined the family coffee business in the City. I was the guest of a godfather in an enormous house in Queen's Gate. We were very near to Hyde Park and I found it a delightfully peaceful place, with the Serpentine, horses cantering round Rotten Row and the distant hum of the traffic in the distance. I soon discovered Speaker's Corner at Marble Arch, where on Sundays we would go and listen to soapbox speakers and also join in the heckling. The main character was Charlie, who talked about nothing in particular but loved all the back-chat. I always remember one heckler shouting at him, 'Charlie, if a cat has kittens on a pillow, are they caterpillars?' Nothing daunted, Charlie switched his subject to cats.

I also began to enjoy the nightlife, especially the entertainments where there was a cabaret or a band. For about five shillings I would have scrambled eggs and a glass or two of lager in the balcony of the Café de Paris and watch the world-famous entertainers perform. Harry Richman, Noël Coward, Florence Desmond, Sophie Tucker (with Ted Shapiro at the piano), Douglas Byng – the list is endless. At the Monseigneur were Roy Fox and Lew Stone, while at the hotels were the bands of Ambrose and Harry Roy at the Mayfair, Jack Jackson at the Dorchester, Sidney Lipton at the Grosvenor House and Carroll Gibbons at the Savoy.

London in the 1930s was certainly a gay place, if one

dare use the word, but there were no gambling clubs and no striptease or nude shows, except at the Windmill, where the girls posed in the nude but were not allowed to move even a flicker. Believe it or not, I used to go there to see a very funny comedian called John Tilley, who did an uproarious act as a Scoutmaster. Of course, I lived in hope of one of the beautiful statuesque girls moving – but they never did.

After three years with my godfather I moved to South Eaton Place to share digs with my school friend William Douglas Home. Yes, London was great fun in those days. As soon as I got out of the Army in 1945 I went back to live there again, starting with a room just off Baker Street – in order to be near Lord's. When I married my wife Pauline in 1948 we started off in a small flat while she looked for a house. My one stipulation was that it should be in St John's Wood, to be near my beloved cricket. She was immediately successful and we have been there ever since. We started about a hundred yards from Lord's and after nineteen years moved to half a mile away. Sixteen years later we moved to our present house, three-quarters of a mile from Lord's and appropriately called Boundary Road.

With my job at the BBC, I have had to travel a tremendous amount both in this country and abroad. I have worked most weekends and bank holidays, and when the cricket correspondent was at the beck and call of the newsroom I had to dash in and do odd pieces about cricket for the news or sports programmes. So I have always lived about ten minutes from my job and I have never regretted it.

St John's Wood is a perfect place to live. All the streets are tree-lined and if, like us, you are lucky enough to have a house and not a flat you will also enjoy a garden. Sitting in our garden, you wouldn't believe that Piccadilly was only three miles away and that you can be on the M1 in ten minutes and at London airport, door to door, in half an hour. It still has a village atmosphere. Neighbours know each other; everyone seems pleased to see you; you can wear any old clothes and find little pockets of shops tucked away between the posh rows of houses. And, of course, when the sun shines I can just pop up the road to Lord's and watch cricket. I am happy to call myself a Londoner.

London was the setting for some memorable broadcasts of *Down Your Way*. For programme number 1,500 we returned to Lambeth, where the very first had come from in December 1946. To mark the occasion we asked the Sun Life Stanshawe Band to play a brand-new arrangement of our theme tune 'Horse Guards, Whitehall' by Haydn Wood. I started them off with the baton and for the first time ever I think listeners heard the signature tune right the way through.

The theme for that special programme was a boat journey down the river Thames from Lambeth Bridge to Tower Bridge. Our guide and skipper for this was PC John Woodhouse of the River Police. Almost as soon as we had got under way he mentioned casually that Admiral William Bligh is buried in the graveyard at Lambeth Palace; he is, of course, more famous for an earlier stage of his career, when as Captain Bligh he was master of the *Bounty* during the celebrated mutiny.

From the river you notice a great many details about London's buildings and bridges that somehow get overlooked from the bank. For instance, as we passed the Palace of Westminster John drew my attention to a set of carvings just above the ground-floor windows. These are the coats of arms of every reigning sovereign from William the Conqueror to Queen Victoria, in whose reign the Palace of Westminster was built.

Further down the river we left the boat at Tower Bridge and I climbed up into the control cabin to find out about the history and working of this most stately of London's bridges. It took eight years to build and was completed in 1894. Since then, any vessel with a mast of 31 feet or more has a right to demand the bridge to be opened. Nowadays they have to give 24 hours' notice, though the bridge must open for them at any hour of the day or night. It takes two and a half minutes from the moment when the traffic lights turn to red for the bridge to open fully and provide vessels passing through with a clearance of 140 feet.

I remembered that on one occasion a bus had actually jumped across the bridge while it was opening and I asked the bridge-master how that had happened. 'Nobody was very proud about it,' he admitted, 'but corners were being cut and there were errors on both sides. Gates weren't shut that should have been shut and various interlocking devices were not actually in operation. This, of course, has all been tightened up since then – but the fact remains that a bus-driver thought he could beat the lights, as it were, and he ended up jumping a three-foot gap. I think he broke all his springs!'

One of the most unusual of all the *Down Your Way* programmes I presented explored what goes on underneath London. In spite of living in London for more than fifty years, I had no idea of what happened beneath the city's 616 square miles. I started the programme in the vaults beneath the Old Lady of Threadneedle Street, or the Bank of England as she prefers to be known. I looked in amazement at the gold bars housed in one particular vault. There were approximately five thousand piled around us, each of which was worth just over £100,000 – and this was just one of several similar vaults. Quite rightly, I wasn't told how many there are in all. The bars I saw and tried to pick up were pretty heavy, each weighing about 28lb. To be acceptable for international debt repayment in London they have to comprise 995 parts gold out of 1,000, the remaining amount consisting of some residual element like copper, silver or platinum.

It amused me to hear the vault described as containing the bank's 'petty cash'. The gold belongs mainly to central banks abroad, along with members of the London market, and it stays in the bank until the customers ask for it to be moved out of the building or into other storage facilities. London, I learned, holds a sizeable proportion of the world's gold, but the largest official reserves are those in the United States of America, where one-third of the world's official gold reserves are housed.

From the rarefied vaults of the Bank of England I moved to the somewhat earthier realms of London's sewers at a point where one of them passes under the pavement opposite Blackfriars Bridge. London has 150 miles of trunk sewers and this was the Fleet Sewer, which carries sewage all the way down from Hampstead. Although there was a fairly acrid smell down there, it wasn't unpleasant, thanks largely to the amount of water used for washing and cleaning which dilutes the raw sewage on its way down from north London. I was very impressed by the safety precautions taken by the team of Flushers, as the sewer maintenance workers are known, who guided us down there. They were careful to report their position as soon as they got out of their van and before anyone went down below ground they tested the atmosphere to check for dangerous or explosive gases.

I ended that programme beneath London in a place where history was made during the war. These were the Cabinet War Rooms near Horseguards Parade. There I met Sir John Colville, who during the war was assistant private secretary to Sir Winston Churchill and his principal private secretary after the war. In spite of great efforts taken to construct these rooms, Sir John said that it was discovered that they would not have been able to withstand a hit by a very heavy armour-piercing bomb. It was therefore decided to add a further layer of concrete above, which Sir John said led to a disastrous incident for Sir

Winston. 'Churchill, being by inclination a builder, thought he knew all about it,' he explained. 'And I remember on one occasion he got so angry that he leaped over a girder and landed plumb in a pool of liquid cement.'

During the periods of heavy bombing during the war the Cabinet rooms were used a good deal for meetings of the Cabinet, the defence committee and the chiefs of staff. 'In the evenings we used to assemble in a small room where they now sell souvenirs,' Sir John said, 'and used that as a mess. We lived off tinned soup, sardines, tinned sausages and an occasional glass of beer if we were lucky. There would congregate the three chiefs of staff, Clement Attlee, Ernest Bevin – all sorts of people. One learned a great deal of what was going on in the war in those nightly sessions down there.'

On the other side of Soho stands the London Palladium, which was one of my favourite haunts as a young man. As befits the world's most famous theatre, it is splendidly appointed and the number-one star dressing-room, where I interviewed Louis Benjamin, the managing director, was absolutely magnificent. This was built specially for Yul Brynner when he played the King of Siam in the run of *The King and I*. As Louis Benjamin said, 'If you're going to live in a theatre for fifteen months, he believed – and we endorsed it – that you should have some comfort.' So they built him a sitting-room, a dressing-room, a bathroom, everything you could imagine.

Louis recalled the celebrated time when the American entertainer Danny Kaye appeared at the Palladium after the war. 'I had the good fortune to be here as second assistant manager,' he said. 'That was just a sensational situation of a show opening to a minor advance booking and the following morning the queues were round the block. Princess Margaret came to see the show and went back home to tell her family how wonderful it was. A secret request came with the message that the King and

Queen wanted to come with the two princesses, but they wanted to sit in the stalls, not in the Royal Box. We tried to allocate four seats in the front-row gangway, but these were already sold. So it fell to me as assistant manager to stop the original owner and offer him seats a couple of rows further back. But the man said that he would only move for the King of England and I wasn't allowed to say who it was. "Look," I said to him, "if you'll please sit where we put you and you're not satisfied with who comes in we'll refund your money completely at the end of the show!" '

For my 600th *Down Your Way* the BBC were kind enough to allow me to invite listeners down my way to St John's Wood, and when, 133 programmes later, I came to do my very last *Down Your Way* we went to Lord's cricket ground, which seemed an appropriate end to my 'innings'. I made my first visit to Lord's in 1927 to be coached and in 1930 saw my very first Test match there. Since the war I have commentated on more than fifty Test matches from the ground. So it's very much a second home for me. Up on the scoreboard they had kindly put 733 for 1, last player 733.

Just at the back of the Pavilion at Lord's is the library which houses the MCC's marvellous collection of books. There is also the Memorial Gallery, which is open to the public. Up on the first floor I interviewed the curator, Stephen Green, while all around us were pictures, memorabilia, treasures, the story of the cricket bat, plates, a lovely bronze figure of Alec Bedser bowling, caps from all the counties and the countries, ties from every cricket club and pictures of all the grounds, all of which he looked after so lovingly.

Among the great collection of cricket bats is the famous one used by Len Hutton when he scored his 364 against Australia in 1938. This has a nice cartoon by Tom Webster on the back showing the Australian wicket-keeper with a

181

beard as long as Moses at the end of the thirteen hours and twenty minutes he was at the crease.

My last interview at Lord's, and my last on *Down Your Way*, was with Denis Compton, who started his career as a young professional at Lord's. He vividly recalled his first appearance at the ground when he walked through the Nursery Gates in 1933 to become one of the MCC ground staff. In that capacity he used to bowl to members and sell scorecards as well as sweeping the ground and pulling the heavy roller out in the middle. Denis told me a lovely story about facing the great Harold Larwood. 'He was off a short run then,' he said, 'but it was the fastest thing I've ever experienced. I'll never forget – he bowled me a short ball, which I somehow hooked for four and he ran down the wicket, shook me by the hand and said, "A wonderful shot, son" – which was very nice.'

Denis chose Frank Sinatra singing 'My Way' as his piece of music, which was a fitting way to sum up his outstanding career. And all in all it didn't seem out of place to play me into the Pavilion, so to speak.

21 The South-East

I LARGELY ASSOCIATE SURREY WITH men in bowler hats carrying rolled-up umbrellas, rushing up to London in the mornings and dashing back again in the evenings – in other words, commuters from this vast commuterland with its large mansions adjoining some of the best golf courses in Great Britain. There are not so many bowler hats these days – it is the fashion to be hatless – but, as we have found in *Down Your Way*, Surrey does tend to depopulate itself during the day, so perhaps there is not quite so much community life as in other counties further away from London.

My first realisation that Surrey existed was when I was given my first bat in 1921 – a 'Force' signed by J. B. Hobbs of Surrey and England. And, of course, the Oval has played a big part in my life ever since – by means of the radio to start with, listening to Patsy Hendren describing the regaining of the Ashes in 1926. In those days he had to be rushed back to Savoy Hill by taxi and I still remember his words: 'The Oval crowd were real glad and all was merry and bright.'

Camberley has wartime memories for me. I was one of the first recruits to undergo training at Sandhurst when it became an Officer Cadet Training Unit during the war. When I visited what is now the Royal Military Academy, Sandhurst, on *Down Your Way* I observed to the adjutant that drill had played a very important part in our training. He told me that it still does. 'I'm the adjutant and I'm responsible for drill,' he said, 'so I must say that I think it plays a vital part. It's really the basis of everything we do. It teaches a young man self-discipline. It teaches him how to react to orders. It teaches him how to hold himself – bearing, turn-out and how to behave as an officer.'

I remember life there being pretty tough. We were always being chased around and didn't seem to have much time to think. That still applies, apparently, especially during the first five weeks when training is very tough indeed. 'It goes on for long hours,' I was told. 'They're up very late and they have to get up very early in the morning. There's not a lot of time to sit down, I'm afraid. The whole aim of the course is to develop, improve and teach leadership in all our officers. This is the thing we consider to be absolutely vital.'

In my day there used to be one passing-out parade a year, but today the Sovereign's Parade, as it is known, is held three times a year, with the salute being taken by either the Queen herself, another member of the Royal Family, a minister or a very senior officer in the Army. The unique element of the Sovereign's Parade comes right at the end, when the adjutant rides a white horse up the steps into the magnificent colonnaded Old Building, where we were talking. I was reminded that the tradition was started by my cousin Tommy 'Boy' Browning, who was the adjutant at Sandhurst in the 1920s and was later appointed the commander of the 1st British Airborne Corps. 'His old groom came to visit me the other day,' his successor told me, 'and he said that the Captain, as he liked to call him, was a very smart officer who took great care of his uniform. At the end of the parade one day it suddenly came on to rain and, instead of going off in the normal way, he thought the quickest way was to go up the steps and under cover, which is exactly what he did, and it's been done ever since.

'We've always used a white horse,' the adjutant continued. 'This particular one has been doing it for several years. He's good at it and knows he's going to get a lump of sugar when we get inside. If I'm lucky I get something rather stronger!'

I found out the origin of another piece of twentieth-century military history during my visit to Farnham, the most westerly of the towns in Surrey. Bill Ewbank Smith, the author of three books about Farnham, proved to be a source of intriguing information. Among several interesting footnotes to history, he told me that the two-minute silence observed at Remembrance Day services originated in Farnham. This was the brainchild of an estate agent by the name of Alfred Agar, who found himself organising a fête to raise funds for the Army in May 1916. In the course of thinking about a suitable symbol for the fête, he hit on the idea of a two-minute silence. Following the fête, the idea was sent to the government, who accepted it as a symbol of world peace. It has been observed on Remembrance Day ever since.

I have several friends in the Cranleigh–Guildford area and have the honour to be an honorary life member of the Shamley Green Cricket Club. This is a charming village between the two towns and the village plays cricket on a green in the centre. It has one snag: there is a right-of-way across the pitch. They still talk of the day when Gubby Allen, ex-England captain and fast bowler, was playing for someone's eleven against the village. He took his usual fast run-up to the wicket but had to stop suddenly before delivering the ball. A formidable-looking lady was pushing a pram, containing a baby and her shopping, right across the pitch. No one, not even an ex-England captain, was going to interfere with her right of way!

About 25 miles due south of Guildford lies the village of Amberley in West Sussex, where I interviewed the tallest man I have ever seen. Ian Spofforth was seven feet two inches and by his own estimate was probably the fourth tallest person in the country. I had to admit being inquisitive about how he coped with everyday matters like beds, doorways and clothes. In each case the answer was that he approached them with commendable common sense and a complete lack of fuss. 'If a bed has no foot-board,' he told me, 'it's no problem. I just stick out. And if it does have a footboard you merely put a further mattress on top to raise it over the level of the footboard.' Doors didn't present a problem either, said Ian, because his eyes were always on the look-out for low lintels, unlike someone of, say, six feet five, who suddenly came across a six-foot-three doorway. To my surprise, everything he was wearing was off the peg, supplied by shops that specialise in clothes for taller people.

Ian's stature won him a place in the film of *Chitty Chitty Bang Bang*, where they wanted a tall person to dance a sort of waltz. But he was also famous for having walked across the river Thames. 'This was on the old Roman ford between St Thomas's Hospital and Westminster,' he told me. 'I stayed within my depth the whole way, but once the water got up to my neck I wasn't really walking. I was just making way with my hands. But I could always stop and put my hands in the air to show that I could stand.'

Sussex is nowadays rather overbuilt and seemingly full of airports and motorways. I first became acquainted with East Sussex in 1921 when I went to a preparatory school at Eastbourne called Temple Grove. So I always think of the downs and chalk cliffs and of the Grand Hotel, Eastbourne, where my parents took me out of school to lunch and tea and we listened to Albert Sandler and his Orchestra. They used to broadcast from the domed lounge in the hotel, which the BBC said had perfect acoustics. Twenty-five years later my wife Pauline and I spent the first week of our honeymoon at the same hotel.

About twenty miles further east along the coast is Hastings, and on *Down Your Way* I visited the old court room in the town hall where a panoramic display of the famous battle is laid out, with all the troops as they fought on 14 October 1066. The 900th anniversary of the Battle of Hastings was commemorated in 1966 by a magnificent embroidery that shows all the stages of English history in 27 beautifully worked panels, each nine feet long. It took the ladies of the Royal School of Needlework in London just over a year to complete. The final panel shows Sir Winston Churchill giving a victory salute on the white cliffs of Dover, but a little further back I spotted something that interested me: the first television broadcast. I was reminded that television was actually invented in Hastings by John Logie Baird in 1924 and the very first outdoor pictures ever seen on a television screen were of people walking backwards and forwards in front of the door of Hastings Town Hall.

Over the years I have been asked to be a member of a great many clubs, but no invitation gave me more pleasure than when I was asked to become a member of Hastings' famous Winkle Club. This came into being in the early 1900s when the fishermen of Hastings, poor as they were, wanted to do something to help the poor children of the district over the Christmas period. They hit on the idea of forming a club and, while they were discussing what sort of emblem they should have, along came someone with a bucket of winkles. That gave them their inspiration. The winkle became their symbol; it had to be carried by every member, who had to produce it whenever he was challenged to 'winkle up' by a fellow member. If he didn't have a winkle on him he had to pay a fine and that is the money that goes to charity. I've certainly been caught often enough for not having my winkle with me!

Kent is one of my favourite counties because of its great connection with cricket. It has some lovely grounds: the Mote at Maidstone; the Neville Ground at Tunbridge Wells, with its rhododendrons; and, of course, the St Lawrence Ground at Canterbury, with stands named after great players of the past like Frank Woolley and Leslie Ames.

Every August the Canterbury Week – not Festival – is a delightful occasion, with marquees for the various Kent clubs and picnics from the backs of cars parked around the ground. There used to be a band, but a visiting player – I believe from Essex – complained that it interfered with the play. There is also the famous lime tree on the field of play. It was at Canterbury that they are said to have had a streaker who rushed past two old ladies sitting in deckchairs. They say that one of them had a stroke, but that the other one couldn't reach him!

The northern part of Kent is overcrowded and commercialised, but further south in the 'Garden of England' there can be few more beautiful parts of the country, with its orchards, hopfields and oasthouses. Especially in the spring with the apple and cherry blossoms enriching the colourful countryside. I once picked cherries there – that delicious brown and white Napoleon species which are very difficult to find these days. Picking has become too expensive and they haven't yet designed a machine to do the job properly. But the hopfields still attract hundreds of pickers every year, many from the East End of London on what to them is their summer holiday.

The coast is, of course, famous for the white chalk cliffs of Dover – such a welcoming sight to the returning traveller. On the north Kent coast is the town of Whitstable, which claims eight world firsts. The first divers in the world went to work in Whitstable in May 1826 when they were engaged to dive on the wreck of the *Royal George*. Among the things they brought up were guns that were cast to form the bronze capital on Nelson's Column in Trafalgar Square. On 3 May 1830 the world's first steam-drawn passenger train went into service at Whitstable a few months before the Liverpool-to-Manchester line was opened. In connection with the railway, the first passenger tickets were also issued in Whitstable and the line also had the first steam locomotive with forward-looking cylinders.

And Whitstable harbour was the first in the world to be served by a railway. The first steam-boat to sail to Australia set out from Whitstable as well. She was the 81-ton *William IV*, which was skippered by a Whitstable man. The town also claims the world's first sea cadets, founded by Henry Barton in 1854. Finally, in 1920 Whitstable had the distinction of building the first council houses in the world, which I found remarkable.

Up in the north-east tip of the Isle of Thanet are the holiday resorts of Margate, Broadstairs and Ramsgate. We used to broadcast a lot of seaside concert parties from Margate in the early 1950s, especially the open-air entertainment at the Oval, an open oval amphitheatre with a bandstand as a stage. It was here that after – or even during – a performance the artists used to go round collecting money from the audience in their deckchairs – 'bottling', it was called. I was thrilled once when I told Cecil Johnson's Concert Party a terrible joke, which they put into one of their cross-talk acts. I remember it got a good laugh on a warm sunny evening.

22 The South

PERSONALLY, I ALWAYS FIND THE county of Wiltshire rather an eerie place, with Stonehenge, the earthworks of Avebury and the cold wildness of Salisbury Plain. Having said that, I only have happy memories of the lovely little village of Lacock that lies midway between Chippenham and Melksham. It was here that my producer Tony Smith and I recorded our first *Down Your Way* programme together. The village buildings represent every architectural period from the thirteenth century onwards. It is spotlessly clean and tidy and, as far as I remember, there wasn't a single television aerial to be seen.

Wiltshire has mainly wartime memories for me, because we were stationed at Warminster for about two years, learning how to handle our tanks on Salisbury Plain, all 92,000 acres of it. In the middle of the war the little village of Imber in the centre of the plain was just being evacuated, so that troops could be trained to fight in built-up areas. When *Down Your Way* went to visit the Warminster Garrison, I learned from the commanding officer that by the end of the war the village resembled any other in north-west Europe over which a battle had been fought. 'The church still stands,' Lieutenant-Colonel Peter Houghton assured me, 'and still remains consecrated. Indeed, a service is still held there on the first Saturday in September of every year.'

Nowadays, Warminster is famous for its many sightings of UFOs and I met Arthur Shuttlewood, a retired local journalist who is the author of a good many books on UFOs. He told me that the first sighting he knew of as a journalist was made on Christmas Eve 1964. Since then,

hundreds of sightings have been noted. 'Mainly unidenti-
fied flying objects,' he told me, 'that normally come above
us at blistering speed, making no sound whatever. The
only sound we've heard is after there has been a landing
of a craft, and there have been several witnessed landings
on the ground. When we've rushed up to the craft it's just
"whooshed" away, very much like the sound of a vacuum
being expelled.' Among the collection of photographs he
showed me I picked out a couple: one that looked like the
shape of an egg, the other like a Mexican's hat. The 'egg'
one, according to Arthur, had been taken by a local photo-
grapher in the presence of police officers and other 'responsible' people. The picture of the 'Mexican' UFO was
from 1965 and was the first photo of the 'Warminster
Thing', as it has become known.

It seemed incredible that Arthur had been able, not
to mention brave enough, to approach these mysterious
objects, but he reckoned he had been within ten feet of
one. 'It dwarfed me as I stood there watching it,' he said.
'It could have been forty to fifty feet across and it hovered
above me.' I asked him if he had ever seen any of the
occupants of these craft. 'We haven't actually seen them
get out,' he admitted, 'but we've had many weird things
happening. Giant figures have been seen walking alongside them. They're translucent shining figures, diaphanous
even. There's no definite structure to them. Yet they're
huge, huge creatures.' One of Arthur Shuttlewood's colleagues had the courage to approach one of these 'men
from outer space' and walked right through it. Now you
know why I find Wiltshire rather eerie!

If I were asked which is my favourite county, I would
have to plump for Dorset. First of all, it offers so much
sheer beauty with its peaceful and unspoiled countryside,
still free from the roar of modern motorways. It has such
variety: the rolling fertile hills, the lush valleys with the
narrow winding lanes, the small valleys and hamlets,

the thatched cottages built of Purbeck stone and the quaint names like Piddletrentide, Affpuddle and Puddletown. Then there are the cliffs round the Isle of Purbeck, matching those in Cornwall for size and grandeur.

I first went to Dorset in 1923 when we lived there for two years, first at Upwey near Weymouth, then at Moreton near Dorchester. Upwey has a famous wishing-well at the end of the long village street and I made many boyhood wishes, most of which have luckily come true. Moreton was where T. E. Lawrence lived and where he was buried after his motor-bike accident. It was here that a kind neighbour called Colonel Parks bet my sister half-a-crown that I would one day keep wicket for England. I'm afraid my sister was never paid! I remember being told about Thomas Hardy and his stories of the Dorset countryside and people, and visiting the famous Abbotsbury swans. And, of course, as a boy I was particularly interested in the Cerne Abbas Giant – the figure of a naked man cut into the chalk hillside, displaying his manliness for all to see.

I also saw much of Dorset during the war. I joined the Grenadier Guards at Shaftesbury, at that time the only town in England without a railway station. We were later stationed in a girls' school at Parkstone. I hasten to add that it had been evacuated, but there were still notices on the dormitory walls where the Guardsmen slept which read: PLEASE RING THE BELL IF YOU REQUIRE A MISTRESS DURING THE NIGHT.

After the war, in the 1950s, we began to go on holiday with our children to Swanage. We had a small cottage in the quarry village of Acton, a great place for fossils – especially dinosaur footsteps imprinted in large slabs of Purbeck stone. Since the 1970s we have had a house on the cliffs at Swanage and we have a fine view of the bay and the monument in honour of King Alfred's victory over the Danes in Swanage Bay in 877. A really delightful place to spend a quiet holiday.

Across the water is the Isle of Wight, with Queen Victoria's Osborne House and Sandown and Shanklin, where comedians such as Arthur Askey and Tommy Trinder started their careers in concert parties on the pier. The other half-mile-long pier at Ryde used to have the best collection of vulgar seaside postcards. To save embarrassment to the buyer, each card was numbered and he just had to ask for the number without revealing the nature of his choice. These have now disappeared.

Yarmouth, on the north-west corner of the island, is the southern terminus of the car ferry from Lymington and for many visitors their landfall on the 'friendly isle'. Short as the distance may be across the water, the Isle of Wight does hold a certain mystery for many from the mainland, judging by some of the questions put to Wilf Eccleston, the Yarmouth information officer. He told me he was often asked for directions to the duty-free shop by people convinced that the island was on a par with the Channel Isles. Another favourite question from visitors was directions for driving in their cars round the Needles lighthouse and rocks. He had another man comment that Henry VIII's choice of location for his castle, right next to the ferry terminal, seemed rather strange. But the one which made me chuckle most was the question as to whether or not visitors were allowed to feed the dinosaurs in the dinosaur park at Black Gang Chine!

My first visit to Hampshire was in 1925, when we went with our tutor in the side-car of his motor-cycle to see Hampshire play Nottinghamshire at Dean Park in Bournemouth, which in those days was in Hampshire, not Dorset. I remember the bald-headed, red-faced Arthur Carr, white handkerchief knotted round his neck, hitting the Hampshire bowling past his rival captain, the portly Lionel Tennyson, standing at mid-off.

193

About eight years later I went to Portsmouth to play cricket against the United Services. During a hilarious evening we were shown over the royal yacht and I was allowed to sit on the special lavatory seat reserved for Queen Mary. It was made of a sort of chamois leather, beautifully soft and warm to the skin.

While at Oxford we used to travel to Winchester every year to play cricket against the college and also against the Greenjackets at St Cross, so that I got to know and love this beautiful city. I have visited it many times since and once on *Down Your Way* claimed the Wayfarers' Dole of bread and ale at Britain's oldest charity, the Hospital of St Cross, the right of any visitor or traveller.

Since the war I have visited and passed through Hampshire many times. With the coming of the M3 it has lost some of its peace and charm, but it still has some delightful villages tucked away in the Test Valley and its fishing and shooting rivals the best in Britain. It is a county of large and prosperous farms and still produces the finest strawberries.

As a county, too, it is steeped in the history of cricket. To mark the occasion of my 500th *Down Your Way* we accepted an invitation to visit the old village of Hambledon, thirty miles north of Portsmouth. Between 1750 and the 1790s Hambledon became the leading cricket club in England. Not only did they lay down many of the original laws but also beat a good many All-England teams. In their early days they played up on Broadhalfpenny Down, about two miles from the village, where the Old Bat and Ball Inn served as the pavilion and headquarters of the club. In the end Broadhalfpenny Down proved to be rather windy, so the club moved to Windmill Down, though I was told that that too could be a bit breezy. Today the club plays at Brooks Lane, which has been its home for more than a hundred years.

I went to the Old Bat and Ball Inn to meet Colin Barrett,

the then captain of Hambledon Cricket Club, and for one of the few occasions on *Down Your Way* I was batting on a familiar pitch, so to speak. I was delighted to find that the modern club still had a strong family feeling about it. Colin's son was in the side; his wife made the teas and his mum scored. It was also good to hear that the majority of players were under thirty years old, which ensured continuity for the future.

In those early days Hambledon played against the All-England side 51 times and beat them on 29 of those occasions. Seeing the monument opposite the pub reminded me too that many of the laws of cricket made by Hambledon Cricket Club are still the same today. They got the width of the bat right, at four and a quarter inches. The weight of the ball is the same. And, of course, Hambledon introduced the third stump after a chap called Lumpy Stevens bowled to the celebrated John Small and the ball went between his two stumps without removing the bail.

There were marvellous characters playing for Hambledon at that time, such as Silver Billy, or Billy Beldham to give him his full name, who was probably Hambledon's most famous batsman. One mustn't forget the spectators either, among them the Duke of Dorset who used to pace up and down, knocking the heads off the daisies with his stick when he was anxious. There are still plenty of daisies on the chalk to remind one of the hours he must have spent walking up and down in the outfield.

Berkshire is now rightly called Royal, with Windsor Castle, Windsor Great Park and Ascot. It is dominated by the river Thames and provides a contrast of towns: industrial Reading, leisure town Maidenhead, Newbury and its racing, and Hungerford with its antique shops and fishing on the river Kennet.

Reading is the capital town of Royal Berkshire and is at the confluence of the Kennet and the Thames. It is a town made famous by beer, bulbs and biscuits, and has often been called the most typical and representative of all English towns. The bulb and seed business and the biscuit-making have left Reading now. Even the huge Courage brewery stands just outside the town boundary. But there is plenty of light industry and micro-electronics to take their place and there is also the BBC Monitoring Service across the Thames at Caversham. Here the staff monitor broadcasts from some forty to fifty countries in thirty languages.

I visited them at the end of 1984, when their energies were being directed towards western and eastern Europe, the Soviet Union, North Africa, Iran and Afghanistan, as well as the English-language broadcasts of other countries further afield such as Argentina, Canada and Australia. There is also an exchange agreement with the service's American counterpart and between them they manage to cover the whole world. About half the monitors are native speakers and the rest are British language graduates. Working an eight-hour day, each one listens to half a dozen bulletins covering news broadcasts, current-affairs magazine programmes, features of political and economic interest, documentaries and programmes on international affairs. From time to time there are major events from certain countries, like the May Day speeches from the Soviet Union. Each monitor records his or her own bulletin and makes notes as it is being broadcast. Then this is taken away to be transcribed. If the item is of sufficient importance a few sentences are typed up and taken at once to the newsroom for immediate transmission to the BBC and government departments, like the Foreign Office, Cabinet Office and Ministry of Defence, and to anyone else who subscribes to the service.

Linda Eberst, Assistant Controller Coverage, showed me around and I asked her whether this centre was ever the only one to gather certain items of news. 'That's really what makes our work so exciting,' she answered. 'One example I can give you would be after 13 December 1981 when martial law was declared in Poland. Correspondents were unable to get their material out of the country and yet we listening in Caversham were able to provide a service to everybody covering exactly what was happening in Poland.' Listening isn't all they do now. In recent years they have started watching Moscow television, which, as Mrs Eberst admitted, does add another dimension to their work.

Among all this sophisticated technology I was amused to see a very comfortable cardboard box in one corner of the Listening Room occupied by a very contented-looking black cat. 'He was a stray we found wandering in the grounds a few years ago,' I was told. 'He was immediately adopted by the staff here and his name is SAM, which stands for Senior Assistant Mice!'

23 The South-West

EVER SINCE THE AGE OF SEVEN I have had many happy memories of Cornwall. We used to go to Bude every summer for our holidays and later lived there for about eight years. And I still go back when I can – partly to visit my parents' grave in the nearby village of Stratton.

I'm afraid food plays an important part in my recollections. After bathing in what was usually a very rough sea we always had saffron buns or cake and I still relish the taste. In the afternoons we used to go on a wagonette drawn by two horses to some delectable places for tea. It might be the old water mill in Coombe Valley, Morwenstow, or Crackington Haven. Sometimes it might be by boat up the canal to Wannacott's farm. The end product was always the same: splits and cream.

The beach naturally played a big part in our lives. We kept white mice and used to dig trails, tunnels and bridges in the sand and then let the mice loose. It used to attract large crowds, who watched them scampering in and out of the tunnels and over the bridges. In the summer there was cricket on the edge of the cliffs. It was very windy and favoured the slow leg-break bowler who could bowl high into the wind. In the winter we would hunt with the Tetcott, a small farmer's hunt. The ground in the valleys was marshy and, as in Ireland, there were banks instead of hedges, which used to cause quite a few problems for the horses and for their riders.

Since those days, I have been back to Cornwall many times. My eldest brother used to live at Port Isaac and Truro and we took our children on holidays to Treyarnon Bay and Polzeath. For me, the main attraction of Cornwall is the magnificent Atlantic coastline with its scenery and views, towering cliffs, large sandy beaches and the giant Atlantic rollers pounding against the shore. The interior is largely without character except for its winding narrow roads and steep hills.

The Lizard Peninsula is a remote and intriguing corner of Cornwall and is the most southerly point in Great Britain. It has sandy beaches, fishing coves, tiny inlets and a generally mild climate. When I was there on *Down Your Way* my visit coincided with the first snow they had seen there for five years, which blotted out some of the spectacular scenery.

Very few precious minerals have been found on the Lizard – not that this seems to have affected its settlement. The first monks to arrive were building their monasteries in the 'meneage' lands as early as the ninth century. Following the Crusades, leper colonies were created all over the peninsula, which according to one theory gave it its name – leper/Lizard.

The Lizard lies 1,300 miles due north from a given point on the coast of Spain and at the spot where you would actually climb ashore if you made that voyage from Spain you can find the flagstaff of the lighthouse. Apart from welcoming you to these shores, this serves the more practical purpose of dividing the Atlantic from the English Channel. Looking out to sea, the great ocean lies to its right, the Channel to the left.

St Keverne, the Celtic missionary, gave his name to one of the Lizard's villages. He is said to have cursed its inhabitants' rather frosty reception by ensuring that no precious minerals would be found within the hearing of the church bells. Today, anyone wandering around the churchyard at St Keverne can get an idea of how terrible shipwrecks must have been in earlier centuries. Two hundred victims from one wreck alone lie buried there.

Devon, by contrast, has a far wider variety of scenery

and countryside; it is, of course, a far larger county. As a boy or young man I never lived or even stayed in Devon. I always seemed to be driving through it or popping over the border to visit beauty spots like Dartmoor, Hartland and Clovelly. But during school holidays, and when on vacation from Oxford, it provided me with some of my happiest cricket. Tavistock, for instance, was the scene of my highest cricket score, when I made 79 playing for Bude. I also used to play at Mountwise in Devonport for the Mount Cricket Club run by an enthusiastic colonel, Bobbie Burlton, and consisting mostly of Royal Navy officers. But my happiest memories were undoubtedly at the little village of Bridestowe, where the present Lord Carrington's father lived. It had a small but beautiful little cricket ground with a small thatched pavilion. The club was called Millaton and consisted of retired clergymen, doctors and solicitors who during the holidays invited one or two young people like myself to join their team.

There are many other places too, such as Exmoor, Plymouth, Torquay, Exeter and Dartmouth. On the north Devon coast is the picturesque village of Lynmouth. Many people will recall the terrible flood disaster that claimed the lives of over thirty people there in August 1952. After days of monsoon-like rain the swollen waters of the East and West Lynn converged on the stricken village in a wall of water forty feet high, sweeping aside many buildings in the centre and carrying the helpless victims far out into the Bristol Channel. When I was there on a glorious September day it was hard to picture that appalling tragedy.

In fact, apart from the now tranquil sound of the two rivers, the only noise of rushing water in Lynmouth that day came from the water tanks of the unique cliff railway, which carries freight and up to forty passengers 475 feet up and down the steep valley wall. Bob Jones, the engineer in charge, explained to me that the railway was designed by his grandfather to work on an ingeniously simple use of the counterbalance principle. Both the cars, connected by a cable that runs up and down the nine-hundred-foot rails, have huge tanks capable of holding two and a half tons of water, which are always filled when the cars are at the top. To set them moving the two drivers release their brakes. If nothing happens, the one at the bottom discharges water until his car is lighter than the one at the top, and away they roll up through the glorious cliff scenery.

The spirit of the sea is ever present in this part of the country, and Tavistock, on the river Tamar, is the birthplace of one of England's greatest seafarers, Sir Francis Drake. I had always thought that he was knighted by Queen Elizabeth, but when I visited Tavistock I found out I was wrong. Apparently, when Drake returned from his circumnavigation of the world, Queen Elizabeth went to meet him, accompanied by the French and Spanish ambassadors. Turning to the French ambassador, she said, 'Have you got a sword?'

'Yes,' he answered.

'Then dub him,' commanded the Queen of England.

In the Queen's Head in Tavistock, I conducted what I think was my most public interview ever for *Down Your Way*. Farmer John Doidge was holding court. He was in his 88th year and had started farming in 1918 with thirty acres. 'I mind,' he said, 'when beer was threepence a pint.' He had greeted me, pint in hand, with a song:

Browny Ale, Browny Ale, thou art my darling.
Oh, it's thee that makes me wear these ragged clothes,
But if I can only get thee to my nose,
Ten to one down she goes.

And indeed, down it went, quick as a flash.

Farmer John had clearly enjoyed every minute of his life, which had not been without adventure. He said he'd been stolen by gypsies when he was a baby. Some people had said it was to spite his father, who had summonsed them for sheep stealing, but he thought they really wanted him to improve their breed. I wished him many happy years in Tavistock. 'Can't expect many more,' he observed. 'Besides, I'm beginning to wonder what I've got to answer for.' The crowd in the bar egged him on to sing 'Paper Roses'. He wouldn't, but suggested I come back at closing time!

The variety of scenery and breathtaking views of Devon are never ending; it must rate as one of the most beautiful counties in Britain. Oh, and I nearly forgot. Devonshire cream! Don't ask me the difference between that and Cornish, nor which I like better. They are both delicious!

The longest stay I have had in Somerset was during the late summer of 1940 when my battalion was stationed at Castle Cary. At that time I was still in charge of a motor-cycle platoon and, looking back now, it is lucky for all of us that the Germans never invaded!

When I was up at Oxford I had an old Austin Seven, and Somerset was another county through which I used to drive regularly on my journey to and from Cornwall. Although it was slightly longer, I used to favour going via Taunton on to the A4, instead of the more easterly route via Honiton, Wincanton and Andover. I used to time my journey so that I could lunch and have a slight rest at the Castle Hotel in Taunton. Remember that the 240-mile journey from Bude to London in my car took something like eight hours! Anyway, luckily the Castle is still there and better than ever.

During my time with the BBC I have done many cricket commentaries from the County Ground at Taunton. But I first went there way back in the 1920s to see Somerset play Yorkshire. It is sad that the only thing I can remember now is that Abe Waddington and Maurice Leyland refused to give me their autographs when they were on their way to lunch.

A thorn tree lies at the heart of one of the many legends surrounding Glastonbury, 22 miles north-east of Taunton. It was here that Joseph of Arimathea apparently settled after fleeing Palestine with a few faithful followers after the crucifixion of Our Lord. Resting on a hill nearby, he stuck his staff, cut from a thorn tree, into the ground and this is supposed to have burst forth into leaf and blossom, which Joseph took as a sign that he should stay to found an abbey.

Leaving aside Joseph's involvement, the ruins confirm that Glastonbury Abbey was an enormous establishment covering a total of forty acres during its heyday. The abbey itself was almost six hundred feet from end to end and the massive tower of which only the impressive archway still stands was over two hundred feet tall.

The other legend associated with Joseph of Arimathea is that of the Holy Grail, the chalice or bowl used by Jesus Christ at the Last Supper. It is said that Joseph brought this to Glastonbury too, although Geoffrey Ashe, the author and authority on Glastonbury and its fascinating history, told me that in his opinion the legend of the Holy Grail was more likely to be a symbolic arrival of Christian values in this part of Somerset rather than the actual grail itself.

Whatever its origin, the legend of the Holy Grail formed one of the key elements in the wider legends surrounding King Arthur, so it wasn't at all surprising to come across a sign in the abbey grounds announcing the site of King Arthur's tomb. In 1191, the bodies of King Arthur and his queen were said to have been found and removed from the tomb in the presence of King Edward and Queen Eleanor. Over the site a very fine black marble tomb was supposed to have been erected. This, of course, has long since disappeared, although during excavations small fragments of black marble were found, indicating that that part of the story may quite well have been true.

As for the thorn, well, there is still a tree there. 'It is not a native of this country,' I was told. 'It is a native of the Near East, which is curious.' Curious indeed and one of the several reasons to visit Glastonbury if you ever have the chance.

About ten miles south-west of Taunton is Wellington, probably best known for its associations with the Duke of Wellington, victor of the Battle of Waterloo. In fact, I discovered he only visited the town once! He was still in France when he was ennobled and wrote to his brother asking him to pick somewhere in the West Country that resembled the family name of Wellesley. Apparently, the brother studied a map and settled on Wellington, with the result that today the Duke's obelisk stands on Black Down to commemorate the fact.

Nestling at the foot of the Blackdown Hills on the banks of the river Isle is the market town of Ilminster. It was there that I met George Walsh, who was then the British snuff champion and the runner-up in the world. There are 460 snuffs manufactured in the UK from the finest of fine tobacco and they can include anything, it seems, from strawberry and raspberry essences to menthol. George's favourite had the splendid name 'Crumbs of Comfort', of which he would take up to 150 pinches a day.

I was curious as to the correct way of taking snuff. 'Tap the box,' George explained. 'Open it up. Take a pinch between your forefinger and your thumb. Tap it on the side of the box. Put it to your nose and sniff. That is, after you've passed it all around to your friends.'

But how do you become a champion? In a nutshell, it is a matter of taking fifty pinches of different snuffs as quickly and cleanly as you can (25 if you're a lady). Each competitor moves down a long table where 25 servers with tiny spoons put a pinch of snuff on the back of your hand for you to sniff, one after the other. Time-keepers and judges are on hand to supervise and disqualify anyone who coughs, sneezes or blows the snuff off his hand. When George won the championship he managed to do this in 60 seconds. What's more, he didn't incur a single penalty point for having any snuff left on his hand or around his nose. Judging by the very mild snuff he let me try, I have a feeling my performance might not have been quite so dignified!

George was a marvellous character. I thought he typified so many of the inspiring and interesting people and activities I encountered in the course of travelling all over Britain, when I went *Down Your Way*.

PART III:
MORE VIEWS FROM THE BOUNDARY

24 Sir Alan Ayckbourn

I FIRST MET ALAN A few years ago when I went to interview him at the National Theatre. He was there in his
role as a director, the play being *Tons of Money*. I knew,
of course, that he lived and worked in what is generally
known as the 'Cricket Town' – Scarborough. It was natural,
therefore, that as soon as the interview was over we should
start to talk about cricket. It soon became obvious that he
would be an ideal candidate for 'View from the Boundary',
especially when he revealed that he used to keep wicket!

I had heard that he used to live in Sussex and had been
at school at Haileybury in Hertfordshire, so I started by
asking him which first-class county he supported.

Headingley, 25 July 1992

ALAN AYCKBOURN I'm a member of Yorkshire. I think you
can't live in Yorkshire for thirty-five years and support
someone else. I've certainly seen them through some lean
times and now I think better times are coming. So I've
clung to Yorkshire. I think I was temporarily a Sussex
supporter, when I was ten.

BRIAN JOHNSTON Slight contrast, really – the Seasiders and
the rather dourer Tykes. And I'm told, which pleases me,
that you are either a wicket-keeper/batsman or a
batsman/wicket-keeper. Which do you like to call yourself?

ALAN I think my wicket-keeping was fractionally better
than my batting, which isn't saying a lot. I used to keep
wicket, but in the last few years I've become a sort of non-
playing manager. I still put a team together – of actors,

mainly. I still challenge people, when I've got enough actors in the company to make up a team.

BRIAN We always talk about this association between cricket and the stage. It's remarkable that so many actors seem to enjoy cricket.

ALAN Well, of course cricket's a huge theatre spectacle. Entering a cricket ground like Headingley here is very like going on stage at Drury Lane, I suppose. There is this enormous walk out, with you in the solo spotlight. The only difference is that you are surrounded by total hostility out there – by people who mean you ill. They mean to send you back as fast as possible. It's also a very great game for teamwork. Although you do sparkle as individuals as batsmen, a fielding team is very much a team and actors respond to this. They like a feeling of clear roles, whether you're a wicket-keeper or a slip fielder or whatever. I think it has a tremendous relationship with theatre, so I'm not surprised.

BRIAN You tell me that you are now forty-five not out – not in age, but in number of plays written, which puts you top of the averages for all English playwrights. You even go ahead of Bill Shakespeare.

ALAN Yes, I wouldn't say in quality, but in quantity, certainly. I've shot ahead of him now. I'm hoping to make fifty. You get depressed when you read that Goldoni apparently wrote over a hundred plays, so I think the Italians still lead.

BRIAN I think *Mr What-Not* was your first play. At what age did you start?

ALAN *Mr What-Not* was my first London play. I wrote that in my early twenties. I had my first big hit when I was about twenty-five. It was some years ago.

BRIAN Michael Hordern in *Relatively Speaking*.

ALAN Absolutely right.

BRIAN With Celia Johnson.

ALAN That's right – and Richard Briers.

BRIAN But what theatrical experience had you had? Did you do any acting before you started writing?

ALAN Yes, I've worked my way through all parts of theatre, really. I started as an assistant stage manager, which is the humblest form of life. I didn't get formally trained, because we couldn't actually afford it. After being an ASM I then went on to become a stage manager, an electrician and at one stage I got involved with sound, which I'm still involved with. Then I became an actor and a director and finally, oddly enough, I became a playwright. All of that experience has helped me.

BRIAN You learned the business. Did anyone particularly help you early on?

ALAN Yes, a lot of people. I've been very lucky. I always say that if in your life you have one or two guardian uncles and aunts – not necessarily related by blood – you're very lucky. I met this incredible man, Stephen Joseph, whose name the theatre in Scarborough actually bears.

BRIAN It was called something else. The Library Theatre?

ALAN It was at one stage but, when he died in 1967, we renamed it the Stephen Joseph Theatre. He was amazing. He encouraged young talent, as I was then, and he encouraged particularly the young playwrights. He had this extraordinary idea that a playwright belonged within a theatre and they weren't sort of mysterious men and women who sent in plays from the Orkney Islands and were never seen. They were actually part of the process of play-making, which was incredibly rewarding and also instructive. If you actually saw your work being done and you saw actors having trouble with it, at least you learned better next time.

BRIAN Did he do the directing to start with that you do now?

ALAN Yes, he directed the company, but, fortunately for me, he was so busy doing everything – he was a great man of theatre – he often left areas which he couldn't cover and he would just grab the nearest person. In my case he said, 'Go and direct the next play.'

BRIAN Is that as easy as it sounds?

ALAN Well, I said, 'Look here, I've never directed. I've been directed. I think I know what not to do, because I've met some pretty bad directors – not yourself, sir, of course.' And he said, 'Just create an atmosphere in which actors can create,' and walked away. And of course that is exactly what one has to do as a director, but how you do it, of course, takes about fifty years to learn.

BRIAN What is your relationship with the actors? Do you leave them a lot to themselves, or do you sort of pop in with ideas?

ALAN Oh, yes, I try to pick up on their ideas. I like it if they initiate ideas and then I hope I bounce things back off them. I think actors like a firm framework in which to work. They like to think that somebody's organising it, if only deciding when the tea breaks happen. Somebody needs to be in overall charge and you have to have someone making group decisions like the style you've got to do it in and the way it's going to be set. That has to be the director's decision. But, obviously, the actor is in pole position when it comes to theatre work and it's very important that they're allowed to motor at full throttle, if you like. You don't want people like me standing in their way. I think I've got to get behind and shove them to get them going.

BRIAN You've got this remarkable way of writing a play. Am I right in saying you sit down five weeks away – it's already been advertised; the title has been done; the bookings have been made and you haven't even written it? How long does it take you from the moment the pen hits the paper to production?

ALAN Well, no more than ten days, probably less, actually.

BRIAN This is terrifying.

ALAN There's a lot of preparation that goes on up top in

my head. I don't make copious notes. I think with writing plays it's very important to get it all down. If you think about a play, it's a group of people all inter-relying and responding and following emotional lines and plot lines and it's very hard to keep in the air, as it were. I feel like a juggler with a lot of coloured balls, throwing them up, and if I actually take too many breaks from it, I drop the lot.

BRIAN One can understand the plot going round, but you've got to put the dialogue down, too. You've got to put yourself in the place of the characters and invent some conversations.

ALAN That's the easy bit. It's the framework, the structure, to try to hold an audience whose attention span these days is getting shorter and shorter. In television now they give them about forty-four seconds before they cut to another shot and we're asking them to look at the same shot for probably two and a quarter hours. So it's a very important narrative structure and that's the toughest thing to achieve, to keep their eyes on the play for that length of time.

BRIAN But aren't the actors and actresses there with their hands out, waiting for the script? The first night coming up and you get the script how many days before?

ALAN Well, nowadays I am a little better. I turned fifty not long ago and I thought, I think it's about time I stopped this. Because it wasn't doing my heart any good, either. My best story is of an actor who was really dyslexic and he was terrified of having to sit in front of his peers reading a script he'd never seen before, and he said, 'Please, please give it to me, even if it's only the night before. I must read it.' When I finished it was four o'clock in the morning and I said, 'I don't think I can give it to him now. He must be in bed.' And the lady typing it said, 'I'll take it round to him. He was most insistent.' And she drove round in the car. There was this house all in darkness, his digs in Scarborough, and she slid the script through the letter box and as it was halfway through somebody grabbed it from the other side. He'd been sitting in the hall till four in the morning.

BRIAN But you don't make things easy for yourself, because I've seen one of your plays where you had four different sets and each one is lit up in turn with different things happening and different families and you have different time-scales. One play, I think, one could choose the finish. What was that one and how many endings were there?

ALAN There was one play I wrote called *Intimate Exchanges*, which actually has sixteen endings, which is rather a lot.

BRIAN Who chose which one it was going to be on each night?

ALAN It was generally the actors. I think the audience would have fallen into disarray with sixteen choices. The idea behind that was to try and remind people – and they do tend to forget – that theatre is live. When we think about theatre and we're always contemplating its demise and it never quite dies, it comes back; we're always talking about what is unique about it. The only thing that is unique about theatre is its 'liveness' – the fact that you get, in a sense, an individual performance every time you go. They don't necessarily change the scripts or even the moves, but the performance subtly alters to an audience and I thought I wanted to emphasise this by saying, 'Look, folks, big things can happen in front of your very eyes. The play can take off in another direction.' Two lots of people came to see a play of mine in Scarborough called *Sisterly Feelings*. One came on one night and saw one version and recommended it to the people in the hotel, who went to see it and saw a different version. When they got back neither realised that there were variations and the most terrible row broke out and we finished up with the man saying, 'Are you calling my wife a liar?' But I think that emphasised the spontaneity of things.

BRIAN One of the nice things is that you use local talent

on the whole up in Scarborough, don't you? Most of your plays have started there with the local talent.

ALAN It's imported local talent. There are very few native Scarborough actors, but, having said that, not just the actors, but the technicians, the backstage crew and indeed a lot of the people working there have sort of fallen in love with it. A lot of Scarborough residents seem to be people who arrived there, like myself, with no idea that it existed and have then fallen in love with it. I think the people who appreciate Scarborough best are probably people from Basildon and Bedford rather than the Scarborians, who are rather dismissive about it.

BRIAN You've been described, I think, as writing middle-class comedies of anguish in people's lives. Do you regard yourself as a sort of comedy writer or is there an under-current? There appears to be, in one or two of your plays, an undercurrent of social trouble, family strife or whatever it is, which is very true to real life.

ALAN I think I regard myself as a writer, really. I think the category of comedy or tragedian is something that's rather invidious. I don't think William Shakespeare ever thought of himself as a comedy or a serious writer. He was both and I would like to think most of us are. It's a tendency these days to try and put people into one little box and say this is a particular type of writer. What's fascinated me – and increasingly so over the last few years – is to try and get at that balance between the tragedy and the comic. And it seems to me that people's emotional enjoyment can be increased – and, of course, theatre is a largely emotional experience – if you can get them reacting on two or three levels. It's both exciting and stimulating for them and for the actors.

BRIAN Do the characters come from your head or are you watching us now and thinking of ideas of characters? Are they based on real people, in other words?

ALAN Bits. I think in the end most characters come from

within oneself. It's very hard to say where you get characters. I think of myself as a sort of large reel-to-reel tape recorder that's always whirring. I'm sure that having spent a very enjoyable morning here in the box I've picked up quite a lot of things, but I'm not going to write a play about *Test Match Special*.

BRIAN Why not?

ALAN Because I think I'd get six libel writs.

BRIAN I was going to come to this. Have you ever been tempted to do a cricket play, or have I missed one?

ALAN There was one called *Time and Time Again* in which one character was fielding on the boundary at sort of deep extra cover and at one point dropped a rather important catch. But I haven't gone further on to the field. Richard Harris wrote a rather good play.

BRIAN Very good – *Outside Edge*.

ALAN I used to think that sport and theatre were not very good bedfellows, that maybe the people who liked watching sport didn't necessarily go to the theatre and vice versa, but I've come to the conclusion that may not be true, because we did a play about rowing the other year and that went terribly well.

BRIAN Can we tempt you to write one on cricket? Go off and in five days will you send me the script?

ALAN I've got somehow to get round not writing it with 22 men, because that's rather a large cast.

BRIAN I think it would be in a dressing room, or it could be in a commentary box. There's a lot of drama goes on here – you wouldn't think it. You may have noticed it this morning.

What's going through your head at the moment? Are you broody?

ALAN I'm midway through rehearsals for what is a bit of a departure for me really. It's a musical, which I wrote with my resident musical director in Scarborough, John Patterson. It's rather fun. Musicals are always tempting to do and they're always full of pitfalls, but I think we're having fun with it.

BRIAN Are you just the librettist, or have you written some of the music?

ALAN I wrote the book and I wrote the libretto and I'm directing it, but the music is John's. So it's rather nice because for once – and it's quite rare – you have a fellow creative initiator alongside you who's able to share the agonies and the excitements.

BRIAN How long did this one take you to write?

ALAN Well, we're a bit short. We went off for a fortnight to Majorca, because we'd read that's what Andrew Lloyd-Webber does. He goes to his villa in the South of France and writes successful musicals. So we thought, We haven't got a villa, so we'll go to Majorca. We went to a hotel in the north and it was lovely. I wrote the book and most of the lyrics and John cracked the music.

BRIAN In the fortnight!

ALAN Yes. I spoke to Stephen Sondheim on the phone and he said, 'How long did it take you?' I said, 'Two weeks.' He said, 'Two weeks!'

BRIAN Of course, Noël Coward used to do this. He even wrote *Private Lives* in a couple of days.

ALAN I don't think speed is necessarily a bad thing. It's not that you have to do it that way, it's just that that's how I paint the picture. I want to get all the ingredients into the frame and the longer you wait the more picky you get.

BRIAN But some of those complicated things you have must take a lot of working out. Do you wait till you actually go into rehearsals and make sure they work?

ALAN No, not at all. It's planned in general broad detail. There's a play of mine that's running in repertory at the moment called *Time of My Life* and this has three time-spans. There is one time going forward quite normally; there's one racing forward two months at a time and there's

217

one going backwards. It sounds complicated, but once I'd got the pattern in my head it wasn't difficult to do.

BRIAN I saw you last when you were directing *Tons of Money* at the National Theatre. How did you like going to the National Theatre, away from Scarborough?

ALAN It was nice, as somebody once said, playing with the big boys' toys. There was a lot more money and a lot more space to work in and I worked in all three theatres. We did *Tons of Money* in the Lyttelton and then we did my own play *Small Family Business* in the Olivier, the big one. Then I finished up having great fun with *View from the Bridge* in the tiny theatre and it was very rewarding. I think I love regional theatre and I like running it and I wouldn't be drawn away from it permanently, but I think you have to test yourself in the big arena and I think it was important to go to the National and say, 'Well, I think I'm quite good in Scarborough, but how am I up against the heavy men in London?'

BRIAN Well, how good are you in Oxford? Because you're a Professor of Contemporary Theatre.

ALAN Yes, the Cameron Mackintosh Professor.

BRIAN That's tremendous, but what does that involve?

ALAN Well, I was a little nervous, because I'm very badly educated. I left school at seventeen and went straight into the theatre, so I missed university. So here I come back as a prof, feeling a bit of a phoney. It's a mixture of some splendid dinners at various high tables. I'm trying to go round them all. I was 'buzzed' on the port the other night. I managed to finish up the bottle at Magdalen. I don't know if that's good or bad form, but anyway I got another free glass. The rest of it is very enjoyable. I've been working with a small group who are directly working to me in a series of tutorials, learning playwriting. I've been doing a lot of lectures, which were a bit frightening, but I think the feeling is very good there at the moment. The students are bright, questioning, but not bolshy.

BRIAN Do you have time to go up to the Parks and see the cricket?

ALAN Yes. And we played a charity game the other day. I put a team together, which thoroughly beat a local eleven, though I did cheat a little, because our wicket-keeper looked suspiciously like Deryck Murray. He came out of retirement. We played on the St Catherine's ground. I stood on the boundary and encouraged the team and kept the morale up.

BRIAN Who were your cricket heroes? In Sussex in those days did you have any special favourites down there?

ALAN Jim Parks, of course, the wicket-keeper there, was wonderful. I'm a great wicket-keeper watcher. I'd like to meet Jack Russell, because I think he's a wonderful wicket-keeper.

BRIAN And I suppose you now have to have some Yorkshire heroes.

ALAN Well, I'm very encouraged by the way the team's turned round and I'm a great admirer of Martyn Moxon.

BRIAN I think he's had bad luck.

ALAN There are some very exciting players in that team now and I do applaud the inclusion of Tendulkar.

BRIAN You were in favour.

ALAN Yes, I was on that side. I did think that we were being ridiculously dog-in-the-manger about it all. There are certain innovations, like that big screen, which I have to shout with everybody else my disapproval of, because it does seem to me that if you're going to have a screen like that up, you might as well dispense with the umpires and just have two cameras. It seems to me just awful. If I thought that my life was run by replays, every time I made a decision it was run back on me, one would become hopelessly inhibited. One Test match I saw here, I left the ground with England 500 to 1 against Australia. As we went home I tore my ticket up for the next day and threw it out of the window, and we all said, 'That's the last time we ever watch England.' We went back to rehearsals and as we were rehearsing people kept sticking their heads round the door and saying, 'You'll never guess what's happened.' Of course it was the famous Botham match [in 1981] and we missed a sunny day's play and, more important, we missed winning thousands of pounds!

25 Max Boyce MBE

IT WAS DAFFODIL AND LEEK time in the commentary box at Trent Bridge on the Saturday of the third Test against the West Indies in 1991. The start had been delayed after a violent thunderstorm had flooded the ground and the luncheon interval had been brought forward. This gave Ron Allsopp and his ground staff team time to carry out a magnificent mopping-up operation, using machines called 'whales'. They did so well that, allowing for an extra hour at the end, only thirty minutes' actual play was lost altogether.

Anyhow, there was no gloom in the box as our guest Max Boyce regaled us with stories in his lilting Welsh accent – stories of rugby matches when 'I was there', or tales of strange events in the valleys. Max has an infectious chuckle and as he reminisced he reminded me so much of my old friend, the late Wynford Vaughan-Thomas. Wherever he was, at a party or in a bar, there was always a crowd around him enjoying his non-stop flow describing things that had happened to him. There was always a strong element of truth in all that he said, but he embellished each story with a few additions of his own, which made it sound funnier than it probably was. So it was with Max, who like so many of our guests had made a long journey, just to be with us for our lunchtime spot. We were especially grateful to him, as he had to rush back to Wales for an engagement that evening.

Trent Bridge, 6 July 1991

MAX BOYCE I was listening this morning on my way here and I heard David Lloyd say something about Wales having done terribly well. I thought, Oh good, Wales have done well in Australia. But he meant the whales – the water-sucking machines drying the ground.

BRIAN JOHNSTON Have you ever seen Wales play in Australia?

MAX Yes, I was out there thirteen years ago. I went on the 1978 tour and I followed them. It was a wonderful tour, because it was the grand slam side, but, of course, they didn't do terribly well out there. There was a wonderful woman from Llanelli out there and she asked me where the Welsh team were staying, because, she said, 'I've made thirty warm Welsh faggots for the team.' She went round to the hotel with these and Clive Rowlands, who was the team manager, accepted them and said, 'The boys will have them for breakfast.' Well, Wales played the Test and they lost, and the next morning the first person I saw was this woman in a Welsh costume with tears running down her cheeks. 'Don't be upset,' I said, 'It's only a game.' 'Oh, Max,' she said, 'do you think it was the faggots?' I was telling the story on Australian television and, of course, a faggot in Australia has got a totally different connotation. They were falling about in the studio when I said that Wales had lost because someone had given them thirty warm Welsh faggots.

BRIAN What about the cricket side of your life?

MAX It was my great love when I was younger and I played from about sixteen in school and then in the South Wales League. Every side had a pro, so it was a good standard of cricket.

BRIAN What sort of a cricketer were you?

MAX Alan Jones, the former Glamorgan opening bat, described me as having the finest temperament of any fast bowler he'd ever seen. My line and length lacked a bit, but I had a fine temperament. I was a fiery opening bowler. I liked it very much.

BRIAN Did you base yourself on Fred Trueman?

MAX Yes, I used to pretend to be Fred.

BRIAN You are Welsh through-and-through. Where were you born?

MAX I was born in a little mining village called Glyn Neath in the Glyn Neath Valley, which is about sixteen miles from Swansea.

BRIAN Was that a mining area?

MAX We had six pits there and there aren't any at all now. The last one closed during the last miners' strike. Very much a pit village – a very pretty village now.

BRIAN Was your father a miner?

MAX Yes. My father was killed in a mine explosion a month before I was born, in fact.

BRIAN But that didn't put you off, because you went into the mines.

MAX I suppose, coming from an area like that, you didn't think of it as being dangerous and hazardous, because all your friends did it and all your family did it. People who've never lived in a mining area would say, 'Why did you go down the pit?' exactly as you've just said. But you didn't think of it, because it was part of the lifestyle of that particular community. There was nowhere else to work. There were no factories. Everyone worked underground.

BRIAN But did you gradually find that you were able to make people laugh?

MAX I never intended to be an entertainer. I started out as a sort of folk singer. I spent ten years underground and five years in engineering and then I bought a guitar and started singing in the local folk clubs. Just upstairs in a pub, and you'd invite professional folk singers down and then the local people would get up and sing a couple of songs. I wasn't doing terribly well and then I started writing my own things. It was the time when Julie Felix was singing about Vietnam. Well, I couldn't sing about Vietnam with any credence, so I sang about the things I knew about, like shift work and the fact that the colliery was being closed. And it struck a chord with people. People could identify with the things I wrote about. Then, gradually, the introductions became longer and it became a bit of story-telling. The songs became more infrequent and now I'll sing maybe only twenty per cent of the time in a performance of an hour and a half.

BRIAN When did your career really take off? In the early seventies?

MAX I was known in Wales from about 1970/71, but in Britain nationally in about 1973. I cut an album in Treorchy Rugby Club. We couldn't sell the tickets – it was fifty pence – because I was completely unknown. So people went into the streets and said, 'There's a lad cutting a record, will you come in, because without an audience it will be impossible.' And they formed the audience and that record went on to sell over half a million.

BRIAN That was your first big hit.

MAX First national success.

BRIAN I remember all these marvellous descriptions of rugby matches: 'I was there'.

MAX That 'I was there' came about actually in a cricket dinner in St Helen's where I was asked to perform for Glamorgan and I'd never performed in an after-dinner context before. And I thought, 'How can I put these stories together?' And the thing that linked them all was the fact that I was there. From there it became a bit of a catch-phrase, so I incorporated it in the stage act. I heard someone talking about Botham's match at Headingley in 1981 and he said, 'As Max Boyce would say, "I was there."'

BRIAN Having mentioned him, what about Ian Botham, the famous pantomime king? He performed with you in

Bradford – a very successful pantomime season. He's a big figure off stage; what's he like on stage?

MAX He was wonderful. I think he'd say himself he struggled for the first week.

BRIAN Well, he would do.

MAX I think if I had to open the batting or come in at number six I'd struggle as well. What I will say about him, he was tremendously disciplined. We'd been friends a long time and I said, 'No, I won't have you,' because I was afraid it might destroy our friendship. I thought he'd be terribly bored, but he absolutely loved it. He was never late and he went round all the local hospitals and signed autographs.

BRIAN Did he sing?

MAX No, he didn't sing. It's not a big part, but the main fact was that it was him.

BRIAN A few mentions of cricket.

MAX England were in Australia and whenever Gower was mentioned we'd have the sound effect of an aeroplane. He'd go, 'Hello, David.' What I was most concerned about was I didn't want to ridicule him. I didn't want him to go with some arty director in another show, who'd make him do stupid things and decry him as a person. So, because I have great admiration for him as a man and as one of the greatest players the world has ever seen, I protected him in that way and I didn't give him any line that would have made him look silly. And he became this very strong king and people could relate to him.

BRIAN Well, I've never known there was a king in *Jack and the Beanstalk*. Was he up with the ogre?

MAX Some people thought he was the giant. I saw the nasty side of the press – 'the fibre-tipped assassins'. I think somebody wrote after the opening night, which went sensationally well, 'The only thing more wooden than Ian Botham was the beanstalk.' But he himself stuck it on the dressing-room door to remind himself. He was measurably better by the end.

BRIAN What about Glamorgan cricket? Have you followed that always?

MAX All my life.

BRIAN Who were your special heroes?

MAX Well, at the moment Hugh Morris is on everybody's lips. I wonder if he'd come from Essex or Middlesex, would he have played more?

BRIAN There's the old Welsh thing – but you've got some very influential people there, Tony Lewis and Ossie Wheatley, for instance. What about the others? Do you ever see Don Shepherd?

MAX Yes, I play a lot of golf with Don. I used to pretend to be Don. Owen Phillips' garage became the Pavilion End and we used to draw white lines on the wall with chalk, and I remember Owen Phillips was the best opening bat in all West Glamorgan. He was in once for twenty-three weeks. And when I finally got him out, he'd say, 'Not out!' 'Why's that?' 'There's no chalk on the ball.' So when I see the action replays and cameras in stumps I think it was a far better day when the reason why you were out or not out depended on whether there was chalk on the ball.

BRIAN Twenty-three weeks! I think that's one for Bill Frindall's record books. You go round the world literally, don't you?

MAX I can only really go where there is huge British involvement, like Canada, New Zealand, Australia or Hong Kong. It's not just Welsh. When people are away from home they flock to see you. If the truth be told, you don't have to be terribly good in Australia, because people go there and they drag their Australian friends along and they laugh at everything. So I've had some great tours of Australia.

BRIAN Can you give us one of your poems? I've been asked to ask you for *The Incredible Plan*.

MAX I'd never be able to remember it and it's about twelve minutes long. But this is a similar poem I wrote when

Llanelli beat the All Blacks in 1973. Again, an occasion
when I'm glad to say that I was there.

'Twas on a dark and dismal day
In a week that had seen rain,
When all roads led to Stradey Park
With the All Blacks there again.
They poured down from the valleys,
They came from far and wide.
There were twenty thousand in the ground –
And me and Dai outside.
The shops were closed like Sunday
And the streets were silent still
And those who chose to stay away
Were either dead or ill.
But those who went to Stradey
Will remember till they die
How New Zealand were defeated
And how the pubs ran dry.
Aye, the beer flowed at Stradey,
Piped down from Felinfoel,
And the hands that held the glasses high
Were strong from steel and coal;
And the air was filled with singing
And I saw a grown man cry,
Not because they beat the All Blacks
But because the pubs ran dry.
Then dawned the morning after
On empty factories,
For we were shtill at Shtradey,
Bloodshot absentees.
But we all had doctor's papers,
Not one of us in pain,
And Harry Morgan buried
His granny once again.
And when I'm old

And my hair turns grey
And they put me in a chair,
I'll tell my great grandchildren
That their grandfather was there.

BRIAN That is great – well done! And these just flow out from you, do they?

MAX I've always been an avid listener to the ball-by-ball. We used to set out on concert tours, with my friend Philip Whitehead who plays up in the Saddleworth League, when there were Test matches on, leaving at ten to eleven, before the ball-by-ball started, and we used to look at maps because we'd hate to miss a ball and the great problem was – tunnels. In the Dartford Tunnel especially you'd miss maybe three overs. So you'd draw out a route plan where there were no tunnels and you'd listen to Brian Johnston. One day it took us five hours to go from Bournemouth to Bath or somewhere! We went the no-tunnel route.

BRIAN You sing and then talk – a mixture?

MAX Yes, a sort of pot-pourri of story-telling with a few songs wedged in between, but they're all true stories that I've embroidered and coloured and added to and they've become routines as such. But they're all born of truth. Some of the most amazing stories are absolutely true. For instance, I was coming back from recording an album in London and I went to find a seat on the train on my own, because I was shattered. I'd been up all night. And who gets on but Stuart Burrows, the tenor. And I said, 'Oh, Stuart, I've had too much red wine last night. Do you mind if we don't chat till we get to Newport?' And he said, 'I've just finished a week of opera myself. I feel the same way.' The train pulls out of Paddington and when we get to Royal Oak a soldier comes into the carriage. The Royal Welch Fusiliers have just come home from Belfast. 'Max! How's it going, Max? Hey, Max, give us a song! Sospan

Fach! Hang on, I'll go and get the boys.' Fifteen soldiers come in now. 'Max, Max, we've brought you some Newcastle Brown!' And they've got a big crate. 'Max, give us a song!' 'We're on a train, it's first class, come on, lads.' He takes off his hat, with the three Welsh feathers. 'If you won't sing for the beer, sing for this.' So I'm under pressure now. 'Oh, lads, I can't sing.' And then Stuart Burrows, arguably the greatest lyrical tenor in the world, says, 'He is not singing.' This soldier says, 'Who are you? His manager, is it?' Stuart says, 'Yes, I'm his manager and he's not singing.' 'Come on, Max, give us a song.' Stuart says, 'He's not singing, but I'll sing instead.' 'We don't want you to sing, we want Max to sing.' Finally they relented and said to Stuart, 'OK, you sing.' Stuart Burrows got up on that 125 train from Paddington and sang 'Waft of Angels Through the Skies'. This wonderful voice ringing through this compartment. And all these commuters were waking up and saying, 'I say, the sandwiches are stale, but the cabaret is awfully good.' And this soldier turns to Stuart at the end and he says, 'Listen, pal, I don't know much about singing, but as far as I'm concerned you're wasting your time managing him!' True story. You couldn't invent that.

BRIAN If you'd been feeling fine, what song would you have chosen?

MAX Strangely enough, when anyone's asked for a party piece, mine has always been 'The Road and the Miles to Dundee', a Scottish folk song. I don't know why, I suppose I can remember it.

BRIAN (with studied innocence) How does it go, Max?

(Max – after a chuckle – sang a verse of the haunting song.)

BRIAN Do you like all sorts of music?

MAX Yes. I like lyrics perhaps more than music, and I was thinking of a cricket link for today and I thought of Dylan Thomas and his wonderful gift of painting pictures with words. The only thing that I know of Dylan Thomas writing of cricket was so vivid a picture that he painted of young kids playing on the beach by St Helen's and another kid who's got nobody to play with and he's stuck, hoping that the family who are playing cricket will ask him to join in. And Dylan Thomas called it *The Friendless Fielder*.

> The loneliness of the friendless fielder
> Standing on the edge of family cricket
> Uninvited to tea or bat.

I wish I'd written that.

BRIAN I didn't know he was into cricket.

MAX He just wrote about anything. He went to St Helen's and he lived near there. He just looked at things and wrote of them. This wonderful descriptive ability. The fattest woman in Neath Fair was described as 'Her eyes like black-currants in blancmange'. It's a wonderful vision. And his grandfather was so wild he was 'Like a buffalo in an airing cupboard'.

BRIAN I wish he'd written about cricket; he could have described some cricketers too. Have you written about a Test match?

MAX No, the only cricket I've written about is when I played for a side called Ponteddfechan in the South Wales League and, unfortunately, back in about 1970, they drove the extension on the Heads of the Valleys motorway right through our cricket ground and that was the end. It was village cricket at its best, and about five years ago we had a reunion match and all the people who ever played for this little village played again. We cut the wicket with a tractor and a five-gang mower and all the old lads came back. Of course, you couldn't bowl fast because it was really wild and, because of the motorway, one boundary was about seventy-five feet. And there were houses, so you could be 'out in gardens'. This guy, Alan Wicks, played and the next day he was playing for a fairly good side at Arundel. And his captain said, 'Tell me, Wicks, are you playing much these days?' 'Yes,' he said. 'I don't know where to put you in. Are you playing well? Did you play yesterday?' 'Yes, I did.' 'How many runs did you get?' 'I got 70.' 'How did you get out?' 'I was "out in gardens".' So he stuck him in at number eleven.

BRIAN We'll have to make that the eleventh way of getting out.

MAX But it was a sad occasion.

BRIAN Yes, awful losing the cricket ground.

MAX And they'd played there for a hundred years. So I wrote a parody of Tom Jones's 'Green, Green Grass of Home' and it got to the speaking bit:

> And as I bat and look around me
> At the four short legs that surround me,
> I realise that surveyor wasn't joking.
> 'Cause they'll bring that ugly concrete highway
> And take away what once was my way.
> I can't believe my green, green field of home.

BRIAN Do you still play a bit of charity cricket?

MAX Yes, I play for the Taverners whenever I can.

BRIAN What length run nowadays?

MAX Oh, it's just as long. But I have a packed lunch halfway now.

BRIAN What's your favourite ground?

MAX Well, obviously St Helen's. I used to go to watch touring sides and my mother used to make me banana sandwiches. And I remember the days when we used to beat Essex before the bananas went black.

BRIAN What about your rugby? Who were the greatest rugby players you enjoyed in Wales?

MAX Probably Gerald Davies and then Gareth Edwards, and Barry John was probably the finest outside half. And there's a wonderful story about when we played golf in a big tournament at the Royal Glyn Neath Golf Club and there was the greatest rainfall for eighty-seven years. After twelve holes it was abandoned because the greens were completely under water. We only had three showers and, because everybody came off the course together, there was chaos in the changing rooms. So this lad said, 'I only live a hundred yards from here. Come down to my house for a bath, Mr John.' 'Call me Barry,' he said. So they go down to his house and Barry's in the bath, having a glass of home-made ale, and this lad's on the phone to his father. 'You'll never guess who I've got in the bath! I've got Barry John!' 'Good God!' he said. 'Whatever you do, don't let the water out. We'll bottle it!'

BRIAN Now, when you leave here, I hope you've mapped out your course so that there are no tunnels on the way, because I hope you'll be listening to us.

MAX I've checked the tunnel route and there's only one in Monmouth, so I'm going to wait until the end of the over and then hurtle through the tunnel at Monmouth so I won't miss a ball.

26 Michael Charlton

MICHAEL CHARLTON WAS UNUSUAL. He was an Australian cricket commentator with a 'Pommie' accent during the 1950s. He also introduced the Australian equivalent of BBC TV's *Panorama* called *Window on the World*. Sadly, for us, he deserted cricket to become a political commentator and interviewer full time, coming over to work in England, where he still lives. He was a splendid contrast to the normal Australian cricket commentator, with a delightful sense of humour portrayed with a friendly chuckle.

He was the ABC commentator over here in 1956, and we started my conversation with him with a clip from his own commentary during the Old Trafford Test – Laker's match. He described a unique wicket: Burke caught Cowdrey bowled Lock 22. It was unique because it was the only wicket Tony Lock took during the match, Jim Laker taking the other nineteen.

Headingley, 14 July 1984

MICHAEL CHARLTON It was remarkable, wasn't it? Two world-class spinners, one of whom gets nineteen wickets and the other gets only one.

BRIAN JOHNSTON Tony Lock's still trying to work it out. Laker got all his wickets from the same end – the Stretford End. Locky bowled from that end as well.

MICHAEL Yes, so it was the same for both. I remember going out to the wicket when it was all over and what I shall never forget is a small circle on a length on off stump in which it looked as if a whole series of two-shilling pieces had been put down – and that was Laker. He'd bowled absolutely on this spot. I thought he was just about unplayable.

BRIAN Well, now, travelling round with the team you get to know all their feelings and inner secrets. Publicly they said the pitch was made to measure for Laker, although in fact England made 459 on it.

MICHAEL It was the same for both sides, wasn't it? There was a lot of controversy about that pitch. I think the Australians thought they'd been taken for a ride. They thought that that pitch at Old Trafford that time was not the traditional one. Some new soil had been put on it and all that kind of thing, but it was the same for both sides. Not a happy tour all round, I think, that one for the Australians. They were on a down-swing that time. I think also that they weren't as well led as they might have been and I think there was a general feeling – certainly my own feeling – that Keith Miller should have captained that side.

BRIAN Let's just remind people that the first Test of that 1956 series was drawn at Trent Bridge, and then the second one at Lord's Australia won.

MICHAEL Yes, Miller won that. Extraordinary figure he was. I remember him as he came off the field throwing a bail to somebody.

BRIAN There's a picture of him; it's been captured and I've seen it in books.

MICHAEL He had a flair for that, didn't he?

(Miller took ten wickets in the Lord's Test.)

BRIAN Then England won the third Test by an innings here at Headingley and then they won the Old Trafford one by an innings and the fifth was drawn. Let's talk about Miller for a second, because you say he should have been captain. How good a captain do you reckon he was?

MICHAEL Well, he was a very fine captain of the state side of New South Wales, because I think he was an inspirational captain. He was not a man to speak coherently and explain things in detail before matches began. He wasn't that kind of player, I think we all know. But he could inspire great loyalty in a side and I think that young side in New South Wales absolutely worshipped him. He could do as he liked and he had great luck of course. I think whatever it was Horatio said about Hamlet, had he been put on he was likely to have proved most royal. He was a most inspiring figure.

BRIAN But he had this lovely, casual approach in everything he did.

MICHAEL Jimmy Burke, who died so tragically, told me of a match we were all at in Newcastle. It must have been a country match and Miller was captain of the New South Wales side, and they walked out in the morning under rather a hot sun. Miller's eyes were shielded against the sun this particular morning and Burke said to him, 'Excuse me, Nugget' – they all called him Nugget – 'there are twelve men.' And Miller, without turning round, said, 'Well somebody bugger off, then.' And just kept on – didn't even look round.

BRIAN Jimmy Burke was a great character. He became a very good commentator, didn't he?

MICHAEL Well, that was long after my time. He was a wonderful tourist, a great mimic, a very amusing boy. He was a happy character when I knew him.

BRIAN And he could imitate somebody throwing when he bowled.

MICHAEL Yes, he had the most dreadful action.

BRIAN I don't think people minded much because it wasn't very effective.

(*J. W. Burke, who played 24 Tests for Australia between 1950 and 1958, committed suicide at the age of 49 in 1979.*)

BRIAN What actually was your period of commentating? We knew you in 1956, when you came here.

MICHAEL Round about 1952 I was doing Sheffield Shield

matches and then I did the 1954 tour, England's tour of Australia – Len Hutton's tour. Then there were some in India.

BRIAN You were there in 1958/59, my first time when I came out to Australia.

MICHAEL Yes, I remember you getting bowled over in the surf at Bondi and Jack Fingleton laughing.

BRIAN Yes, someone shouted, 'There's one out the back,' or something. What's it called? I was 'dumped'.

MICHAEL You were dumped, yes. I remember you striding heroically into the surf and appearing like a torpedo about five minutes later, belching sand and salt water.

BRIAN You were a bit extraordinary to be a commentator in Australia, because you had what they used to describe as a slightly Pommie voice.

MICHAEL It's always difficult to explain, but my parents were New Zealanders and we were always brought up very strictly at home not to speak the colonial twang, as my father called it. So it's an environmental thing, largely, coming from my father. We always called England 'home'. In fact, when I came here in 1956, they wanted me to sound more Australian. They were a bit disturbed by that.

BRIAN But you were a bit different. The average Australian commentator is not quite as light-hearted as we are and certainly you were light-hearted. You saw the fun in it.

MICHAEL Too often, perhaps. Yes, I always looked for that myself. I think it's the most marvellous witty and amusing game. We were brought up, of course, in the Bradman era and they always said about him that he'd be trying to get a hundred against the blind school. It was a serious business in Australia. I think Don Bradman's seriousness of purpose rather overlaid it, you know. It sat upon its soul like a mountain for many years.

BRIAN Why did you give all this up, then, because you obviously love cricket so much?

MICHAEL Well, I very much ask myself that. The best years

I had were undoubtedly going round the world with cricketers and cricket teams. I loved it and I felt quite tearful coming back here this morning. I haven't been here, to this ground, for twenty-eight years. I had the most marvellous time. I suppose because of the rather puritan background, I wondered, at the age I was – mid-twenties – if one was going to go on doing this for the rest of one's life. Oddly enough, it was through cricket that my life was pretty much changed to politics because I was in Delhi once, doing a Test match there on the Australian tour – Richie Benaud's tour – and I sat next to Nehru, the Prime Minister of India. And I interviewed him on the strength of this later and I got a bit of a taste for this and I ended up doing that ever after.

BRIAN Why did you decide to come over here? We're very glad you did.

MICHAEL I was invited, Johnno. They asked me to come and I've been here ever since.

BRIAN I want to take you back now to perhaps one of the most exciting matches you ever did. The tie in 1960 at Brisbane.

MICHAEL I brought my tie to show you. Especially for you I wear it.

BRIAN That's the famous tie. Is it everyone who was there who can wear it?

MICHAEL Any one of the players or correspondents who were there can wear it. It's a rather unimaginative thing, as you see. It's the West Indies colours and the gold and green.

BRIAN What's this insignia?

MICHAEL Well, you might well ask. Fingo designed this – Jack Fingleton – and it's a golden tied knot. It's the tie for what must be – I don't know, a lot of water's gone down many rivers since then – the greatest Test match ever played.

BRIAN I think it must have been. And yet the strange thing

is, we hear very strange stories of how – it wasn't you – but one of the Australian commentators who was on at the end didn't realise what the result was and I think said it was a draw, and the next day had to go back and do a cod commentary for the archives with some people applauding in the box.

MICHAEL Well, I've not heard that. We all left the ground in the dawn next morning. Nobody went to bed that night – players, public or the travelling press. There was confusion at the end. It was the last over, last day and the last couple of balls of the Test match, and you know those huge tropical sunsets in the north in Australia – it was like a scarlet ribbon. It was quite hard to see the scoreboard. And the scoreboard panicked, because of all these run-outs at the end, because you very nearly had completed runs. Everybody had their hands on the trigger. Everybody was saying, 'It's all over. They've won.' And it wasn't won, because all these hairline decisions for run-outs were being given. I'd done the commentary period just before the Test match ended, the penultimate twenty minutes. Clive Harburg did the last session and I was down on the field just as they came off. Joe Solomon thought the West Indies had won and Worrell, the captain, thought they'd lost. It was quite confusing. The ABC scorer kept his head. He was marvellous. He had it right.

BRIAN No names, no pack drill, but certain well-known commentators and ex-Test cricketers writing for newspapers had left the ground and heard the result when they arrived by air in Sydney.

MICHAEL They had indeed. There were those – and we dare not speak their names, even now – who left before the last hour or so, assuming that Australia were going to win. It would have been a remarkable Test match even if it hadn't had the finish that it did. There was a wonderful innings by a glamorous young Australian in the first innings – O'Neill made 181. There was an absolutely superb innings by Sobers – 132. And there were two shots in that innings in particular. He hit something through mid-wicket – a pull shot, but the trajectory of that shot I can still see. It never rose more than about five feet above the ground. I thought it must have been like that at Trafalgar on Nelson's ships, with a cannonball carrying away the rigging. It went straight over the fence like a rocket and it mowed down the crowd. Then he hit something that hit Colin McDonald at very deep mid-off on the shoulder. An off-drive off Benaud, I think, and it hit McDonald on the left shoulder as he put a knee down to field it and it hit the sight board. That was Sobers. Anyway, it all came down to this: Australia had to get 233 to win in 300 minutes and it looked as if they would do it easily.

(*A seventh-wicket stand between Benaud and Davidson had taken the Australians from 92 for 6 to 226 for 7.*)

And it got down to this last over at four minutes to six, I remember, in this blood-red sunset and almost hysterical excitement. Australia had to get six runs off eight balls and there were three wickets to fall, and Benaud had batted marvellously throughout the afternoon. I was talking to Richie, whom I hadn't seen for years, only this morning and he said that Frank Worrell went over to Wes Hall, who was to bowl this last over, and said, 'No bouncers, Wes.' So the first thing Wes Hall did was to bowl a bouncer and Benaud hooked it – and I have Richie's authority to say this: he said it should have been a six, but he got a top edge and it went miles high and Alexander, the wicket-keeper, caught it marvellously over his head.

(*Benaud was out for 52; Australia needed five runs to win off six balls. The new batsman, Meckiff, was nearly run out taking a bye off his second ball. Four needed off four balls.*)

Wally Grout hooked the next one from Hall – skied it to mid-wicket. Now, Wes Hall was soaked with sweat. He was bowling like a hurricane and his shirt was flapping all over the place. I remember the umpires kept having to stop him and tell him to tuck his shirt in, because this billowing sail, this spinnaker, was obscuring everybody's view. The umpire couldn't see. Anyway, Wally Grout skied this to Rohan Kanhai at mid-wicket and Kanhai had all day and all night to get underneath this, except that Hall, who was doing all his own fielding, changed course and I swear he was doing fifty mph. He galloped across and he barrelled into Kanhai, knocked him flying and it went to ground. They got a single. Three were needed off three balls. The four thousand people who saw this are the members of the most exclusive and boring club in the world.

BRIAN I've never heard it in such detail.

MICHAEL So Meckiff let fly at the next ball from Wes Hall and he hooked him far out to deep mid-wicket, on the far mid-wicket fence, and again you could hardly see in this terrific sunset.

BRIAN A four would have won the match.

MICHAEL Of course. And they rushed off. They took the first two. Wally Grout turned for the third and Conrad Hunte – he was a beautiful player, Hunte – he threw. It must have been the throw of a lifetime. He was travelling round the boundary, right on the boundary line. He scooped it up and he threw it over the top of the stumps and Grout was flying for these last few yards. He hurled himself along the ground. He skidded on his stomach – out by half a foot, something like that. He got up covered in red dust and people were hysterical by this time. Kline came in and he hit the first one to forward short leg, and Joe Solomon threw Meckiff out from side on. And so there was this enormous confusion, you see, with people running around. I think the official attendance that day was four thousand, and I shall never forget, like Colonel Maitland at Waterloo – you must know this, Johnno, as a Guardsman: 'Stand up, Guards!' – that crowd stood up as one man and they came over that fence like a wall and they rushed the pavilion. Frankie Worrell came off and I remember him saying, 'Man, this is a game for cool fools.' And Bradman, who was below us, he had a newspaper in his hands and the thing was in tatters, it was twisted so much. Like a stage magician with a torn paper act.

BRIAN And the celebrations that night.

MICHAEL The West Indians sang calypsos all night. The crowds were out in the streets. I've never seen anything like it.

BRIAN Well, happy memories, and how could you really have left that for a world of interviewing kings and prime ministers? Is it fun?

MICHAEL Well, yes it is, but it's a different kind of amusement.

BRIAN Do you get a few laughs?

MICHAEL I wouldn't say there are many laughs, no. I would say it's a fairly detached sort of amusement. It's not the generous, carefree, likeable world that you all happily reflect here.

27 Leslie Crowther CBE

O N 3 OCTOBER 1992 LESLIE had a horrendous car accident. His Rolls Royce veered off a motorway into the embankment on the side of the road. It turned completely over, with Leslie still inside. Miraculously – thanks, no doubt, to the solid bodywork of the Rolls – he was able to get out and, still conscious, was even able to crack jokes with his rescuers. However, after being taken to hospital he had a severe relapse and went into a coma, which was to last for six weeks. He was transferred to Frenchay Hospital in Bristol where he underwent two operations on his brain. At first, when he came out of his coma, due to a tracheotomy he was unable to speak, but he could write things down.

There are two delightful stories about this. His wife Jean opened a letter addressed to him from Number 10 Downing Street asking if he would agree to accept the award of a CBE. She whispered into his ear that he must sign his acceptance and it was the very first thing he wrote. On another occasion one of his daughters was exercising his brain by asking him to identify and point at various shapes – circles, squares etc. She felt he was not concentrating so reprimanded him gently, saying, 'Come on, Dad, concentrate, and try harder.' He immediately reached for his pencil and paper and hastily scribbled just one word: 'Bollocks'. Recovery was under way! *(Sadly, Leslie died in September 1996 at the age of 63.)*

I suppose a lot of people remember Leslie as a presenter of *Crackerjack*, or think of his famous 'Come on down!' in the quiz show *The Price is Right*. But, of course, he was far more than that. He was one of the top five stand-up comedians in the country, performing in cabaret, panto-mime and especially as an after-dinner speaker. He had a fund of stories and jokes, usually topical, and was a great ad-libber with any interrupters. Aside from his work he was a tremendous worker for charity. In 1991 and 1992 he was president of the Lord's Taverners for whom he made nearly 350 appearances at various events, every one requiring a speech from him.

When he joined us in the box at Old Trafford in 1985 it was a wet day, so we had a rather longer session than usual during 'Rain Stopped Play', though he had to leave us in mid-afternoon to go back to Blackpool where he was appearing twice nightly in *The Price is Right*. I mentioned his quick wit as an ad-libber. You will find proof of this with his final remark of our conversation!

Old Trafford, 3 August 1985

BRIAN JOHNSTON I got you to sign something just now and you did it with your left hand. Are you a left-hander at cricket?

LESLIE CROWTHER I'm a left-handed bowler. Fred Trueman, who is godfather to our son, Nicholas, describes my bowling as left-arm 'blankety-blank' over the wicket, which is very accurate. But I bat right-handed.

BRIAN So where did you start your cricket? When did you first become interested in it?

LESLIE I first became interested at the Scarborough Festival when I was in a show called the Fol-de-Rols, which was a concert party, as you know. The Australians were playing and Neil Harvey was over and so were Keith Miller and Ray Lindwall and all that lot.

BRIAN Sounds like 1953.

LESLIE That's right, it was. I went along and I suddenly saw all these magical people in real life, as it were, and I became totally besotted and I've followed cricket ever since.

BRIAN Did you play at school?

LESLIE I did, but I was very bad. I wasn't any good at any kind of sports. I had a very strange illness called meningitis.

BRIAN You were lucky to get away with it.

LESLIE In the late 1940s I was very lucky to get away with it. They diagnosed it as scarlet fever and I was shoved in a scarlet fever ward, so I had to be cured of scarlet fever before they could start on the other.

BRIAN You wear glasses, so that would have affected your cricket – the fact that you're short-sighted.

LESLIE Oh, very short-sighted, yes, but nothing affects my cricket. It's always been bad.

BRIAN So when you started in 1953, which team did you take up as your favourite?

LESLIE England. I thought that was a good team to take up. I didn't bother with a county, just went straight for the country. Lately, of course, I've been following the fortunes of Somerset, because that's where we've moved and it seems a fairly good team with people like Richards and Garner and another chap called Botham.

BRIAN You're near sunny Bath, are you?

LESLIE Yes, about three miles. The Bath cricket festival, of course, is great, now they've sorted out that wicket.

BRIAN It's lovely, isn't it? So who were your heroes after 1953 on the English cricket scene?

LESLIE Oh, Peter May, Ted Dexter, Tom Graveney, Ken Barrington – the really elegant strokemakers. You were saying earlier that cricket and the theatre are very aligned and that there is something in common with the two professions, and there is. The thing about cricket, although some people call it a slow game, it's a very, very dramatic game and every player gets his entrance and his exit –

very often sooner than he wants to – but it's a dramatic game and I love it.

BRIAN There is this affinity and it's partly because cricketers enjoy meeting people from the stage.

LESLIE That's right. When I was in a thing called *Let Sleeping Wives Lie* at the Garrick Theatre, there was a nervous tap on the dressing-room door one evening and Johnny Gleeson was ushered in. And apparently, when he came to England to play in that marvellous series with that incredible bowling that nobody could fathom, he went to every single West End show and introduced himself shyly to everybody.

(J. W. Gleeson toured England in 1968 and 1972 and played in 29 Tests for Australia, bowling an enigmatic mix of off- and leg-breaks.)

BRIAN Back in Australia he was a farmer and used to have to go 120 miles each Saturday to play in his game and he didn't see any theatre. I remember talking to him about it and he literally went to everything when he came here.

LESLIE He absolutely adored it and so we got to know him very well. There was a wonderful moment in *Let Sleeping Wives Lie* with Brian Rix – who, as you know, is potty about the game – Leo Franklyn – wonderful chap, mad about cricket – and myself and Bill Treacher. There was a Test in the West Indies when all England had to do was draw the last match to win the series.

BRIAN That was Colin Cowdrey's tour in 1968. Jeff Jones came in to bat for the last over and held out.

LESLIE That's right. We had a dresser who was a wonderful guy – gay as a brush – and we got him with a blackboard and chalk at the side of the stage, chalking up the score. The audience must have been absolutely baffled.

BRIAN That was one of the best matches I've seen. At one time there was no chance of Jeff Jones ever having to bat, and the night before he had a very good night out and he wasn't quite prepared for it. It didn't matter, because he didn't hit the ball with the bat. Every single ball hit him on the pad. There were six appeals for lbw. He thrust his leg out and it was the most marvellous last over. It won the series and we had great celebrations in the English Pub in Trinidad that night. Did you ever play for the Stage?

LESLIE No. I am an old stager. I play for the Lord's Taverners. I've got a photograph of the late and great Kenny Barrington saying, 'Thanks for helping with my benefit and for taking the greatest catch off my bowling I've ever seen.'

BRIAN That's rather nice. Wasn't he lovely, though, Ken? In your career, which do you prefer? Standing up in front of the curtains? Is that your favourite?

LESLIE Anything is my favourite, I don't really mind. In a farce or a play or after-dinner speaking, a variety act, cabaret, pantomime – that's great, because you've got the lot there. Everyone thinks pantomime's easy, and it's the most difficult convention.

BRIAN Can I reveal, for the first time in public, that last week I was rung up and offered the part in pantomime of Alderman Fitzwarren this winter.

LESLIE You're joking! Oh!

BRIAN And I think it was going to be at a very nice theatre. I said I'd rather be Baron Hardup, but he said, 'No, you've got to be Alderman Fitzwarren,' and unfortunately this January I've already mapped something out. It's a thing I've been dying to do all my life.

LESLIE You'll have to wear tights, you know, if you're Alderman Fitzwarren.

BRIAN What Fitzwarren fits me. But pantomime is hard work, isn't it? You've got to do those twice-daily things.

LESLIE Oh, yes. You clock in at two and clock out at half past ten at night.

BRIAN Have you ever managed to bring cricket into your act?

LESLIE I've got masses of cricket stories. The first time I

met Fred, in fact, I was doing a cricket ballet. There was a ballet-dancing wrestler called Ricky Starr, so I did this burlesque. If you can have a ballet-dancing wrestler, why not a ballet-dancing cricketer? I did this thing from *Swan Lake* and ponced about in tights and a box and pads. Sheila Burnett was behind the wicket as the keeper. This was in the Fol-de-Rols.

BRIAN Where are you from originally?

LESLIE In fact I'm a Nottinghamshire man, born in West Bridgford, or bread-and-lard island, as it's called.

BRIAN Not so far from Parr's Tree, then.

LESLIE No, in fact Parr's Tree fell down when I was staying at the Bridgford Hotel, which is now council offices. I was in pantomime and there was this horrendous storm. Down went Parr's Tree and I went down in my pyjamas and dressing gown, got this hacksaw from the night porter and a torch and I climbed over into Trent Bridge. And I still have a branch of Parr's Tree.

BRIAN They turned the rest of it into cricket bats, which they sold at enormous profit, but yours is the genuine branch.

LESLIE There is a poem in the Long Room – or square room, really – at Trent Bridge. It was written in 1938 to mark the centenary of cricket at Trent Bridge, and it goes like this:

So small a space, so lost this slip of earth,
When we spread out the map that spans the shire
Only an oasis in a city's dearth,
A spark still left in long extinguished fire.
But men have gathered here and given their praise
To many a battle, many a Notts-shire team,
Stored up great sunlit deeds, then, going their ways
Have seen Trent Bridge for ever more in dream.
They helped to build a game, those cricketers,
The Gunns and Shrewsbury, Daft and Flowers,

Batting and bowling down the golden hours
On this hallowed turf. Surely today
Their ghosts come back where once they loved to play.
No cricket ground had nobler visitors.

BRIAN That is super. Now, who wrote it?

LESLIE Thomas Moult.

BRIAN I must tell you, he wasn't reading that. Are you good at memorising lines?

LESLIE Well, yes, because I started out as a straight actor – a lot of people think I still am!

BRIAN You've managed to snatch an afternoon today, but how often can you get away to watch cricket?

LESLIE My agent has arranged it very badly this year, because we started round about the time of the first Test and we finish working long after the sixth Test is over.

BRIAN You had a match at Blackpool, though.

LESLIE Oh yes. And what is amazing about coming up here to work is that if you're living down south you do tend to forget, unless you're reminded of it – and there's no reason why you should be, because it's not publicised in the papers – the fact that the Lancashire and Northern and Bradford Leagues – all these leagues – are unbelievably strong, play the most wonderful cricket and all have as a pro a Test cricketer who just doesn't happen to be playing Test cricket for his country at that moment. There was this cricket festival at Blackpool. It was Geoff Boycott's World XI and an International XI and I just went along and, sure enough, there were 22 players plus about eight reserves all of whom were Test cricketers from Sri Lanka, Pakistan, India, Australia. David Hookes was playing; it really was quite remarkable. I was asked to adjudicate the man of the match on the Sunday and there was no doubt about it that it was a guy called Sivaramakrishnan. He was turning the ball square.

BRIAN When the Indians come over next year, will you

come and coach us in how to say that, because you've got it rather well. I'll call him 'Shivers'.

LESLIE It'll be 'shivers' anyway.

BRIAN You're wearing the MCC tie.

LESLIE The old ham and egg. It took me nine years of impatient waiting to get it and I've worn it ever since. I bought it seven weeks ago and I've worn it as a pyjama cord – I just love it.

BRIAN At one time it was not done to wear that tie until the great Lord Cobham became president of MCC in the mid-1950s and he said, 'What is the point of having a club tie if nobody wears it?' And he began to wear it, and now everybody does. I think it's very good.

LESLIE I think it's a great honour to be a member of that particular club and to wear the tie. I'm not saying that sartorially it is the greatest choice of colours, but it's a smashing tie to wear.

BRIAN A great honour to be in the club.

LESLIE You're in the club, are you? You'll make Fleet Street!

28 Eric Idle

WE HAVE HAD A NUMBER of comedians as our guests in 'A View from the Boundary' – Michael Bentine, Brian Rix, Willie Rushton, John Cleese, Leslie Crowther and Max Boyce. They all seem to love cricket and it's often the one thing in life that they take seriously. I am not so sure, however, that our guest at Trent Bridge, Eric Idle, did so. In fact, after meeting him I could not discover what he did take seriously, except perhaps for comedy itself – which, strangely, is a very serious business.

Mind you, I am probably wrong in classifying Eric as a comedian. He is so many other things as well – writer, guitarist, composer and film star. At the time he was living in a large house in St John's Wood, not far from me, but only a penalty kick or so from Gary Lineker, then one of the Wood's other most distinguished inhabitants.

On reading through the transcript of our conversation I suppose I should also award him the accolade of 'singer'. I also found fascinating his description of how *Monty Python* was put together. I told you comedy was a serious business.

I began by asking him about the tie that he was wearing.

Trent Bridge, 9 June 1990

ERIC IDLE This is actually a Pembroke College tie – which I borrowed from a garage attendant on the way up.
BRIAN JOHNSTON You were at Cambridge.

ERIC Yes. I put this on to remind you, so you would mention it and people would think I wasn't quite so eccentric.

BRIAN Did you perform at cricket at Cambridge?

ERIC No, I wasn't half good enough for that. I just performed on the stage. I wasn't even good enough to play for Pembroke.

BRIAN But you achieved a certain prowess there, because you were president of the Footlights. There must have been some famous names.

ERIC When I got there Tim Brooke-Taylor was president and I had to audition for him and Bill Oddie. John Cleese was there and Graham Chapman. The Frost (*David Frost*) had just left.

BRIAN What do you do when you go to an audition?

ERIC We did a very bad sketch. I went with some other people who laughed all the way through and giggled and I didn't laugh. They thought, therefore, that I must have been funny.

BRIAN What has been your cricket connection? What county do you follow?

ERIC Warwickshire. I lived quite a lot of my early life there. The first game I ever saw was about 1953, Warwickshire against Australia. Freddie Gardner and Norman Horner opened the batting, I think, and I used to have one of those books and used to do all the dots and all that on the Rea Bank.

BRIAN Oh well, Frindall's getting a bit past it. Would you like to come and do it for us?

So you went and watched. What about actual playing?

ERIC I was at school at Wolverhampton and we had a cricket pitch and I became a wicket-keeper, because I realised fairly early on that you had gloves on. This was obviously much better. Also I tended to go to sleep on the boundary, and if you're wicket-keeper you know pretty certainly that it's coming in your direction every ball.

BRIAN It's essential to keep awake.

ERIC And much easier, because something's always about to happen. I broke my nose keeping wicket, which is why I have this rather handsome and eccentric profile.

BRIAN I thought it was a very distinguished nose. I was getting rather jealous about it.

ERIC It depends which side you look at.

BRIAN Keeping wicket can be quite dangerous. I was standing up to a moderately fast bowler and the batsman snicked it on to my nose. It's painful, isn't it?

ERIC It's very painful.

BRIAN What it does reveal is that both you and I stood up at the wicket. They don't nowadays, which is very cowardly. I know you're always travelling all over the world. Do you follow the cricket at all?

ERIC I love watching cricket, yes. Wherever England are losing abroad, I'm usually there.

BRIAN What about the film career? We've all seen you in *Nuns on the Run*. Was that fun to make?

ERIC It was an hysterical film to make. We spent most of the six or seven weeks dressed as nuns, walking round west London.

BRIAN What did you have on underneath?

ERIC We had our trousers and jackets. It was freezing. So you can whip it off and leave for home at once or nip into the pub quickly.

BRIAN Are they quite comfortable with that thing across your forehead?

ERIC They're horrendously uncomfortable. They're tight and only your face protrudes. You can't hear anything and you can't see anybody. If they approach you from behind it makes you jump. You can understand now why nuns take a vow of silence.

BRIAN What about old Robbie Coltrane, is he funny?

ERIC Coltrane is hysterical. And he is huge. He's a very big man.

BRIAN What do you like to be called? Writing is your basic business.

ERIC Well, it was my basic business, but for the last five or six years I seem to have been doing nothing but acting. I like to be called a comedian, really.

BRIAN In *Monty Python* you started writing, did you? And then you wrote yourself some good stuff, I suppose.

ERIC The whole thing about the Footlights is that you write and act. Nobody else is going to write for you, so you're virtually forced into writing for yourself. And we were very lucky. When we came down from Cambridge we got co-opted by Frost who dragged us off to write for him. We were writing his ad-libs for about ten years.

BRIAN Do you mean to say you've written some of Frost's jokes?

ERIC Some of Frost's best jokes. He still uses some of mine.

BRIAN You're the chap I've been wanting to meet for years.

ERIC I can let you have a few after-dinner jokes, partially used.

BRIAN What were all these people like, Michael Palin, Terry Jones and the late Graham Chapman?

ERIC Chapman was a mad, pipe-smoking eccentric.

BRIAN John Cleese said you used to sit round the table and discuss the next *Monty Python* and all go away and write something completely different from what you'd agreed to write. Was that roughly it?

ERIC Usually, yes. You can't really map out comedy. It just has to come and you have to say, 'Well, that works and that doesn't work.'

BRIAN How disciplined was it? Because it looked zany and inconsequential.

ERIC It was completely disciplined. We worked from about ten till five solidly and we never ad-libbed a word. It was always completely scripted. We did all the ad-libbing in the writing sessions, so we always knew exactly what we were going to say. The Footlights motto is: *Ars est Colare Artem*.

BRIAN Oh, quite. You needn't translate for me, but for the sake of the listener, would you mind?

ERIC I will translate. It's 'The art is to conceal the art', which is true, I suppose, of most activities in life.

BRIAN Why do I always think of the sheep in *Monty Python*?

ERIC Well, we always used to drop sheep on people's heads when things were going a bit slow.

BRIAN Why did you select sheep? Because they're harmless characters?

ERIC Well, they're very boring – sheep. They stand around all day not doing much and then being eaten. It's hard to sympathise with them, isn't it? So being dropped on people's heads on television is relatively a stage up for a sheep.

BRIAN How long ago was *Monty Python*? It seems so recent.

ERIC It started over twenty years ago.

BRIAN And how many series did you do?

ERIC We did about forty-five shows in all and we finished in about 1973, so we're already history.

BRIAN And then you made films.

ERIC We made films until about seven years ago, and since then nothing really.

BRIAN And how different was it doing the telly and then films?

ERIC In television everything can go in, because you're going up to the last minute. Filming is so slow and you've got to get the script right. We'd always take two or three years to write the script and re-write it and re-write it. So it's all much more prepared and there's much less room for spontaneity to add things at the last minute.

BRIAN You took the mickey out of the establishment always.

ERIC That was our job at the time, and now we've become the establishment.

BRIAN Have people taken the mickey out of you?

ERIC Oh, absolutely yes.

BRIAN How many people copied *Monty Python*? It's been copied in various degrees, hasn't it?

ERIC It's like a cricket team. We were the team at that time and now there's the current team. They remember you when they were kids and they say, 'Oh, that's why we became comedians.' In the same way, I imagine, as cricketers today say, 'We became cricketers because we saw Mr Trueman bowl.'

BRIAN I always hoped that the film you did called *The Life of Brian* was named after me.

ERIC As a tribute, of course. I think you actually appeared in one of the sketches a long time ago.

BRIAN Oh, I did – Peter West and myself. You took the mickey out of us. Are you a team man or are you happier performing individually?

ERIC I am much happier in a team. I think essentially as a comedian I'm a wicket-keeper.

BRIAN But you have floated off into different films and things.

ERIC Even in a film it's a team activity, really. I would never want to be a stand-up comic or just on my own.

BRIAN Have you ever done that in cabaret or anywhere?

ERIC The cabaret was at Cambridge. We used to do that at weekends and make quite a good living out of it.

BRIAN Are you a good stand-up comic?

ERIC No, hopeless. I'm terrible. I can write other people's jokes and one-liners, but it doesn't appeal to me. I like to hide behind a character and put on some make-up, or in Peter West's case I had a whole bald head to put on.

BRIAN You tended often to be in drag.

ERIC (with a sigh) I had the best legs, it has to be said. But with *Python* we'd just divide up the parts and whatever was going we'd grab. So usually by the time Cleese had taken all the bullying parts and the slapping cars and the hitting people about the head parts and Jones had taken the smaller parts, there were only a few women left, so I used to end up with those.

BRIAN Going back to Warwickshire, Freddie Gardner, who you mentioned, was a great character, although he didn't appear to be one on the field. Did you mingle at all with the players?

ERIC I think I saw them in Stratford once, but the only player I met in the early days was Tom Graveney, who was my great hero.

BRIAN He's the ideal chap to have watched.

ERIC Wonderful batsman.

BRIAN You don't see so many like him.

ERIC Well, I think Gower's in the same mould.

BRIAN He's outstanding. Now, I believe you play the guitar. The fingernails, of course, are beautifully manicured. Do you use a pleckers – a plectrum?

ERIC I have a plectrum, yes.

BRIAN Is that cheating or is it allowed?

ERIC It's totally allowed. Anything is allowed, I think – unless you get caught at it.

BRIAN Do you play for fun or just for yourself? Have you done it professionally?

ERIC I've done it semi-professionally. I came out of a fridge in *The Meaning of Life* and sang a song about the galaxy. I sang a catchy little ditty [in *The Life of Brian*] on the Cross, *Always Look on the Bright Side of Life*, which I wrote.

BRIAN What about your voice? You've just performed Co-co in *The Mikado*. Did you enjoy doing that?

ERIC I loved doing Co-co. I did it at the English National Opera and then last November I went to do it in Houston, Texas.

BRIAN The Doctor produced you – Jonathan Miller. Was it very different from the orthodox?

ERIC I said to him, 'What are you going to do with *The Mikado*?' And he said, 'Well, I'm going to get rid of all that Japanese nonsense for a start.' Which is very good, since it's set in Japan. He made it entirely black and white, with dinner jackets and thirties style. A cross between Fred Astaire and the Marx Brothers.

BRIAN Did you do one or two of the traditional twiddling dances, which they used to do in Gilbert and Sullivan?

ERIC Well, I had to do quite a lot of dancing. I had seven songs and about four or five dances. You get 'Tit Willow'; you get 'A Little List' – I used to re-write the list every day for the performance. I used to put whoever was in the news on the list that night and the chorus used to face me upstage and look at me, so that I'd always try and make them laugh.

BRIAN You were unlucky in a sense in that you missed the great music-hall period.

ERIC There was a bit of that around when I first started. I went to see Norman Evans in Manchester, and Morecambe and Wise were just young comics then. Rob Wilton – that wonderful man with 'The Day War Broke Out' – I saw a bit of that. There were still music-hall acts.

BRIAN Have you ever modelled any of your female parts on Norman Evans?

ERIC He was very *Python* – he was huge.

BRIAN And he did that marvellous act like Les Dawson does today, with no teeth.

ERIC Well, I think Lancashire comedians are probably the best and certainly were the funniest.

BRIAN Oh, yes. If you just go through them from Tommy Handley to Arthur Askey to Ted Ray – they're helped a little by the accent. If you tell a story in a Lancashire accent it sounds a bit funnier than if I tell it. You never saw Max Miller, did you?

ERIC No, but I adored his records. I used to play them regularly. I never saw him live and he wasn't allowed on television, was he?

BRIAN He was the great insinuator. He never quite got to

the point and left it to people's imaginations. Nowadays people go a bit further.

ERIC He used to let the audience complete the joke, which is very clever. 'You're the sort of people who will get me into trouble! Now then, is this Cockfosters? No, madam, it's Max Miller's.'

BRIAN Oh, that one he didn't leave to the imagination. What about alternative comedy, as they call it? Do you think sometimes they go a little too far? Or do you think you can't go too far?

ERIC I think it's the job of comedy to go just that bit too far. It's just to stir people up and make them laugh a bit and I think you have to go a little bit too far to do it. Then the line keeps moving as life continues. *Python* looks quite staid now – conservative.

BRIAN But the essential bit of your comedy was to shock, I think.

ERIC Well, yes, partially. It's too easy to do that. We tried not to rely on just pure shock. There's a limited return on it. You can't just shock and keep shocking. So we'd always try to provide good laughs.

BRIAN What about *Baron Münchhausen*? That's a good film.

ERIC It's a lovely film. It was one of the most nightmarish experiences of my life. I had to have my head shaved. I was bald for six months. I was in Rome, being hung up in tanks, being blown up and suspended from the ceiling, and it was total hell.

BRIAN Can you stay bald for a week, or do little tufts of hair start growing?

ERIC They have to shave it every day, otherwise it becomes like velcro and you can run into the wall and stick to it with your head.

BRIAN And how long did it take to recover from it to the fine head of hair that you've got now?

ERIC I am terribly butch, so it grew back quite quickly.

BRIAN Will you do anything for art, then?

ERIC Anything for a laugh is what I was accused of. Art? Yes, I think you have to. If you're doing something you have to plunge yourself totally into it to get it right.

BRIAN You live in St John's Wood. Will you be going round the corner to Lord's this summer?

ERIC Yes. I hope to see Mr Gower occasionally.

BRIAN He is great fun to watch. You probably like him because he's artistic – the touch player.

ERIC That's what the game's about for me. It's what makes the difference between that and baseball and anything like that. It's the class shot. You can't describe it; it's a thing of beauty – the good cover drive.

BRIAN I was delighted to hear that you've written a play about cricket. It's one of my ambitions. You have produced a musical comedy – not for the stage.

ERIC We wrote it originally for the stage and then we thought it would do very nicely on radio. It's called *Behind the Crease* and it's about the three things the English like most: sex, royalty and cricket – not necessarily in that order. I've written it with a friend of mine called John Du Pre, and we did it with Gary Wilmott playing a West Indian hotel owner and I play a seedy journalist.

BRIAN A cricket writer? Or one who sits by the pool and takes notes of what goes on that shouldn't?

ERIC Exactly. It's all about entrapment. Which, of course, never happens.

BRIAN No, no. It wasn't, of course, based on any tour in the West Indies.

ERIC No, it just came to me while I was on holiday in the West Indies one year.

BRIAN Is it easy to compose a cricket song?

ERIC We did a lovely song which went:

Oh jolly good shot,
Oh well played, sir,
Oh well let alone,

Oh he's hit him on the bone!
Did it hit him on the head?
No, it hit him on the leg.
I think the fellow's dead,
No, he's getting up again.
Oh it's just a bit of rum,
No, it's hit him on the bum.
Is he out? Is he out? . . .

We should have had fifteen people singing this – very tightly.

BRIAN That was very good – quick moving. Is there a wicket-keeper's song? Why he missed a stumping, perhaps – a wicket-keeper's lament?

ERIC There should be a wicket-keeper's lament. Gary Wilmott is playing this hotel-keeper at the Nelson Arms – 'We turn a blind eye to most things.' It's set in 'the Wayward Isles', which I rather like. I play the seedy reporter who's trying to get something on this English cricketer called Brian Steam, who's a fast bowler. There's a seedy journalist's song, 'Strolling Down the Street of Shame':

I saw a judge outside a judge's quarter
Messing with another judge's daughter.
I said, 'Hello, hello, me lud,
I'd keep this secret if I could,
But I have a moral duty as a reporter.'

BRIAN Very good. It seems to be all sex so far.

ERIC It's mainly sex. There are one or two bits of cricket in there.

(*And, finally, Eric was persuaded to finish with a reprise of 'Oh Jolly Good Shot'.*)

29 John Kettley

THE WEATHER PLAYS A VITAL part in cricket. Ask Dickie Bird, he knows! So we thought that it was about time we had someone who could forecast for us whether rain would stop play. We were lucky to find that the youngest of the weather forecasters was also a very keen cricketer, and needless to say it was raining when he joined us in the box at Old Trafford.

I think they do a super job with their live, off-the-cuff commentaries on local showers, high winds and depressions. I have never heard them make a gaffe as we (occasionally!) do at cricket. But in the days when they used magnetic devices to put letters or logos on the weather board one of them did slip up once. He was sticking letters all over the board showing where there would be RAIN, WIND, SHOWERS or FOG. As he tried to put FOG on the board, the F came unstuck and fell to the ground, leaving OG over south-east England. He finished up with: 'So the outlook for tomorrow is still unsettled, with some strong winds – and I'm sorry about that "F" in fog!'

Old Trafford, 29 July 1989

BRIAN JOHNSTON Well, if you presented this weather, you know what you can do with it. You are from Yorkshire.
JOHN KETTLEY Born in Halifax.
BRIAN Are you a committed Yorkshireman?
JOHN There's no choice – I am a Yorkshireman. I never lived in Halifax, I was just born in hospital there and lived

in Todmorden. Many people will know that Todmorden is just about twenty miles from here. It's the border town. Administratively, of course, it's under Lancashire, in some respects, but not others. We're the only Yorkshire team in the Lancashire League. We've always been known as the border team, but there's no doubt about it: anybody who lives there is really a Yorkshireman.

BRIAN So did you learn your cricket there?

JOHN I'm still learning my cricket, Brian. It's very difficult to put it together sometimes, but yes. I did start as a very young boy. In fact, I was taken round in my pram by my dad when I was a baby – all round the ground at Todmorden.

BRIAN What sort of cricketer are you? What's your forte?

JOHN I laughingly call myself an all-rounder, which means to say that, if I fail with the bat, I've still got a second chance. So I do a bit of both – a bit of batting and a bit of bowling.

BRIAN You've brought these Lancashire League handbooks along with you. One's for 1961 and one's for 1956.

JOHN Well, the 1956 one you'll see me appearing in – I was only four at the time, but I was taken round by my dad and saw all these really good cricketers. Everton Weekes was playing at Bacup at that time. But *Lancashire Cricket League*, priced ninepence in 1961, is the first one I really remember. I was doing a lot of scoring in those days.

BRIAN Some wonderful pictures of some young people who played in the league there – Hughie Tayfield, Everton Weekes, Harry Halliday.

JOHN I played in the league – mainly second and third team, it must be said. I only ever played in the first team once. It's the story of my life, really. I was selected for the first team in about 1969 or 1970. Peter Marner was the pro who used to play here and went to Leicestershire.

BRIAN Hit the ball well.

JOHN Certainly did. But that game I was selected for it

rained all day long. The game was called off about four o'clock. My card playing improved.

BRIAN It counted as being in the first team, anyhow.

JOHN Oh, I think it did, but nobody remembers, of course.

BRIAN But you still play cricket in charity matches. You're in much demand. Have you got a regular team?

JOHN I play for a village called Ardeley, which is very near Stevenage.

BRIAN My sister married the son of the people who used to live at Ardeley Bury. It wasn't a great cricket ground. I played cricket there against the village.

JOHN We've actually lost our ground now. We were kicked off it last season. We now use a recreation ground at the next village called Walkern. It's actually a football ground in the winter. 'Variable bounce' is the most accurate way of describing our pitch.

BRIAN How often are you doing the weather?

JOHN We have three shifts. One morning shift, broadcasting domestically, and then we have the afternoon shifts: one into Europe and one into BBC1 and BBC2. The broadcast for Europe many people here wouldn't ever have seen, because we're broadcasting to Superchannel on the satellite and we're also broadcasting to the forces in Germany.

BRIAN How long does the preparation take?

JOHN We've got a poky little office and we have a camera in there. We put the whole lot together and we do our own graphics. We sit at the console all day long; that's why we're all blind.

BRIAN Do you make all the marks on the maps?

JOHN Yes, we do everything. We couldn't possibly go in there cold one morning at seven o'clock and do a broadcast at ten past, because we have to get all this information together and put it into graphical form.

BRIAN I watch your hand with fascination because you have a little clicker.

JOHN That's right. We change the picture when we want

to. That's the wonderful thing about it – we control our own destiny.

BRIAN So how long did it take you to learn about the weather? Is there a weather school?

JOHN We have a college at Shinfield Park near Reading. We are employed by the Met Office, of course, and we go down there for refresher courses. I must be due for another one if it's raining on a Saturday at Old Trafford. We go down there for several weeks at a time on courses, just to see what the latest research is doing and whether we can actually still do it properly.

BRIAN And the actual things you say – those are your own words?

JOHN Absolutely, yes. We don't have a script or anything like that. There's no autocue. We don't read anything. We just make it up as we go along. It's got to agree with the forecast coming out of headquarters – the engine room at Bracknell. They're providing us with the latest computer information, which says, for instance, if a band of rain coming across tomorrow is going to reach Manchester at five o'clock in the afternoon, and we can't go on and say it's going to arrive in Manchester at three o'clock, other-wise we'd get our backsides kicked. But essentially we present the weather as we wish. We present it in the nicest possible way to explain the situation to the public.

BRIAN Are you allowed to crack any jokes? What's the best joke you've cracked?

JOHN I can't remember jokes, Brian. But I do like to be fairly light-hearted on television. I think if your own per-sonality comes across, that's the main thing. I was told when I did my first audition in BBC Midlands back in 1980, 'Nobody's invited you into their lounge, so you've got to go in there and be pleasant. You mustn't upset anybody. Be yourself and don't try to copy anybody else.' It was a great temptation, when I first started down in London, to copy who I thought was the best – that was

Jim Bacon at the time. But, what's the point? You can't be another Jim Bacon. You've got to be your own personality.

BRIAN Is there a Big Brother listening and watching who rings up afterwards and says, 'Not bad, Ketters, but if I'd been you I'd have said a little bit more about those storms coming in from the east'?

JOHN Yes, we've got our people at Bracknell who monitor everything. I think they record every broadcast and it is quite strict, but on the whole they do trust you. They've got to trust you – they're the people who put you on in the first place.

BRIAN I'm sure you get 99 per cent right, but has there been a 1 per cent where you've made a most terrible bloomer, said it was going to be the most glorious day tomorrow and it's pelted down all day? Don't be afraid of revealing – Big Brother's not listening.

JOHN It does occur and I think the public know that we're not trying to get it wrong.

BRIAN Where were you before the famous 1987 storm? Were you on that night?

JOHN I was on the breakfast time of the storm, travelling in to do it at four o'clock that morning. The A1 was like a chicane. There were trees all across the road and, of course, there were no traffic lights working in London that morning, so it was a really hairy journey. We were in Lime Grove in those days and everybody was standing outside with candles when I got there and a great cheer went up. 'Here he is. The man who's responsible for all this.' There'd been a power cut inside the studio, so we went up to Television Centre to do the broadcast from a little annexe. I was due to start on the air at five to seven and my shift finished at nine. I was doing updates with no graphics at all about every twenty minutes about how the storm was going. And I was still there at two o'clock in the afternoon, doing little updates.

BRIAN People do tend to blame you, don't they?

JOHN Yes, they do, but it's like expecting the bus to be on time. Everybody knows the bus is always late. It's just an old-fashioned thing that's carried on for ever.

BRIAN We talk of long-distance forecasting. Had I come to you in May, would you have forecast this glorious summer?

JOHN Oh, I did. I'm sure I told you that. I had a hunch, actually – because it was an odd year, 1989 – that it was going to be a good one. And we'd had two very mild winters. It was only a hunch, and I would not have dared go on television and say so.

BRIAN And I believe you said, if you remember, 'except on Saturday 29 July, when it may drizzle during lunchtime at Old Trafford'.

JOHN Well, we should have played this Test a week ago.

BRIAN Now, you are one of the few people who've been mentioned in a hit at the top of the pop charts.

JOHN It was a rather boring title called 'John Kettley is a Weatherman', which is open to debate. But it could have been the end of a wonderful career and the start of a new one. But I never really got into the music industry. It was a band called the Tribe of Toffs who wrote to me in about February last year and said they'd got this song together. I questioned whether it was a song at all.

BRIAN Can you remember the words?

JOHN There weren't many. 'John Kettley is a weatherman. John Kettley is a weatherman. And so is Michael Fish.' Since that day Michael Fish thinks the song is about him.

BRIAN Now, let's go back to Yorkshire. Who have been your real favourites there?

JOHN He's not here at the moment, but when I was a kid Freddie Trueman was my hero. And then, I must admit, even though things were a little unsettled at Yorkshire in recent years, Geoffrey Boycott became a hero as well.

BRIAN Well, he was a marvellous player. You could admire the technique.

JOHN Since then it's been difficult to have heroes, because they're not really performing as we'd like them to perform. But they're a great bunch of lads and nothing would give me greater pleasure than to see Yorkshire a fine side again.

BRIAN Do you go and watch them?

JOHN When they pop down south. I went to Lord's last year for the county match on a Wednesday afternoon. It was a nice day, but there weren't many people in the ground. I was walking towards the pavilion and David Bairstow saw me, so I had to go and join them in the dressing room. That particular day Yorkshire were having a bad time of it and Kevin Sharp was the twelfth man, but he had done something to his back. He really was in a bad state and he was on antibiotics. So that day I almost went out subbing.

BRIAN Would that have been the climax?

JOHN That would have been absolutely wonderful.

BRIAN Walking along the street, do people stop you and say, 'What's it going to be like for our fête next Saturday week?'

JOHN Yes. It's nice in a summer like this. People ask about wedding days and they think you know months and months ahead. I think about it first and then I'll say, 'Yes, it looks as if it's going to be OK. I think the temperature – not as high as it is now, of course – about 21 degrees – 70. A bit of cloud, but yes, it should be fine.' Because that stops them worrying about the weather.

BRIAN When you work out the centigrade and Fahrenheit thing, it doesn't quite work out the way I do it, which is to double it and add thirty.

JOHN No, but it's not far away. We do tend to remember all the conversions now, with years of practice.

BRIAN At 33 centigrade, what is it?

JOHN Ninety-two.

BRIAN Under my method it would be ninety-six.

JOHN The bigger the number, the more out it will get. But

16–61 is a good one to remember. You just reverse the numbers: 16–61.

BRIAN What happened then?

JOHN Oh dear. This is the end of a promising interview.

BRIAN 1661?

JOHN Not *in* 1661, Brian, 16 Celsius is 61 Fahrenheit.

BRIAN I was thinking something might have happened to Charles II then.

JOHN There's another one: 28–82.

BRIAN Oh, I'll be able to do that. What are the finer parts of the British Isles as regards weather?

JOHN Apart from St John's Wood, of course, the south coast of England is probably just about the driest. But the east of Scotland usually does extremely well – surprisingly well. They do get this horrible 'haar' effect off the North Sea, this low cloud and cold wind sometimes, but they actually get very good shelter from the Grampians.

BRIAN Are we too unfair? There's always the joke about rain at Old Trafford.

JOHN Well, they get about thirty-five inches of rain here a year, I think, off the top of my head. It is cloudier up here in the north-west of England, but the rain isn't necessarily all that heavy. The Lake District probably bears the brunt of most of the rain. That's why it's so green. But I thought you were going to ask me about this England team.

BRIAN Well, do you have a quick solution?

JOHN It would be nice if there was more pride put back into English cricket by having people wearing caps, like the Australians do.

30 Professor Sir Bernard Lovell

IN THE MID-1980s I VISITED Jodrell Bank when doing a *Down Your Way* in Cheshire. I was amazed at the gigantic size of the revolving bowl of the telescope. It was not until I had finished my interview with Sir Bernard about Jodrell Bank that, over a cup of tea, I discovered his great interest in cricket. He had not only been a good cricketer, he had also carried out a number of highly technical experiments to try to help umpires in making their decisions. He emphasised that he was only trying to help them, not to usurp their powers. They are, and probably always will be, the final arbiters on all decisions.

None of his aids has so far been used in this country, partly due to the large expense involved. We now have a referee at all Tests, and overseas there has been a third umpire watching the television replays who can be called on if either umpire is in doubt about a run-out or a stumping. The difference between this and Sir Bernard's successful experiments is that his method involves direct and more or less instantaneous contact with the umpires.

With the third umpire watching a monitor, decisions have taken up to 30 seconds as he watches several replays. Personally, so long as TV and the big screens on the grounds show replays, I think the umpires should be given Sir Bernard's aid to decide at least on run-outs and possibly stumpings. I hope you will find our conversation as fascinating as I did.

Old Trafford, 6 June 1987

SIR BERNARD LOVELL I was given permission to take equipment to Jodrell Bank in 1945. It was very remote then and we were allowed to stay for a few weeks with these trailers. That was in December 1945 and we're still there. We started building the big steerable telescope in 1951/52. Before that I'd been building bigger and bigger aerials on the ground to try and do certain things, and then the desire to make one of these devices completely steerable arose and that led to what you now see in the Cheshire Plain. We began operating in 1957 and this year we shall celebrate the thirtieth anniversary of its first use, which is really quite remarkable, because no one believed that it would be any good. In fact, I had the greatest difficulty in persuading people either that it would last as an engineering structure for fifteen years, or that it would be useful scientifically, and now it's busier and more in demand than it ever has been.

BRIAN JOHNSTON Now, don't be modest about it: is it one of the great telescopes of the world?

SIR BERNARD I think it is. It's still one of the largest and I think remarkable as a scientific instrument because of its longevity. It cost us £600,000 to build and you may remember I got into a lot of trouble because of overspending. Now you couldn't possibly build it for less than £20 million. So it's one of the great investments of science.

BRIAN What's the greatest achievement you've seen in your time there? What gave you the most pleasure?

SIR BERNARD I think the answer must be, oddly enough, the detection of the carrier rocket of the first Sputnik in 1957, for the simple reason that it was the only instrument in the world that could do this by radar and it was the episode that got me out of trouble.

BRIAN Because it justified the expense.

SIR BERNARD Well, some solution to these problems then

had to be found, because this was the first inter-continental ballistic missile. But, on the astronomical side, the fascinating thing is that if you go round the place today, you'll find the students and the staff working on maybe ten different projects and the things they're working on were entirely unknown when we built the instrument in the 1950s. They've been the result of recent advances. So I think the great advantage of the instrument is that it has been so adaptable both to modern techniques and to the new discoveries that have subsequently been made, and today it is a front-line instrument.

BRIAN It is a very fascinating thing to see. It revolves completely round, does it?

SIR BERNARD That's right – about 3,500 tons, revolving with great precision on the railway track, just taking out the motion of the Earth. And of course the bowl, which is about 1,500 tons or thereabouts, is rotated on those columns, which are as high as Nelson's Column.

BRIAN What achievement that hasn't been achieved would you like to do?

SIR BERNARD Well, I'd like to put the telescope into space. There's no problem in principle, but we're talking about billions of dollars. One of the next major developments in the subject with which I'm concerned is to put a large radio telescope, like the one at Jodrell, in orbit round the Earth and link it to the Jodrell telescope and to others round the Earth. This would give you the equivalent for some of these experiments of measuring the sizes of these remote objects in the universe with a telescope which had an aperture, instead of the 250 feet of our Jodrell telescope, of ten thousand miles.

(Although the United States have subsequently put the Hubble telescope into space, it is an optical rather than a radio telescope. There are hopes that a combined American/Russian project may put a radio telescope into orbit and there are Jodrell Bank scientists involved in that project.)

271

BRIAN So that's played a big part in your life. Now, let's come to cricket. You were educated down in Bristol, so did you play cricket as a boy down there?

SIR BERNARD Oh, very much so. I spent – I was going to say 'wasted' – but I nearly failed all my exams because of my enthusiasm for cricket.

BRIAN We're not modest on this programme; how good were you as a boy?

SIR BERNARD Well, I played for the university. I played as a bowler, but I made a few runs. I then got more interested in work, but I did play during the critical period of my first degree in Bristol. I played for three different teams, including the university. Nowadays, if one of my students told me he was doing that, I would have no time for him.

BRIAN And did you see some Gloucestershire cricket in those days?

SIR BERNARD Oh, very much so, yes.

BRIAN Who particularly?

SIR BERNARD Hammond. I think I must have seen Walter Hammond play more or less his first match for Gloucestershire. One of my earliest memories is not of Gloucestershire but of seeing Hobbs make his hundredth hundred. That was in Bath, because the boundary between Gloucestershire and Somerset was close to my home. But I was a fanatical Gloucestershire supporter and indeed remained so until I became closely involved here at Old Trafford. Nevertheless, Somerset was also a great interest and then they had these tremendous hitters, Earle and Lyon.

BRIAN G. F. Earle – Guy Earle.

SIR BERNARD His bat looked like a toy. I thought of him yesterday, watching Botham. He was much bigger than Botham. But Hobbs – I think that is my earliest memory. I must have been a boy of about ten.

(Sir Jack Hobbs made that hundredth hundred at Bath in

1923. At the time only W. G. Grace and Tom Hayward had ever reached that landmark.)

BRIAN He was brought out a glass of champagne or ginger ale.

SIR BERNARD Something like that – by Percy Fender – and I believe given a cheque for one hundred guineas. But Hammond was really the person that was so marvellous to those of us who were young.

BRIAN I was lucky enough to see him make his 240 at Lord's against Australia in 1938 and I don't think the modern generation really appreciate how tremendous he was.

SIR BERNARD No, the cricket you see here is stodgy compared with that. His elegance was quite amazing. I remember one day Gloucestershire were playing Kent and I think either Freeman or Woolley got him out before he had scored and I was quite miserable. I almost went home for the rest of the day.

BRIAN When you came up here, then, what about Lancashire cricket?

SIR BERNARD Well, I came to Manchester and joined the university in 1936 and I discovered that the university was quite close to this ground and I used to get a bus down to the entrance. Where we are now, on top of this executive suite, is more or less on the site of the old galvanised shed. One used to pay sixpence to get in there. I saw quite a lot of cricket.

BRIAN Any particular Lancashire player you'd picked out?

SIR BERNARD Well, Cyril Washbrook I remember. I've talked to him today and he's full of praise for some of the young people we might get in a few years' time. I remember him not only as a batsman, but also his fielding at cover point, which was quite spectacular.

BRIAN And you have some sort of office here?

SIR BERNARD Well, I was very lucky to be made one of their vice-presidents about five or six years ago. So that's a very nice arrangement.

BRIAN Now, you've taken tremendous interest in the various technicalities of cricket and are trying to help the umpires. We can start with an easy one, because we can see it. There is your light meter, which looks like the top half of a clock. There are two of those on the Wilson Stand. How do they work?

SIR BERNARD We have a photosensitive element, which is transformed by some rather simple electronics into a small motor which drives that clock. The photosensitive element is more or less focused on the region of the sightscreen and there you see what the light is. It doesn't pretend to be absolute, but it's relatively accurate.

BRIAN When it's up at twelve o'clock, is that perfect light?

SIR BERNARD No, the perfect light is when it's hard over at a quarter past. These are really crude experimental models. We've got a manufacturing design, but at the moment the TCCB are sitting on that, deciding what to do about it.

BRIAN People always say that you can't have a common thing like that, because the light on each cricket ground is different.

SIR BERNARD Well, of course they're different. But then you adjust this to suit the particular ground and from experience. You can't be absolute, because the umpire has to decide whether he offers the light to the batsmen. It depends on the speed of the ball and all that sort of thing. It gives them a guide. You see, in the beginning, I thought it would be interesting to make a permanent recording of the light, and about six years ago I had a light meter over the pavilion with a recording device and the intensity of the light came out on a paper chart. This was fascinating, because the conclusion one came to very quickly was that the umpires were rather consistent in the time at which they offered the light to the batsmen, but they were extremely inconsistent as to when they came back again. Very often the light would recover to what it was when they went off and another ten or fifteen minutes would elapse before they came back again. Now you have the recording here continuously. These are very sensitive. A cloud comes over and you will see them . . . in fact, at the moment the light is better at the Warwick Road End than it is at this end. But I doubt if a batsman would notice that. These models won't last for ever, because they're very experimental; the sort of thing that scientists do with some bits and pieces. Every time I come here I look with some anxiety to see if they're still working. They're all right at the moment. They are the result of a sort of evolution. In the beginning we had a radio link which became interfered with, I think, by BBC television transmissions and things like that. But now we've overcome that and they're very reliable.

BRIAN And I think it's terribly good for the public. They can at least see just what is being done to them.

(The light meters continued to function efficiently until the end of the 1992 season when the old Wilson Stand was demolished to make way for a new one. They were rebuilt on the Red Rose and Executive Stands, so that they were in line with the pitch.)

SIR BERNARD I started the light meters off, but then I was asked by the TCCB to investigate the possibility of electronic aids for umpires other than light meters.

BRIAN When I came to see you in your office at Jodrell Bank, you'd just had a meeting with two umpires and you asked them a simple question: how could you best help them?

SIR BERNARD David Constant and Don Oslear. They were very nice and they said that the things that worried them were, on the lbw law, whether the ball really would have hit the wicket if the batsman hadn't been in the way.

BRIAN Which they can't tell.

SIR BERNARD They said, 'Look, we can tell you whether the ball has pitched in the right place or whether it's going to go over the top of the wicket, if you can give us some indication if it would have hit the wicket.' Well, this was a fascinating problem – a very difficult one. The TCCB financed a feasibility study with a firm we knew in the south-east of London and this study was presented to the board last summer, and I heard recently that they decided to do nothing about it. It is rather expensive.

BRIAN What does it involve? Is it cameras?

SIR BERNARD You need very sensitive cameras of the type you use on your television and the computational problem is quite difficult.

BRIAN And at each end of the ground you'd have to have two?

SIR BERNARD You'd have to have four cameras to do this and the communication with the umpire would be quite simple. One would show lights on a board, for example.

BRIAN And would that be instant?

SIR BERNARD Absolutely instant.

BRIAN The ball hits the pad, there's a shout of 'How's that?' How long would it be before he could say?

SIR BERNARD This is one of the problems, that the computation would have to be done at very high speed. You can't keep the umpires waiting. But this problem is solved and each installation would cost somewhere between £100,000 and £200,000. Incidentally, doing this, one becomes aware of the immense power and accuracy of the human eye. People say that computers can do everything. The umpires are jolly good. You have to do a very expensive design of equipment to give an answer equivalent to what the eye can do. The other problem that interested the umpires was caught behind. I asked some of the Test match cricketers and some of them were most unhappy that they had been given out erroneously on many occasions because they hadn't touched the ball. We have also solved that. This means inserting something in the bat and a few weeks ago here at Old Trafford I tested what I thought was going to be the final development model. I tried it in the nets and the first ball the whole thing more or less disintegrated. It's a very sensitive device.

BRIAN Inside the handle of the bat, would it be?

SIR BERNARD That's right. And from there you transmit a signal to the umpire. He has an earphone.

BRIAN That does sound good. Are you going to do it again?

SIR BERNARD Oh yes. The TCCB are still interested and the problem is mine and that of the firm who are doing this. We have to produce this final model so that it will withstand the impact of the bat on the ball.

BRIAN What do the bat manufacturers say?

SIR BERNARD Well, we haven't asked them, but it's a very small device – something about as big as your little finger. The miniaturisation of modern electronics is quite astonishing.

BRIAN What about the other controversial one, which shows up on these big screens they have in Australia – the runouts. They can be very difficult to judge with the human eye.

SIR BERNARD Well, that's very easy. The device that would do the lbw decision could easily do that as well. That would be an easier problem than the lbw decision. This would be an electronic decision from the video responses of the cameras as to where the bat and the crease are in relation to the ball hitting the stumps. But you're quite right, this is another thing that worried the umpires. A lot of things are easy if you're prepared to spend money.

(A straightforward experiment with a third umpire watching video playbacks of run-outs and stumpings was introduced for the South Africa v. India series of 1992/93. Light meters which show the worsening light on a series of illuminated lamps, rather than Sir Bernard's system, have been introduced on most first-class grounds in England, although this system was tried at Old Trafford several years ago and discarded in favour of the more accurate clock-type meter which will continue to

operate there. The lbw and caught-behind devices have been shelved because of expense.)

SIR BERNARD I think if these devices ever went into use, there would be many more decisions against the batsman, because the umpires always give him the benefit of the doubt.

BRIAN Which is right.

SIR BERNARD Which is right, but I think the batsmen would probably be rather annoyed, because they would be given out legitimately, but they might not think so. But I do think it would save a lot of these irritating uncertainties. Of course, the umpire's decision is always final. There never has been any suggestion of taking the decision away from the umpire. It's a matter of giving him some assistance in the things he really needs.

31 The Rt. Hon. John Major

A	T ALMOST EVERY TEST MATCH from 1988 onwards, John
	Major was a regular visitor to the *TMS* commentary
	box. It was always on a Friday and he was usually
accompanied by his cricket-loving friend Robert Atkins,
who later was to become Sports Minister. He would stay
about half an hour and took an interest in all that was
going on in the box. He also showed his expert knowledge
on all aspects of cricket – tactics, techniques, records and
so on. In fact, after our talk together on the air, he said he
had hoped that I would have asked him what he thought
of the modern game and what changes he would like to
make to its laws and playing regulations. (This was in
1990, so perhaps it was a gentle hint that he would like to
do another 'View from the Boundary'!)

When he first came to visit us he was Chief Secretary
to HM Treasury. Then he had a brief spell as Foreign
Secretary and by the summer of 1990 he was Chancellor
of the Exchequer. After he became Prime Minister at the
end of November 1990, his visits to our box became rarer.
This was partly due to his crowded programme of duties,
but also to security, especially at grounds like Old Trafford
where he had to walk round the ground to get to our box.
In 1992, his duties were particularly arduous as he had a
six-month session as president of the European Community. But he did find time to do a short interview at
Lord's, during which I chided him for allowing European
affairs to interfere with cricket, and another by telephone
to the Oval while he was at the Barcelona Olympic Games.

Cricket has been lucky to have had a number of cricket-
loving Prime Ministers: Stanley Baldwin, a member of

MCC; Clement Attlee; Alec Douglas-Home (he played twice for Middlesex); Ted Heath (a keen Kent supporter who gave a splendid reception at Number 10 for Ray Illingworth's victorious team on their return from Australia in 1971); and of course John Major.

I have one happy memory of John Major off-duty in 1992. Paul Getty opened his lovely cricket ground on his estate of Wormsley on the Buckinghamshire/Oxfordshire border. The opening match was Paul Getty's XI against MCC, which the Queen Mother and John Major attended. He spent a large part of the day behind the pavilion bowling to a number of boys aged between four and ten. If ever a man looked happy, he did. I'm not sure whether he bowled any of them out with his slow-medium deliveries, but it did show what a great relaxation cricket can be, away from the stresses and responsibilities of a Prime Minister.

Lord's, 28 July 1990

BRIAN JOHNSTON When did your interest in cricket start? You were born in Merton, so you were qualified for Surrey.
JOHN MAJOR I was qualified for Surrey in everything except talent. It really started when my family moved to Brixton and I was about ten. I was within walking distance of the Oval and that was at the time Surrey were beating everyone, generally within two days – that marvellous team that won the championship from 1952 to 1958 inclusive. It was, I think, probably the best county side I ever expect to see. They were truly magnificent, and I watched them whenever I could.
BRIAN Where did you sit at the Oval, under the gasometer?
JOHN No, I sat on the other side. I sat at square leg with the batsman at the Pavilion End, in the popular seats there, and by pure habit I used to go there for years after as well.

BRIAN What chances did you yourself get of playing cricket? Were you coached?

JOHN I played a bit at school. We had quite a good cricket team at school. I played for them and I played a bit of cricket after school as well. I played a bit in Nigeria when I first went there at about twenty to do some banking. But my cricketing days came to an end after a motor-car accident in Nigeria when I was twenty or so, and I haven't played since.

(This interview came before the 1991 meeting of Common-wealth Prime Ministers in Zimbabwe when Mr Major opened the batting with the then Australian Prime Minister, Bob Hawke, in a match to mark the occasion.)

BRIAN So we were robbed of – what? A fast bowler, or what would England have had if you'd been fit?

JOHN You were robbed of an extremely mediocre medium-paced bowler.

BRIAN Banking in Nigeria sounds an interesting job.

JOHN Yes, it was. It was certainly that. The greatest enthusiasm that most of the people had there was for the weekly cricket match. They had their priorities absolutely right.

BRIAN It does happen all round the world. So when you watched that Surrey side, were there any special favourites you picked out? Was it the bowlers you liked – Bedser, Laker or Lock?

JOHN Oh, they were tremendous. It was such a superb team and they were so varied. I always thought Alec Bedser bowling was rather like a galleon in full sail coming up to the wicket. Last evening, Brian Rix said to me that he'd been batting a few years ago against Alec Bedser in a charity match and he'd said to Alec, 'Let me have an easy one to get off the mark.' And he said Alec couldn't do it. He couldn't bowl the bad ball. And I can well believe it. But the rest of the team were superb. I used to time, with an old stopwatch I had, how long it took the ball from leaving Peter May's bat to hitting the boundary. It wasn't long.

BRIAN Ah, those famous on-drives.

JOHN And I think that Tony Lock was the most aggressive-looking bowler I ever saw – and fielder.

BRIAN And a little lesson in leadership, too, because old Stewy Surridge was a tremendous leader. He was a very forceful leader, too.

JOHN He was. I met Stuart Surridge for the first time about six weeks ago. It was a very great thrill. I remember thinking as a boy, when I watched him standing there, round the wicket, where he fielded absolutely magnificently, that he was one of the few men I've ever seen who could scratch his toes while standing upright. He had these amazingly long arms and he just caught everything – truly wonderful.

(Stuart Surridge died two years later in 1992 at the age of 74.)

BRIAN Very brave he was, but then they all were – Micky Stewart and Locky walking in when he was fielding at backward short leg, which not many short legs do.

JOHN Some of Lock's catches are still unbelievable, even in retrospect. You just didn't know how he got there and how he held it.

BRIAN But when did you see your first Test match? Do you remember that?

JOHN Well, I remember the first Test match I listened to seriously. It was an Indian Test match and it was in 1952, when India were 0 for 4 in the second innings.

BRIAN We had a certain gentleman – Fred Trueman – in here just now, who was not unconcerned with that.

JOHN He took three of the four wickets. It was an astonishing scorecard.

BRIAN But have you been able to go to Test matches much?

JOHN I've been to quite a few – a good deal fewer than I would wish to have gone to, but, yes, I've been to quite a few over the years. I saw a bit of the last Test match in 1953 when the Ashes came back and I saw some of the 1956 series.

BRIAN I wonder, when you have all these conferences, are you ever brought in notes with the latest score?

JOHN Certainly in the period I was Chief Secretary and we had great negotiations with colleagues about spending matters, the meetings did used to break up for critical parts of the Test match, to watch it. My then secretary, who was a Surrey member and a fanatical cricketer, used to send in notes to say the Test match had reached a critical stage and we used to break up and watch it. Nigel Lawson (*the former Chancellor of the Exchequer*) is also a great cricket supporter – a great Leicestershire fan – and we used to sit there, with Nigel in the chair, his fellow ministers, lots of extremely important mandarins and others at the other side of the table and a piece of paper would come in that would be passed gravely round the table. It was the Test score; it wasn't the markets, I promise you.

BRIAN Did you just nod as though it was important financial news?

JOHN Well, over the last couple of years, some of it was very grave.

BRIAN Are quite a few members of the Cabinet keen followers?

JOHN The best cricket player in the Cabinet is probably Tom King. He is a good cricketer.

BRIAN He also keeps wicket, I think.

JOHN He keeps wicket as well. Peter Brooke is a walking *Wisden* and knows a great deal about cricket.

BRIAN We could put him against the Bearded Wonder (*Bill Frindall, of course*) and he'd stump him, d'you think?

JOHN Well, I think as a non-gambling man I might put my money on the Bearded Wonder, but not by much. Peter

Brooke knows a great deal about it and there are a number of others.

BRIAN I suppose, because you were injured, you haven't been able to play for the Lords and Commons.

JOHN No, I'm afraid that motor accident ended my playing days. I wouldn't run too well now, otherwise I would love to play.

BRIAN They play some very good cricket. It mingles up the parties, too. They don't seem to bother about the politics.

JOHN Indeed not. Bob Cryer, the Labour MP for one of the Bradford seats, is a very fine left-arm slow bowler. There are some good cricketers right across the Commons.

BRIAN What's the first thing you read in the papers in the morning?

JOHN I do read the sports pages every day. I tend to read Matthew Engel when he writes cricket. That is the first thing I turn to in that particular newspaper. (*Matthew Engel was appointed editor of* Wisden *in 1992.*) I much miss the fact that Jim Swanton doesn't write quite as regularly as once he did. I thought he was supremely good, and I much enjoy reading Tony Lewis. But I do turn to the sports pages at an early stage in the morning.

BRIAN Are you great on the literature of cricket? Have you got a big library of cricket books?

JOHN Well, quite big, yes. I do read a lot of cricket. I've been trying to get hold of a book on cricket that Richard Daft wrote a long time ago – way back in the 1870s or 1880s. Richard Daft's great grandson, incidentally, is the Cabinet Secretary, Robin Butler – another fine cricketer. The Civil Service has some extremely good cricketers. But I haven't been able to find that book in old bookshops. Robert Atkins has a copy, which he jealously guards and lends to me occasionally.

(*As a result of this broadcast, Mr Major received a copy of the Richard Daft book.*)

BRIAN What other great cricket writers in the newspapers do you remember especially?

JOHN In the evening papers, when one used to go out and see how Surrey were doing and whether the game would go into a third day, I remember reading E. M. Wellings a lot.

BRIAN He wrote a lot of very good sense – and played for Surrey, too.

JOHN And, of course, in terms of literature, like everybody, I've read a lot of Cardus.

BRIAN Which is absolutely marvellous stuff. He and Arlott and Swanton – and Robertson Glasgow, did you ever read him?

JOHN I've not read a lot of him.

BRIAN Well, if you can get any of his little vignettes about players, they were absolutely brilliant. He was the chap who said, 'Hammond, like a ship in full sail', which was a perfect description of Hammond going to the wicket.

JOHN I wish I'd seen him bat, too.

BRIAN But I suppose you don't get a lot of time to read, do you?

JOHN Well, I do, actually. Whatever time I go to bed, I tend to pick up a book for half an hour or forty-five minutes, just to wash away the rest of the day, and it is often a cricket book.

BRIAN I hope that doesn't send you to sleep.

JOHN Well, I go to sleep, but it's not the book.

BRIAN Young James, your son, is he a good cricketer?

JOHN He's a better footballer, and for the reason that there isn't as much cricket at schools as there ought to be. The point about cricket in schools is that it takes such a long time-span. That's the real difficulty, and whereas I think the staff are willingly prepared to give up an afternoon for a football match to get the pupils there, play the game and get them back, it is a good deal longer for a cricket match.

BRIAN Are you a quick learner? I mean, you had to switch

suddenly to the Foreign Office. How did you brief yourself in that short time, because you appeared terribly knowledgeable when you went to conferences immediately afterwards.

JOHN Well, you're very kind to say so. You read a lot and hopefully recall. It's really a problem of total immersion. It's the same in cricket in many ways. I'm sorry to name-drop, but I bumped into Arthur Morris today – a very great player – and he remembered hitting Wilf Wooller for four fours off the first four balls of a game down in Glamorgan. And I said, 'That was a bit extravagant.' And he said, 'Not as extravagant as the field that had been set,' which he then described to me. So I think these things just stick in the mind. He, forty years on, remembers the field placing.

BRIAN If you ask Fred Trueman about any of the wickets he took or the innings he played, he'd tell you exactly. He's got a marvellous memory.

JOHN Yes, it's a great gift.

BRIAN Are you great on music?

JOHN I like music very much and I go whenever I can, which isn't as often as I would wish, with Norma. She's forgotten more about music than I'll ever know.

BRIAN And besides cricket, any particular hobby?

JOHN Well, I read a lot; I'm very fond of the theatre; I go and watch a fair bit of football and athletics if I can – most sport.

BRIAN John Major, thank you very much. You're a cricket fanatic and a man after our own hearts, and I hope you'll continue to listen to us.

JOHN Brian, I will. I wouldn't miss it for the world.

32 Peter O'Toole

MENTION PETER O'TOOLE AND, IN spite of the many different parts he has played since, on stage or in films, most people probably picture a white Arab figure in the desert as Lawrence of Arabia. An unlikely sort of cricketer, you might think. On 14 June 1992, Peter played for Paul Getty's XI on his beautiful cricket ground at Wormsley. The opposition was Tim Rice's Heartaches. At his own request, Peter went in first and scored a stylish 5, including a fine stroke for four through the covers. When Getty's XI fielded Peter bowled five tidy overs of leg-breaks at a cost of only 14 runs.

I had first met him in 1991 in Paul Getty's box at Lord's, where I learned of his passion for cricket. During the winter, when not working, he goes every Monday night to the Indoor Cricket School at Lord's, where he and Don Wilson became firm friends. In the summer, whenever he is free, he coaches young boys on Friday nights at the Brondesbury Cricket Club. So he is not just a celebrity who turns out for occasional charity matches. He plays and practises whenever he can and is a completely dedicated devotee of the game.

With his tall, languid frame, his handsome, craggy face and immediately recognisable, somewhat husky voice, he does not look like the average cricketer. But he is one, and it was a real joy to meet someone who is so famous in their chosen profession, but who would probably much prefer to be thought of as a cricketer.

On the Saturday when he was with us, we had had a riveting morning's play, in which the West Indies, after looking comfortable enough at 158 for 3, had suddenly declined to 164 for 6.

The Oval, 10 August 1991

PETER O'TOOLE I'm often asked why cricket means so much to me. And it's this high drama. Tufnell comes on – takes a wicket. Botham returns – takes a wicket. Viv Richards, the great king, delays his entrance. Delays and delays and delays. Finally comes on with a couple of balls to play before lunch to a standing ovation. And, of course, he could have been out first ball.

BRIAN JOHNSTON Have you ever had an ovation like that? That lasted the time it took him to get to the wicket.

PETER And I believe he was deeply moved – and who wouldn't be?

BRIAN Well, Bradman says he wouldn't be, because when I asked him whether he had tears in his eyes when there were three cheers when he went out in his last Test, he said, 'No, no,' but I bet there were really.

PETER I saw Bradman play at Headingley in 1948 and he scored 33, having threatened to score a century the evening before, and as he walked back to the pavilion there were no tears. He looked extraordinarily grumpy and very, very thoughtful, in a huge cap and walking very slowly indeed.

(*Bradman did make a century – a match-winning 173 not out – in the second innings of that Test Match.*)

BRIAN Before we go on with the cricket, I'm colour blind, but I gather those are green socks.

PETER They are green socks.

BRIAN Now, why do you always wear green socks?

PETER Because my daddy was very, very superstitious and wouldn't allow me to wear anything green on a racetrack, so my way of being disobedient was to wear something green that he couldn't see.

BRIAN He was not unconnected with the bookmaking business.

PETER He was a bookie.

BRIAN Were you a runner?

PETER I was a runner, but not exactly an official one.

BRIAN When did you first start playing cricket?

PETER I was reared in the north of England, so cricket for me began in Yorkshire – where else? I remember the first real turn-on for cricket for me was being taken to the news cinema over and over again to watch Hutton's 364, here at the Oval in 1938, when I was six. And the great joy and cheers in the cinema are very clear to me. Then, towards the end of the war, I remember in Roundhay Park Sir Learie Constantine and Arthur Wood.

BRIAN Great wicket-keeper.

PETER They put together Sunday sides and there was an Australian team and we little boys could be chosen as ball boys to stand on the boundary, and one of my great moments, in fact my greatest moment still in cricket – even though I wasn't playing – was when I was standing at long-off. Constantine scored 50 off eighteen deliveries and he whacked the ball over the ropes and it fell into my hands. I remember this huge man just beaming and waving his bat. It was a lovely moment.

BRIAN Now, what about the talent? We're never modest.

PETER Well, I think this is about my mark, the blind cricket we're watching here.

(A demonstration of the game was taking place at the Oval during this interval.)

BRIAN Come on, now, you're better than that. If one goes to the Lord's indoor school during the winter you can be seen there.

PETER True. I love to turn up and play. I love to be with cricketers. I'm not any good any more. My hope – wish –

nowadays is to be involved in a stand. If I can plug up one end and let somebody else do the scoring and occasionally pop in a little single and charge up and down the wicket.

BRIAN Have you got the Trevor Bailey forward defensive?

PETER Yes, I've got that, much to the amusement of all my chums. When I say 'play' it's an overstatement. What I do is creak out to the square and hope to plonk a little timber on the ball. I hope to turn my arm over and get a maiden or perhaps a wicket.

BRIAN Leg tweakers or anything?

PETER I have a delivery which is really, really special. It does absolutely nothing.

BRIAN That's very good.

PETER From leaving the hand to pitching – nothing at all. This confuses many batsmen.

BRIAN But you do go into the indoor school. Who do you play with there? You go once a week, roughly.

PETER Well, I usually go with young chums whose delight is to try to knock my head off. They love it. They see this silly old fool turning up and padding up and they love to fling down the leather and try to take my head off.

BRIAN I saw someone I know who is a member at Brondesbury and he says that every Friday night you go and coach the boys there.

PETER Well, that's a delight for me. Again, I'm with my standard – under nines. I love to ... less coach than encourage.

BRIAN Do you give them a demonstration of your strokes?

PETER No, I'm the bowling machine and the umpire.

BRIAN This is great, because we've got to get at the young, haven't we?

PETER This is why Brondesbury is such an extraordinary club. If you go there on a Friday night it's one of the most delightful sights in cricket. The entire field is filled with little boys. The nets are filled. There are something like a hundred little things in white there and it's a lovely sight.

BRIAN It's a great credit to the club that they get them there.

PETER My job is not to coach. I don't want to say, 'Look, get your foot to the ball.' I like just to cheer them up and encourage them. Cricket is in the hands of the young.

BRIAN Do you play with odd actors and people still?

PETER I play for a club called Lazarusians.

BRIAN I don't really know that one.

PETER Well, you may. We're not doing too badly.

BRIAN What sort of people do you play?

PETER We play some high-class stuff. We've played North-amptonshire professional coaches and drew with them and we won against Sandbach.

BRIAN And where does O'Toole bat?

PETER He opens.

BRIAN Against all the hostile fast bowling. What do you look like in a helmet?

PETER Well, we were playing in Northamptonshire and a distinguished pro, who was in the other side, insisted that we all wear helmets because the pitch was bouncing. So I went into the pavilion and was given a helmet and I couldn't find my way out of the pavilion. I stumbled around and I couldn't see where the door was. I'm sure I looked like a Dalek. So I took it off.

BRIAN And you can't hear, either. What about the bowling, then? Do you get any wickets?

PETER Sometimes I get a wicket or two. I get a few maidens. For me, one run is now what six runs meant when I was a boy. One wicket now means a five-wicket haul. If I do a piece of decent fielding I'm very happy. If I take a catch I'm delirious, and as long as I don't become a passenger with the team I'll keep on playing.

BRIAN Are you good at sprinting round the boundary?

PETER Oh, that's a great sight. I'm greatly encouraged by my team, who say, 'Go on! Go on! Off he goes!' and I puff and pant.

BRIAN I think we last met in the box at Lord's, watching a Test match. Do you go quite a bit?

PETER I always do watch as much cricket as I possibly can wherever I go in the world, be it the West Indies or Australia. I was in Australia for Christmas, watching. Which brings me to the subject of David Gower. I have the solution. David will go to live in the West Indies until he qualifies as a resident and then he will play for the West Indies and come back here at the age of 37 and tonk everybody round the park.

BRIAN I think he'd have to live there a bit longer after having played for another country. He's obviously a hero of yours. Who are the past heroes you've had?

PETER Well, Hutton was my god until along came a tall, handsome man called Flying Officer Miller, and to this day he's my cricketing god. I met him in Sydney about a decade ago and we had a long, long chat about the old days. I remember watching him play a long innings. I don't know where or when, but I remember his back foot like a stanchion. He was moving out to everything. He was everything I wanted to be when I was a boy.

BRIAN When he played slow bowling sometimes, he nearly did the splits because his back foot was static at the crease and he stretched forward. Can we talk a little bit about yourself, because you don't appear to have come from an acting family. How did you get into acting?

PETER Looking back on it now, there seems to have been an inevitable logic to it all, but there wasn't. I really stumbled into it from one thing to another. Somebody got ill in an amateur production and I took over. And then someone said, 'You ought to do it professionally.' Then I thought, Well, shall I try this? Then I got a scholarship to the RADA and it went from there.

BRIAN And you got the scholarship, so I'm told, for rather sort of barging in and making a nuisance of yourself.

PETER It's not quite true, but what is true is that I'd spent the night in Stratford-on-Avon, watching Michael Redgrave play King Lear. Then, looking for somewhere to sleep – I had no money – I slept in a field with a chum and we'd covered ourselves with what we thought was straw, but it was indeed merely the cosy to a dung pile. So when we'd thumbed a lift into London, we weren't exactly fragrant, but the lorry driver dropped us at Euston station.

BRIAN Very quickly, I should think.

PETER Even that was a bit terrifying. It was a lorry carrying beer barrels and we were standing on the barrels. We got off at Euston, aiming for a men's hostel, where we had booked a bed, and I passed the RADA. I popped in and started talking to the commissionaire at the door. We were looking at a bust of Bernard Shaw and the commissionaire and I were telling stories about Bernard Shaw when Sir Kenneth Barnes came along and joined in the story-telling, and one of my stories may have intrigued him.

BRIAN I should think the smell did.

PETER Well, my companion said, 'You will be removed from there, O'Toole, by a person with a clothes peg on his nose.'

BRIAN They tell me your bagpipes played a big part in the first film part you ever got, in *Kidnapped*. Is that right?

PETER That's right.

BRIAN Did you actually have to play them in the film?

PETER I did. It was my friend Peter Finch who was in it. There was a part for Rob Roy MacGregor's son, who had a bagpipe competition with the part that Peter was playing. And Finchy had said, 'There's only one actor I know who plays the –– bagpipes.'

BRIAN Well, this is useful. For promising people who want to go on the stage, go and learn the bagpipes; you might get a part from it. Now, *Lawrence of Arabia*. One or two others turned the part down.

PETER Did they?

BRIAN Weren't you told? You snapped it up as soon as it came along.

PETER I felt I was in the slips and the ball came my way. I thought, I'll have that one.

BRIAN You were on a pretty sandy wicket for a long time.

PETER Very – and with Omar Sharif, another good cricketer.

BRIAN Did you have any games of cricket?

PETER We did. In the middle of the desert in 120 degrees, to the astonishment of the Bedouin, who hadn't got the foggiest what was going on.

BRIAN Did they field for you?

PETER No, they didn't, but they looked at the ball with great suspicion. Then one of them picked it up and thought this was a wonderful weapon and they were flinging it about.

BRIAN Did it take an awful long time to do?

PETER It took a couple of years. It became my life. It was more than just a film; it was a huge adventure. It was everything that a young twenty-eight-year-old man could wish for. I was out in the desert in the Holy Land, working with a genius – David Lean – with a superb company of actors.

BRIAN Quite a few in the cast, to say the least – thousands.

PETER I need a scoresheet, or I'll leave someone out. I was like a young matador – another bull would come in. 'Who's this morning?' 'Anthony Quinn.' 'Who's today?' 'Alec Guinness.' 'Who's today?' 'Anthony Quayle.' 'Who's today?' 'Donald Wolfitt.' 'Who's today?' 'Claude Raines.' 'Who's today?' 'Arthur Kennedy.' 'Who's today?' 'José Ferrer.' It was astonishing.

BRIAN Not a bad team, that. Isn't it extraordinary how many actors love playing cricket?

PETER Yes, there is an affinity between this game and ours. Well, think of C. Aubrey Smith, who captained his country.

BRIAN That's right, only one Test match he played and he captained England. Did you ever play in Hollywood?

PETER No, but Hollywood, as you know, has a cricket team.

And lots and lots of West Indians are going to live in California. Down in the Valley they're setting up cricket matches. So it may take on. In America, you know, they call cricket 'baseball on Valium'.

BRIAN Jonathan Agnew and I disgraced ourselves yesterday by corpsing. Are you a corpser?

(This was the day after the infamous 'leg over' incident.)

PETER Hopeless – pathological.

BRIAN Have you had any experiences on the stage or in a film where you simply couldn't go on?

PETER Oh, yes. Twice I've been in productions where the curtain has been pulled slowly down. One of my favourite moments was in Brighton in a play, which was not very successful and was not going to have a long life. It was a complicated play, set on a strand, with the corner of a little beach-side cottage and the back of the set was the sea. Lots and lots of gauzes and lights and complicated things to make it look like the sea and, indeed, I entered from the sea with Sylvia Syms, in our bathing costumes.

On the beach was a lovely man called Nicholas Meredith – no longer with us – a great giggler, and his first line was, 'Good morning, Roger.' I was Roger. Then he had to erect a deckchair, which is never easy. It's a tricky old business. Your fingers get trapped. And I remember the line very clearly, because I heard it for seven or eight weeks. 'Good morning, Roger. There's something about a deckchair – austerity, poise and comfort. The austerity is an illusion; the comfort is achieved only with difficulty and the poise we leave to Pamela.' Well, he would do that line erecting a deckchair and not once did he get the deckchair up. Nick had a habit of twisting his hair into little spikes. This meant, 'I am not giggling.' Then, when he coughed, this meant, 'I am certainly not giggling.' So there was Nick, twisting these huge spikes on his head and coughing away. And after an agonisingly long time of not getting the deck-chair up he left behind this crumpled mass of timber and canvas and said, 'I am going to post a letter,' and walked into the sea.

The only thing I could think of was, 'I did not do this. This is not me.' So I hid behind a palm tree. Nick was floundering around looking for a letter-box in the sea among the gauze and electricity at which point everything went potty – sparks and flashes. And on to the beach came a fireman in a brass helmet with an axe. And, of course, the curtain came down very, very slowly. The producer immediately looked at me and wagged his finger. But it wasn't me.

BRIAN You've done a fair bit of Shakespeare. *Hamlet*, for instance.

PETER That was funny, too. I came on stage at the Old Vic to play Hamlet and I'd been down below with a stage hand, trying to pick a winner. I walked on to the stage and I knew that Noël Coward was out front and he was sitting in the front row with his friends. And I said, 'To be or not to be, that is the question.' I heard a snigger. 'Whether it is nobler in the mind' – snigger – 'to suffer the slings and arrows' – snigger. I thought, what am I doing? And I had a quick glance down to see if my fly was open. Finally, there was real proper laughter throughout the entire audience and I didn't know why. At which point Rosemary Harris came on as Ophelia and I put my hand to my forehead and realised I was wearing twentieth-century horn-rimmed spectacles. How should I get rid of them? So I said to Rosemary, 'There should be no more marriages!' And I flung the specs at her.

BRIAN That's great. And your Macbeth got a few laughs. Was it meant to?

PETER Not really. Again, the chief cause was this awful sense of the ridiculous. As Banquo appeared, drenched from head to foot with blood, down the Waterloo Road came an ambulance and you could hear the siren clearly.

I caught Brian Blessed's eye and I'm afraid we were both giggling.

BRIAN The great thing is, you've had fun all the time.

PETER All the time. And I hope it continues.

33 Harold Pinter OM

I HAD NEVER MET HAROLD PINTER before he joined us at the Oval for the third Test against India in 1990. I had always heard how keen he was on cricket. Indeed, his sole recreation recorded in *Who's Who* is cricket. Funnily enough I never came across him in any of the many charity matches in which I have played. At the Oval he was accompanied by his lovely biographer wife, Lady Antonia Fraser, who was wearing what I think I remember calling 'a smashing hat'.

Incidentally, it is now perfectly easy for a lady to visit our box at the Oval because ladies are allowed in the pavilion, even for Test matches. It was not always so. On one occasion some 25 years ago a high-up at the BBC had had a very good lunch with a lady friend and decided to go down to the Oval to watch a Test match during the afternoon. He paid at the gate for both of them and then asked where the BBC commentary position was. He was told that it was on the roof at the top of the pavilion, but that ladies were not allowed into the pavilion. Nothing daunted, he noticed some BBC engineers climbing a ladder up the side of the pavilion and decided to follow them. Precariously, he started to climb, he in his black Homburg hat, his lady friend in a picturesque Ascot hat and wearing a rather short, flimsy summer dress. The members in the stand below watched fascinated. There was a stiff breeze blowing and the higher they climbed, the higher was the lady's skirt blown up over her thighs. All eyes were on her; no one was bothering with the cricket. There were gales of laughter and loud applause as they finally reached the roof. How much she had revealed I'm not sure, but I think it was lucky that she was not wearing a kilt! The Surrey Secretary, Brian Castor, was not too pleased, and there was a lot of apologising to be done by the hierarchy of the BBC. It wouldn't happen today. Ladies can come up to us in the orthodox way.

But to get back to Harold. I am ashamed that I have never seen any of his twenty or more plays that he has written for the theatre, not even his most famous, *The Caretaker*. I have, of course, seen plays he has written or directed for films, TV and radio. He does, and is, so many things these days that I am amazed that he finds any time at all for cricket. But he does and, as you will gather from some of his observations, he has a surprisingly deep knowledge of the game.

The Oval, 25 August 1990

BRIAN JOHNSTON You were brought up in Hackney in the 1930s. Not the sort of playground, I would imagine, for someone who enjoys cricket.

HAROLD PINTER Oh, we had cricket. When I finally went to Hackney Downs Grammar School during the war there was lots of cricket. We played as much cricket as possible, and I also went to Lord's a great deal during the war. I started to go to Lord's in about 1944, but really in 1945, when the Victory Tests were taking place and I saw Keith Miller and Wally Hammond and Hutton and Washbrook. Compton was still in India, but it was a very exciting period.

BRIAN But you were also evacuated during the war. Did you get any cricket in the country?

HAROLD Oh, yes. I was evacuated to Cornwall, right down in the south – Carheays Castle, in fact, with about twenty-six other boys. We played cricket there. Cricket was very much part of my life from the day I was born.

BRIAN Were your parents keen on cricket?

HAROLD No, no, there was a general feeling about cricket. In the 1930s the whole of England loved cricket, I think, at all levels. That was my impression as a child, anyway.

BRIAN And your skills as a boy – what were you, a batsman?

HAROLD Yes, a batsman. I'm sixty next month, but I still regard myself as a promising batsman.

BRIAN Who have you played for?

HAROLD Well, I've really only been associated with a wandering side called Gaieties for the last twenty years. That was originally a theatrical club started by Lupino Lane. I started to play in about 1969 for Gaieties. It was called Gaieties because Lupino Lane was working at the Gaiety Theatre – nothing to do with other kinds of Gaieties.

BRIAN The theatre is, alas, no more – on the corner there in the Strand.

HAROLD It was originally a stage side, but now it's still very active and we have a strong fixture list. I'm the chairman now. I skippered the side for about five years in the 1970s. I'm still very, very involved in it. In fact, I'm also the match manager, I have to tell you.

BRIAN You stand a good chance of going in first and getting the opening over, don't you?

HAROLD No, they wouldn't let me do that any more. We don't have a theatrical thing any more. Our last few games of the season are Oxted, Ashtead and Roehampton, and we're going to play a club in South Wales.

BRIAN That's getting serious – Roehampton. You're a member of MCC. Did you get in as a playing member?

HAROLD No, no. I don't know how I got in, but I became a member in the 1960s. The changes at Lord's are very interesting. I remember very well I happened to be in front of the pavilion when Freddie Titmus was playing, and before the game he walked in front of the committee room and looked inside and there was Freddie Brown and

Gubby Allen and he said, 'Good morning, sir.' And Freddie Brown said, 'Morning, Titmus.' That doesn't happen any more.

BRIAN There was the business of initials, too. An announcement was made at Lord's once. It said, 'On your scorecard, for "F. J. Titmus", read "Titmus F. J.",' because they'd put him down as an amateur.

HAROLD Wouldn't do at all.

BRIAN Do you support Middlesex? Are they your side?

HAROLD No, I've always supported Yorkshire. I don't know why – actually I do know why, because Len Hutton was my hero from 1946.

BRIAN A good man to pick.

HAROLD He still is, really, though I've never met him. I could watch him bat for ever. I thought he was the most wonderful batsman and I did as much of that as I could – following him all over the place. So Yorkshire became my side.

BRIAN I thought you had associations somehow with Somerset.

HAROLD No. I was lucky enough to play with Arthur Wellard. He actually played for Gaieties. He played in the 1970s when he was in his late sixties. He was a wonderful man, a great cricketer.

BRIAN Was he still hitting sixes?

HAROLD Oh, yes. He could really give it a tremendous whack. He was my teacher, actually. He was very rigorous with me. I produced the odd six.

BRIAN Now, Jeffrey Archer told me he read an article by you about Wellard. He said it was one of the best articles he'd ever read.

HAROLD Well, that's very kind. What always impressed me about Arthur was that his life really was cricket. He would hold a cricket ball as if it was a golf ball, his hands were so big, but the point really was that he'd lived a life that was really happy, playing cricket.

BRIAN I was lucky I saw him playing in the Lord's 1938 Test match.

HAROLD Where he got 38.

BRIAN Well done – and Denis Compton helped save us in the second innings.

HAROLD Arthur bowled Badcock, you know, and he gave me the stump.

BRIAN Big hands. Alec Bedser's got huge hands and Alan Davidson had big hands, but Arthur Wellard's were real Palethorpe sausages, weren't they? The fingers and the huge palms.

HAROLD But he was an inspiration to the club side, you see. And then he umpired when he couldn't get the arm over.

BRIAN He took a few wickets for you umpiring, did he?

HAROLD No, never. He wouldn't do a thing like that at all. 'Not out,' he'd say, and that was it. And 'You're joking,' he'd say.

BRIAN I know he played on fairly small grounds, Frome and ones like that, but he did hit I don't know how many sixes.

HAROLD Well, he twice hit five sixes off successive balls.

(Arthur Wellard died at the end of 1980, aged 78. Until Ian Botham's 80 sixes in the 1985 season, Wellard held the top four places in the record list of sixes hit in a season: 66 in 1935, 57 in both 1936 and 1938, and 51 in 1933.)

BRIAN What had he got? He was very strong. He must have had a super eye.

HAROLD He had a wonderful eye, and he told a wonderful story of when he was on the Lionel Tennyson tour of India in 1936. He hit the biggest six off Amar Singh. He said it was going into the Ganges, but something stopped it at the top of a stand. He said, 'I really got hold of that ball.' And on that tour was Joe Hardstaff, who I thought was a wonderful batsman. In fact, watching Azharuddin the other day – I'm not old enough to remember Ranji or Duleep – but I thought Hardstaff had that grace.

BRIAN Well, he was like Cyril Walters or Tom Graveney, it didn't matter if he was defending or not – rather like David Gower. When you see him just stroking one through the covers, it's lovely to watch. You go to Lord's; do you come to the Oval a bit?

HAROLD Yes, I'm a member here, too. It's a great ground.

BRIAN Now you don't play, you watch, do you?

HAROLD I don't play much. Oddly enough, it's the fielding. The eye's gone. I used to be really able to catch. I had quite a good eye, but that's become very blurry now.

BRIAN How do you mix it with your writing? Could you write a play sitting in the dressing room? Or did you have to take time off to do the writing and play cricket another time?

HAROLD You find it's like a good old stew, you throw a few things in. I've always enjoyed the range of life that I've been lucky enough to experience.

BRIAN Have you written a play about cricket?

HAROLD No, but in a number of films I wrote I managed to get a cricket scene in, like *The Go-Between*. There was a very important cricket scene in that.

BRIAN Oh, that was lovely.

HAROLD And another film I wrote, *Accident*, I got a cricket scene in.

BRIAN Are you tempted now to sit down and write a nice cricket play, because there's room for one.

HAROLD It's not an easy thing to do. I've thought about it a bit. I think the real cricket action goes on in the dressing rooms, you know. All the real aggro. This is amateur, of course; I've never been in a professional dressing room; I don't know what it's like. People – particularly foreigners – tend to say cricket is a peaceful game, like a ballet. Obviously it's not. It's a very, very violent activity, I think. A lot of people are bowling very hard and trying to hit the ball hard and the feeling is incredibly intense. The thing that always continues to amaze me about cricket is that every game possesses tremendous tension and drama.

BRIAN It's the team drama; it's the individual drama. Imagine the scene now when Gower goes back. Is he left alone to sit and mope? Knowing him, he'll probably be smiling.

(David Gower, after missing the previous winter tour to the West Indies, had only returned to the England side for the second half of the season. He had not had notable success and now, with his selection for the forthcoming tour of Australia very much in the balance, he had been out for 8. On the final day of this Test, though, he was to add to the drama with a superlative 157 not out to save the Test against India and secure his tour place.)

HAROLD That phrase 'bad luck' covers an awful lot, doesn't it?

BRIAN With the pat on the back from the skipper, 'Bad luck.'

HAROLD That's it. But I think the aggravation and the disappointments are so profound, aren't they?

BRIAN Do you enjoy captaining? There's something about it. I used to enjoy captaining teams. I think it adds tremendous fun working things out.

HAROLD Oh, I found it very tough, because everyone knows if it goes right you're fine. When it goes wrong there's only one person that's to blame and that's you. I actually resigned my Gaieties captaincy on the spot one day on the field.

BRIAN Oh no!

HAROLD Yes, I did. Because I took a bowler off and said, 'Thank you very much, Mac, that's it.' And my vice-captain, who was one of my greatest friends and still is, said to me, 'You're taking him off, are you?' I said, 'That's right,' and he called me a short, sharp word, so I said, 'That's it!'

BRIAN Talk about tension in cricket.

HAROLD So I then said, 'OK, Chris, you're the captain.' This wasn't a democratic election. 'You're taking over.' And the next game I played under him – it was at Ashtead – they were 174 for 2 and he came to me and said, 'What do you think I should do?' And I said, 'I haven't the faintest idea.'

BRIAN No more responsibility.

HAROLD Absolutely. 'Sort it out for yourself.' It was a wonderful moment of relief, I must say.

BRIAN Is there anything about the modern game you'd like to see changed?

HAROLD Someone was saying, I think, this morning in one of the newspapers, and I entirely agree – this is a detail, but it's rather important – with the helmet situation, you can't actually discern the batsmen. My world was the world of Hutton, Bradman and Miller and they were all absolutely individual.

BRIAN They were people you could see. We have asked Micky Stewart, in fact, to ask his players to come out holding their helmets, so people could at least see who these zombies are before they put their helmets on. They say it's difficult to fit it on. It's a pity for the game, but then you and I don't have to go out and face the bouncers.

HAROLD No, that's right, but when Griffith and Hall were bowling – they were pretty quick too – people weren't wearing helmets. Brian Close didn't wear a helmet; Dexter didn't.

BRIAN I once asked Bradman if he came back now if he'd wear a helmet and he said he would, but I reckon he was being polite. He didn't wear one against Larwood.

HAROLD I was very lucky to see Bradman. I saw him in 1948.

BRIAN Were you here for the famous dismissal?

(Don Bradman was out second ball for a duck at the Oval in his last Test innings.)

HAROLD I certainly was. I was here for Hutton's 30 when he was caught by Tallon off Lindwall.

BRIAN Down the leg side. I think he was the only chap who got to double figures. We made 52.

HAROLD That's right, 52 all out.

BRIAN You've got a retentive memory for these things.

HAROLD Yes. I was thrilled to meet Keith Miller and Denis Compton a couple of weeks ago and I asked both of them a question I've been meaning to ask for many, many years and I've never had the opportunity. Was Bradman caught by Ikin for 28 at Brisbane in 1946?

BRIAN Was he out? Well, Wally Hammond thought he was.

HAROLD Well, Miller and Compton also thought he was. Miller was the next man in. He was just reaching for his gloves and suddenly he saw that Bradman wasn't walking.

BRIAN This was one in the gully and it was a question of whether it touched the ground or didn't.

HAROLD And, of course, Bradman went on to get 187 and 234 in the next match.

BRIAN And if he'd failed in that match he might have given up, because he wasn't a very fit man.

HAROLD Yes, but he didn't.

BRIAN To go back to the war, when you went to Lord's, the matches involved teams like the Home Guard and that sort of thing.

HAROLD Absolutely, but at the end of the war – I was a boy of fourteen at the time – I heard a report that the Americans were going to play baseball at Lord's. And I rang Lord's and asked to speak to the Secretary of the MCC. I said, 'I'm ringing you as a schoolboy and I feel that this report that the Americans are going to play baseball at Lord's is the most disgraceful thing I've ever heard.' And he said, 'Don't worry, my dear fellow, I don't think you should take these reports too seriously. I don't think we're actually going to allow it to happen.'

BRIAN Let's just talk about your acting. Do you enjoy that?

HAROLD Oh, yes. I enjoy acting. But the trouble with acting was that I couldn't play cricket when I was young, because

I was moving about so much in rep. And I was in Ireland, but I took my cricket bat there with me and we played a bit on the meadows over there.

BRIAN But you've now gone to the other side of things, directing. Do you enjoy that?

HAROLD Oh, yes, I enjoy the activity, but there's nothing I enjoy more than being at the Oval today. That's the truth.

34 Ian Richter

ONE OF THE REWARDS OF being a commentator on *Test Match Special* is the number of letters we receive, not just from this country, but from all over the world. They come from many different sorts of people of both sexes and of all ages. It may sound presumptuous, but it does give us the feeling of being the centre point of a vast cricket-loving family. It still gives me a special thrill when Peter Baxter puts a small card in front of me which reads: WELCOME WORLD SERVICE. The thought of speaking to people thousands of miles away in so many countries and different environments creates a little extra drop of adrenalin.

You can imagine, therefore, how pleased we were when Geoff Parker of BBC World Service Sport told us that he had received the following letter, which read: 'As you know I'm confined out here and have been for some time, one of my great comforts is listening to the ball-by-ball commentary, and I have been delighted to hear England's win at Headingley, after a long 22-year wait.' The letter was headed 'Baghdad' and signed by Ian Richter, who had been arrested by the Iraqi police in 1986. He was held for five and a half years in jail just outside Baghdad until his release in November 1991. He was right on the ball about England's win against the West Indies at Headingley in June 1991. It was England's first home victory against West Indies since 1969, when Ray Illingworth's team also won at Headingley.

I'm afraid the weather was not too good when he joined us in our commentary box high up on the stand at the Stretford End.

Old Trafford, 2 July 1992

BRIAN JOHNSTON It's marvellous to see you and to congratulate you on the way you got out of that predicament. It must have been dreadful.

IAN RICHTER It's wonderful to be here, even in this weather. I've had enough sun in the last few years. I could do with a bit of rain, but I don't like it interfering with my cricket.

BRIAN I've had a report from the naval and air force attaché from Baghdad *(who had rung the BBC that morning when he heard Ian Richter was going to be our guest).* A chap called John Marriott, who said you were a very fine cricketer, that you were a wicket-keeper who went in first. So you're a sort of Alec Stewart. He said you were also a fine squash and hockey player. Is all that right?

IAN Yes. In my younger years I did play hockey for South Africa and played cricket for South African Universities and Western Province once. I have two first-class matches to my credit. Not a lot, but I've always had a deep love for the game and it did help me enormously during my early days of solitary confinement – getting into little exercises like picking world cricket teams.

BRIAN That was mental exercise. What about when you were playing out there before you were arrested? What sort of cricket did you have?

IAN Very little in Baghdad – but fun cricket. We used to play for the Embassy side against various nationals. We played an Indian side or a Pakistan side every now and then, and occasionally we'd come across a side from a company with a very large contract, one that had enough players to put together a team. The Indians and Pakistanis used to bring on one or two surprises from time to time and it was a variable pitch.

BRIAN What sort of pitches were they? Matting?

IAN No, we had a grass pitch. The British Embassy in Baghdad is delightfully set right on the river Tigris and I think the Iraqis have been trying to move them out for several years now, but been resisted. It's a glorious setting, with many trees, and it's a grass wicket of variable bounce.

BRIAN Did you ever hit a six into the river Tigris?

IAN Yes, I did manage one for which I had to forfeit several beers.

BRIAN Since coming back here have you had any cricket?

IAN Yes, I was kindly invited by the Free Foresters to play against my son's school at Ampleforth, so it was a wonderful arrangement and we had a glorious day during the festival weekend. It was quite glorious to be playing cricket again. I was so impressed with the way Don Wilson looks after all the boys there. He doesn't push them too hard, doesn't destroy their natural talent and at the same time he guides and keeps them going.

BRIAN Can you remember what your final World XI was that you selected over the five and a half years?

IAN Well, I found it so difficult defining periods. Originally I started with the post-war period, then narrowed it down to people I'd either seen or heard of. There were two or three sides; I could never actually settle on one, but I guess it would be something like Greenidge and Barry Richards opening the batting. At three we could have had Kanhai or Greg Chappell or Vivian Richards. I would have looked at Graeme Pollock possibly at four, having a slight South African background. Clive Lloyd at five, maybe. I had great difficulty in choosing the all-rounder – Procter, Botham.

BRIAN What about your bowlers?

IAN So many: Wes Hall, Griffith, Lindwall, Miller – four wonderful bowlers – Fred Trueman.

BRIAN You have to include him, although he's not in the box.

IAN And Geoff Boycott was first reserve, if Richards and Greenidge hadn't got a hundred by lunch.

BRIAN So you're going to get him to bring out the drinks. He wouldn't like that.

IAN Wicket-keepers too was a difficult choice. Knotty possibly.

BRIAN You say you received the ball-by-ball. How did you actually get it?

IAN For the first three years I was in solitary, so I had virtually nothing. But eventually I got a radio and I started playing with it, and I managed to get a copy of *London Calling*, which announced that they were having a ball-by-ball service, and I tuned in quite fruitlessly one morning. I then, quite by chance, discovered that if I listened to a certain frequency, once it finished, shortly after lunch UK time, if I twiddled the knob a little further to the left I would pick up the South Eastern wavelength where it was being beamed to. It was rather faint, but if I cocked an ear to one side and told everyone to shut up – I was quite fierce about that – I would have four or five hours' cricket. So it was wonderful.

BRIAN Let's just work back a bit. How did you get a set?

IAN Well, it took a lot of pushing. As you can imagine, it was not something the Iraqis were terribly keen on doing. I think my wife got hold of three. The third one got to me after various people had intervened along the way and that made a huge difference to my quality of life.

BRIAN And did your Iraqi guard put on the headphones and listen to the commentary?

IAN Er – no. They're not the keenest of cricketers.

BRIAN Let's go back to the beginning. First of all, you are South African.

IAN Yes, born there and came over to Britain in 1972 after I got my MSc in chemical engineering, and I've been here ever since.

BRIAN So why did you go out to Iraq?

IAN We had sold a large water-treatment plant to them – drinking water – and the requirement was that we had to set up an office out there within twelve months of signing the contract. So it was a career move, really. I wasn't an expatriate as such. It seemed a good step forward to move out of engineering into management and so I accepted the chance and went out for three years. I was asked to stay another year and was asked to stay another year and then, actually on my departure to come back, the grey faces arrived.

BRIAN Were you on your way to the airport?

IAN I was at the airport.

BRIAN With the plane outside waiting to take you back to the old country? What did they do?

IAN It was frightening, really. They came up to me and they said, 'Your passport's out of order.' So I said, 'I don't think it is.' And they said, 'Well, come with us to the old airport.' And I thought something was wrong when five goons jumped into a Mercedes with me, because not many people have Mercedes in Baghdad, apart from privileged people. We drove well past the old airport and I was refused access to my wife, and I said, 'Where are we going?' They drove me to a piece of wasteland and said, 'Lie down on the floor.' That was terrifying. I thought I was going to be executed then. You hear these stories. In fact, all they were doing was preventing me seeing where they were taking me, but I didn't know that. Then I arrived at the great Majabrat headquarters. I guess it's like the KGB head-quarters in Moscow. It's a sort of dark place.

BRIAN And were you then questioned?

IAN I was questioned for three days. They tried to associate me with one person, failed to, and then a second, then a third.

BRIAN What were they accusing you of?

IAN Various things. One was bribery, second was espionage, and as they kept on trying, the more desperate they got.

BRIAN Without offending any of them, I should have thought that bribery was rather a normal thing.

IAN Well, no, it's strictly forbidden out there. As I was not a director, I had no ability to sign foreign currency cheques so it was fairly far-fetched.

BRIAN Who were you accused of bribing?

IAN The Mayor of Baghdad, who was not our client at the time. Our client was something to do with the Ministry of Housing, which was nothing to do with him. They quickly found out that he was nothing to do with me, and I think all in all I had been held as a hostage for this chap who's over here who had assassinated an Iraqi Prime Minister some years ago.

BRIAN Did you have a sort of trial?

IAN They left me alone after the three days for roughly nine months. That was a challenging period, too. Day after day in the darkness.

BRIAN Were you in solitary?

IAN Yes. That was a difficult period.

BRIAN In the dark. Take us through a day. One just can't imagine it. Do they shove food through at you?

IAN A cup of tea in the morning, a cup of tea in the evening. I went on hunger strike for the first two weeks and refused to eat what they were giving me. I'll never know, if I'd had the courage to keep going, whether they'd have let me go on. But eventually they called me in and they were very upset. They said, 'You've got to eat something. We're going to bring you a roll from outside. Will you eat that?' I said, 'Well, I'll see what the roll is.' And eventually hunger got the better of me and I started eating the roll. But the first two or three months were difficult, because I didn't know what was happening. I kept thinking that help was at hand any moment. But then I just realised that you had to get on with life by yourself.

BRIAN Were you visited at all? Did the ambassador come and see you?

IAN They were trying desperately to get access to me, but it wasn't permitted. I had the pillar of using my mind and that was either developing a mathematical equation for a shadow on the wall or picking a cricket team.

BRIAN What things did you have? Pencil and paper?

IAN No, absolutely nothing. No light. It was just a blank cell. I slept on the floor.

BRIAN Absolutely unbelievable. What do you think of all day? Choosing your World XI?

IAN Yes. You invent a business. You see how it would do in Britain or how it would do in Saudi Arabia. It was very important to keep the mind going.

BRIAN Did you get any sense of time?

IAN I had no watch and couldn't detect time through the light. The only way I kept track of the days was through the tea in the morning and the tea in the evening. I had a passion to keep track of the days. It was a real thing with me.

BRIAN And no news from outside whatever?

IAN No. After about three months I was shown to the British chargé d'affaires, but I wasn't allowed to speak to him and he wasn't allowed to speak to me. It wasn't easy for a year and a half to two years, but then things got slightly better.

BRIAN You're throwing that away – it wouldn't be easy for a week or a day. What were the Iraqi guards like?

IAN Well, at first they were fierce. It was a difficult situation. I don't think they have much regard for human life and they were desperate to extract information from people they held, so they used various techniques in so doing. After that, when I was transferred to the main jail, I think I was discriminated against for some while, but eventually my discipline and daily routine appealed to them, I think, and we gradually made friends. They weren't the people who had arrested me; they were just normal prison guards.

BRIAN Did they talk to you?

IAN At first they were terrified, because Iraqis are really discouraged from speaking to foreigners, but gradually they plucked up courage and saw that I had two arms and two legs and two eyes and went running every now and then – 'The mad Englishman who likes this, but he doesn't like that.'

BRIAN Where were you allowed to run, though?

IAN Well, that again took about three years, but eventually I persevered and I said, 'I want to run round that dusty football pitch you've got out there.' And they said, 'But no one runs here.' So I said, 'Well, I want to.' It was wonderful, running, because it took me away from the maelstrom of Egyptians and Sudanese and the cigarettes and the spitting, and it was just a bit of peace.

BRIAN But how were you physically? Your legs must have been completely weak to start with.

IAN They weren't too bad, because in solitary after two months I realised no one was going to get me out of this and I had to survive myself and I got stuck into the exercises then. So I used to leap about doing star jumps and press-ups, and occasionally I'd get a knock on the door saying, 'What the hell are you doing in there?' But generally that kept me going and I did find physical exercise important mentally, too. The two seemed to go together.

BRIAN Now, what about the Gulf War? Did you know when it had started?

IAN Yes.

BRIAN Did their attitude change?

IAN It didn't. They were surprisingly good to me during the war. Whether that was because I'd built up a relationship and a respect before that, or whether they were just hedging their bets on how the war was going to go, I don't know, but they were very good to me during the war. The war itself was difficult to handle, because there was a desperate shortage of food and water, so we really had to struggle to survive.

BRIAN Were you bombed at any time by our planes?

IAN Yes. Funnily enough there was a strike of lightning and thunder the night before the war started and we all thought, 'Oh, God, this is it.' But they came the next night and there was an army camp round us, which got plastered. But for the first day or two you get frightened of bombs and then you get used to the noise. You get a bit blasé about it and get this feeling that it's not going to happen to you.

BRIAN Did they try the propaganda and say how great Saddam Hussein was? Presumably they worshipped him.

IAN Well, they had to worship him, but gradually, after the war, when there was this insurrection, I was amazed how many people came to me and said, 'This man has ruined our country.' That took a lot of saying to a foreigner. It could never have happened before the war.

BRIAN And you were made more comfortable, were you? Did you have a better cell with other people?

IAN It was very crowded when I first left solitary and was brought to the main prison. I was in a hall about forty metres by sixty metres with about sixty people in it, so it was very crowded – a bit like a goldfish bowl. After five years, yes, I was given a cell of my own, and that was marvellous. I put up a big sign, saying ENGLISHMEN ONLY. PICCADILLY CIRCUS. KEEP OUT.

BRIAN What a relief. And your wife went out to visit you regularly?

IAN Yes. Shirley had come back to Britain after six or nine months, having been refused permission for a while, and then led this marvellous campaign. She was absolutely wonderful. She came regularly until the invasion of Kuwait, when, of course, we didn't see each other for a year. Then she came out with ITV and there was this most extraordinary interview. I thought she was coming out, but I'd no idea of the time, and I walked into this room and there were all these cameras and Jeffrey Archer was there. So it was a sign that things were going well, but I'd been through so many disappointments I didn't take it as a sign at the time. But the fact that they did allow a TV crew in was good.

BRIAN And how did you actually hear the news that you were going to be released?

IAN The Russian ambassador came to see me three days before I was released and he said, 'Ian, I'm terribly sorry relations between Britain and Iraq are particularly bad at the moment. Sadruddin Aga Khan's coming out, but I really wouldn't bank on him. He's going to try, but things are just terribly bad at the moment.' So I said, 'Oh, well, thanks for that.' He was a super chap. The Russians were marvellous to me after the war. They found me and helped me.

BRIAN Did you interest them in cricket? One day they're going to play, aren't they?

IAN They got into rugby in quite a big way. So then three days passed and nothing happened and I went out and ran a half-marathon to get rid of my pent-up fury at not being released, and I had a shower, which was a bucket of water and a ladle. And a guy came to me and said, 'You've got five minutes to leave.' And I said, 'As I've spent five years as your guest, you can give me a bit longer.' He said, 'No, there is a press conference. We've got to be there.' I think Saddam Hussein would have killed him if he hadn't got me there in five minutes. So I grabbed a shirt, borrowed a tie and unfortunately lost all my letters, but I preserved my books – particularly the cricketing books, which people had sent me. Towards the end I got most of the *Wisden*s.

BRIAN I suppose you had to catch up, didn't you? Those years when you were in solitary you didn't get the cricket scores.

IAN I missed 1986 to 1989, basically. So I missed a period when we lost a few.

BRIAN And you read of the successes of various new people. That must have been fascinating – a new breed of cricketers.

IAN It was. Lamb had come and gone and come back again and gone again and come back again and, yes, a whole new breed had come through.

BRIAN And as soon as you were released, where did you go?

IAN I went to a hotel and I had twenty-four hours with Prince Sadruddin and his team and then flew back with his plane.

BRIAN He did a good job, did he?

IAN Marvellous guy. Shirley met him during her visit to Iraq three or four months before I was released. She went to see him and he promised to help, and many people who said that helped in their own ways, but Prince Sadruddin kept in telephone and fax contact with her weekly thereafter.

BRIAN Would you ever go back there?

IAN I don't think so. I think I've probably donated enough of my life.

BRIAN So are you working for a firm here?

IAN I've come back to my old group company. Not the firm itself I worked for; they were sold off to Thames Water when the water industry was privatised, but I'm in the same group.

BRIAN And now you're starting a cricket tour. You said you were playing for the Free Foresters. How many did you make? How many stumpings?

IAN Twenty-six. One stumping and two catches – and the next match I got one and dropped two catches.

BRIAN That's roughly the way cricket goes. So who are you going to be playing for now?

IAN Well, I have Emeriti in a week's time.

BRIAN This is the club formed by the Catholic schools, roughly – Downside, Ampleforth?

IAN And they had to include St Aidan's in Grahamstown, where I was brought up – a Jesuit school. I'll be playing for a number of sides and Don Wilson wants me to play one or two over the bank holiday.

BRIAN It would be nice keeping wicket to him. You'd get a few stumpings.

IAN When I came back I spent the winter up in Yorkshire and he allowed me to play with the first-team squad at their indoor nets, and he bowled to me and he's a wonderful bowler. He just twiddled it over and stretched me forward and a little bit more forward each ball – lovely to see.

BRIAN It sounds to me that if we were all put into solitary confinement we'd all become better cricketers. How did you pick it all up, after five or six years, picking up a bat again or putting on the gauntlets?

IAN I think a moving-ball game is instinct – squash or tennis, that's all come back to me, too. But I can't hit a bloody golf ball.

BRIAN But did it affect your eyes? There you were in darkness. What happened when you suddenly saw the light?

IAN I was worried about that, but it seems fine.

BRIAN So you can still see the ball. The other thing, having trained running round that football field, you've now run in the London Marathon here. You must be mad. What was your time?

IAN Four hours thirty minutes, less ten minutes to get to the start, so I claim four hours twenty. When we came back we were interviewed by a lot of people and after one day we said, 'Right, that's it.' Somebody from a running magazine rang up and said she wanted to do an interview. I said, 'Sorry, those times have passed now.' And she said, 'But I'll get you into the London Marathon and I'll get you kit.' The kit disappeared towards my children rapidly, but she got me into the London Marathon and the Red Cross, who'd helped Shirley a lot while I was away, asked me to run for them.

BRIAN So you got some money for the Red Cross. How did you feel when you crossed the line?

IAN I felt pretty grim at about twenty-three miles, when we got to Tower Bridge for the second time, but, as luck would have it, I bumped into Shirley, who'd spent three hours looking for me, and that sort of raised me for the last three miles. Yes, it was fun to finish.

35 The Rt. Rev. and Rt. Hon. Lord Runcie of Cuddesdon

I HAD ALWAYS HEARD THAT the Archbishop of Canterbury liked pigs and bred them with great success. This was confirmed when I interviewed him at Lambeth Palace for *Down Your Way* shortly after he had become Archbishop in 1980. I was met at the palace by none other than Terry Waite, who took me to meet the Archbishop. During the interview which followed I also learned of his love of cricket, and I subsequently met him several times in various boxes at Lord's. He, somewhat naturally, was always asked to the president's tent during the Canterbury week. This probably led to the apocryphal story that I told him towards the end of his 'View from the Boundary'.

There is also another story which I did not dare to tell the Archbishop. It's of two visitors to Canterbury having coffee in a café. One of them spotted a grey-haired man with horn-rimmed glasses sitting at a corner table. He said, 'I swear that's the Archbishop of Canterbury sitting over there.' His companion replied, 'Don't be ridiculous. Of course it isn't.' 'Right,' said his friend, 'I bet you a quid that it is. I shall go and ask him.' He went over to the corner table and after a brief conversation returned looking very red in the face. 'Well, what did he say?' his friend asked. 'He told me to mind my own —— business and to —— off!' He handed over his one pound to his friend, who said, 'Thanks. But what a pity. Now we shall never know whether or not it was the Archbishop.'

After a session in the commentary box in his company, it was much easier to understand how, in the Second World War, the Archbishop had been a successful tank commander in the Scots Guards. He came over as a very strong character with a delightful sense of humour, neither of which could perhaps be sensed during his many TV appearances on state or ceremonial occasions.

(Lord Runcie died in July 2000 at the age of 78 after a long battle with cancer.)

Lord's, 22 June 1991

BRIAN JOHNSTON How long was your reign as Archbishop of Canterbury?

LORD RUNCIE Ten and a half years.

BRIAN That's quite a long innings.

LORD RUNCIE It's enough – for me.

BRIAN Well, you're looking very well on it now in retirement. What are you doing?

LORD RUNCIE I'm settling down and watching a bit of cricket occasionally. I've been in America, delivering some uncontroversial lectures. I hope I didn't undermine my successor. And I've been opening things and launching things and I've got a variety of occupations, some ceremonial and some on which I want to focus. I'm going to be President of the Classical Association, which is quite formidable, but there is an old association between the classics and cricket, I think, as a civilising element in national life.

BRIAN You've got some rather grand title – the High something.

LORD RUNCIE Yes, I'm the High Steward of Cambridge.

BRIAN What on earth does that involve?

LORD RUNCIE Well, it doesn't involve a great deal. It doesn't carry any emoluments, but it's a very ancient title and ceremonial figure in the university and it was once held by people like Thomas More. Now I walk in processions, and actually last week I made my debut as High Steward and walked behind Prince Philip as Chancellor. One of the people who was getting an honorary degree, an East European mathematician of great distinction, turned to me as we were robing and said, 'Vot does ze High Steward do?' And I said, 'Well, he's rather a ceremonial figure, you know.' And then, trying to make it more exciting, I said, 'I walk behind the Chancellor and, of course, I suppose, if anything happened to the Chancellor . . .' 'Oh,' he said, 'I see you are a kind of Dan Quayle.'

(Dan Quayle was then Vice-President of the USA.)

BRIAN Well, how did the 'kind of Dan Quayle' start? You were born in Liverpool. Did you go to school in Liverpool?

LORD RUNCIE Yes, I went to Merchant Taylors, which is in Crosby, between Liverpool and Southport, and learned to love cricket there.

BRIAN Did you play cricket a lot?

LORD RUNCIE Yes, I was very keen on cricket. It was my first love, I think, in sports. I was not a great cricketer, but I captained the school in a lean year.

BRIAN Look, we're not modest in the box. What did you do well? Did you bat?

LORD RUNCIE Yes, I was an opening batsman – pretty steady – and a poor bowler. I've always been a poor bowler. I played what I suppose may be my last game last year, the Archbishop of Canterbury's XI v. the Governor of the Bank of England's XI, and in order to jazz up this charity match they persuaded me to bowl an over. Of course, even in my heyday I've never been a bowler and it was a rather disastrous moment, particularly as the television cameras happened to be there at that moment. And for weeks and indeed months afterwards people would say to me, 'That was a spectacular wide you bowled on television.' That was the first ball.

BRIAN You got through the over all right?

LORD RUNCIE I managed to get through the over. I actually bowled against Colin Cowdrey and one ball scarcely reached the stumps at the other end.

BRIAN So you had the powers of leadership as a boy – you were selected as captain.

LORD RUNCIE I don't know who selected me, but I was actually captain and we used to play around the various schools. Our most distant one was playing in the Isle of Man against King William's College. I think that's where I made my best total. I think I scored a century.

BRIAN You made a hundred! I never did.

LORD RUNCIE I've got this in the back of my mind. The unfortunate thing is that, although I've been parading this story and I did have very happy memories of the Isle of Man, I've got to go there to present the prizes at their Speech Day in the autumn. I'm not sure if they've invited me because of my great century in the past or whether they're going to disabuse me of this illusion by showing me the scorebook.

BRIAN I'm sure you wouldn't say you'd scored one if you hadn't. So, living in Lancashire, did you support Lancashire as a cricket side?

LORD RUNCIE Liverpool had two games a year.

BRIAN At Aigburth.

LORD RUNCIE Wonderful Liverpool name that, Aigburth – Saxon name. They were interesting games, because you had the tourists once and a county match the other. I used to set off with my sandwiches and I saw Wally Hammond, playing for Gloucestershire, and Cyril Washbrook, and I also saw Bradman and George Headley. So before the war, when I was at school, Aigburth was a place of pilgrimage.

BRIAN Were Hallows and Makepeace around?

LORD RUNCIE Yes, they were playing, and the Tyldesleys.

BRIAN Ernest Tyldesley and Richard Tyldesley – a rather rotund character who bowled slow leg-breaks.

LORD RUNCIE And a very gentlemanly captain, P. T. Eckersley.

BRIAN He was killed in the war, wasn't he?

LORD RUNCIE Yes, a fine man. And there was a lot of cricket

around Liverpool. The Liverpool Competition brings together Bootle and the Wirral, or did in my day.

BRIAN So, what did you do before the war?

LORD RUNCIE I just went up for a year to Oxford at the beginning of the war and then I went away to the Army and came back in 1945.

BRIAN We were both in the Brigade of Guards. You were in the Scots Guards; I was in the Grenadiers. I got in because we decided before the war started we might try to get into the best regiment. We went and drilled in the summer in our black Homburg hats and city suits at Wellington Barracks. How did you get in?

LORD RUNCIE Well, it's a long story. I got in because the Scots Guards had lost a lot of officers in the Western desert.

BRIAN This was in 1942?

LORD RUNCIE Yes. I was going into a Scottish regiment. My father was Scottish and we came of a Scottish family and I was at Oxford in the Officer Training Corps and they put into my mind the idea of becoming a Scots Guardsman. And I said, 'But I haven't got a private income.' And the adjutant said across the room, 'I think in wartime, you know, it wouldn't matter greatly. It's more important that we have soldiers these days.'

BRIAN As long as you've got a few polo ponies. And you were a tank commander. We were tanks, too. So, you commanded a troop?

LORD RUNCIE A troop of tanks, under the command of people like Willie Whitelaw.

BRIAN You're a splendid couple, you and Willie Whitelaw. No wonder we won the war!

LORD RUNCIE We soldiered together. The Scots Guards weren't mad keen on cricket. I couldn't persuade the tank crews much. I always remember a day when we were in Normandy and it was a very fine day. We'd cleaned the tanks and so on and I suggested to the sergeant, 'What about a game of cricket?' And this Glaswegian looked at me witheringly and said, 'Crucket? Yon's a daft wee girlie's game!' So I didn't get much cricket in the Army.

BRIAN So when you came out of the Brigade of Guards, what did you decide to do?

LORD RUNCIE Well, I wasn't too sure. I had at the back of my mind, but not very much at the front of my mind, that I might one day be ordained, but I went back to Oxford, where I'd started, in the early years of the war, to read Classics. I went back and read ancient history and philosophy and finished off my course in 1948, when I went – it sounds rather unadventurous – across to Cambridge.

BRIAN Yes, two universities. A bit greedy.

LORD RUNCIE Yes, and I stayed there a bit, although I was ordained after two years and went up to Newcastle. I then came back and taught in Cambridge for a time. Then I married a wife who was the daughter of a real criceter. He was the Senior Fellow of a college of which I was at that time the Junior Fellow, which was rather a crafty move, I think. It's called endogamy – marriage within the tribe. He was a man called Turner – and this is the only bit of homework I've done for this conversation, I've looked him up in *Who's Who* – he played for Worcestershire forty times between 1909 and 1921. I went to a Worcester diocesan festival shortly after I became Archbishop of Canterbury in 1981 and it was held on that marvellous cricket ground beneath the cathedral. It was an open-air service and I wasn't sure then about my father-in-law's cricketing past, but I risked saying at an early stage in the sermon, 'My unbelieving father-in-law would have felt that at last I had been preaching on a sacred spot.' And by the time I'd finished the service, the cricket officials, who'd been watching and suddenly leaped into action when I mentioned this, produced for me his average over the years. His bowling average and his batting average. I thought that was a good example of dedication.

BRIAN Can you remember what they were?

LORD RUNCIE Modest.

BRIAN How long did you have a parish for?

LORD RUNCIE Well, first of all I was in Newcastle and only for a short time was I in a parish, because I came back to teach. But when I'd left teaching in Cambridge I went to be principal of a college just outside Oxford for ten years, between 1960 and 1970, and during that time I was also vicar of the parish of Cuddesdon, a place to which I'm devoted. And for me being in charge of that parish, though it was tiny but full of character, was, perhaps, more significant than running a college. I learned more and was rather a Pooh-Bah in those days, because I was chairman of the parish council and chairman of the sports committee.

BRIAN Were you selected to play for the village, though?

LORD RUNCIE I played cricket for the village against the college and I played cricket quite a bit during those years, because there was, for example, in the neighbouring village of Garsington a famous manor house. The squire of Garsington was somebody called John Wheeler-Bennett and every year he had a tremendous occasion when the Squire's XI played the village at Garsington. And the Squire's XI was a mixture of real cricketers, local characters and royal equerries. It was free drink for everybody and the village really turned out. It was a weekend, so he had a house party. Then there was always a service on the Sunday, and I remember that if you were recruited to preach before the village and before this cricketing house party, it was traditional to get up some striking text appropriate to the occasion, like 'Ruth came down with a full pitcher.' The man who won, having regard to the sociability of the previous afternoon, was the man who ultimately became the Dean of Lincoln and rejoiced in the name of Oliver Twisleton-Wykeham-Fiennes. He discovered a text in Chronicles which was 'The lords of the Assyrians were drinking themselves drunk in the pavilion.'

BRIAN What was your text, do you remember?

LORD RUNCIE I think mine was fairly unadventurous. It was, I think, in Kings – Saul: 'Give me a man that can play well.'

BRIAN Well, I think Gooch would say that. Are you in favour of cricket-playing vicars? I have a friend, John Woodcock, who has the gift of giving the local vicar his job and he sets a great importance on the religious side, but he does always ask him, 'Do you play cricket?'

LORD RUNCIE Well, I think it's a good qualification. Obviously I think the spiritual qualifications are the ones that really matter, but it's a symbol of something rather good. It's the same with the Classics. I remember, in years gone by, meeting once Isaiah Berlin, the great Oxford savant, and I had a cricket bag in one hand and a copy of Plato under my arm and he was delighted. I was an undergraduate at the time and he stood in the middle of the pavement and said, 'Ah! What we all stand for, what we all stand for!' In my experience, I have to say that cricketers form a very good ingredient in the clergy in any diocese. There was in the diocese of St Albans in my days a very old-fashioned, rather eccentric clergyman who I remember once saying that until clergy give up their modish obsession with synods and return to their traditional activities of cricket, bee-keeping and siring Nelsons, we shall have no improvement in the morals of this country.

BRIAN You talk about bee-keeping, what about pig-keeping, which is your big hobby?

LORD RUNCIE I've got, perhaps, too much attention over that. My pigs are looked after by a splendid farm for mentally handicapped people and I'm interested in that. It's Oast Farm Trust, and I have a few black Berkshire pigs.

BRIAN They win prizes, though.

LORD RUNCIE We've got a secret weapon in a man who lives near the community who is an international expert on pigs. He gives advice and the pigs win prizes and I get this notoriety and indeed a spurious reputation of being a distinguished pig-keeper. We've got a very fine sow called Portia who won the Kent Show two years ago, then she had a year off for motherhood last year.

BRIAN Would she rival the Empress of Blandings? Do you go and poke her with a stick? Pig owners generally do, don't they?

LORD RUNCIE My Portia is a black Berkshire pig, which the Empress of Blandings was, although it's sometimes depicted as a pink pig. I could prove to you from the texts of Wodehouse that she was a black Berkshire pig.

BRIAN To come back to cricket, when you were in Canterbury, did you go to the county ground to watch?

LORD RUNCIE I wish I could say that I did. I only really was able during the last ten years to have two days that I kept particularly, and that was to have a day at the Lord's Test and a day at Canterbury cricket week. I think Canterbury cricket week is something that nobody can match.

BRIAN There was an occasion there – I don't know if you know – when you were sitting on the right hand of Mr Swanton when he was president. On his left was the Duke of Kent, and do you know what the chap walking past said? 'Who are those two people sitting with Jim Swanton?'

LORD RUNCIE I can well believe that. I've had some wonderful conversations with people there who were my boyhood and young manhood heroes. Like Leslie Ames – I miss him a great deal. We always used to have a little talk about George Duckworth, his old rival at Lancashire, and he was always so generous.

BRIAN Who else were your heroes in the cricket world?

LORD RUNCIE The first real bat I had had LEN HUTTON on it, and it's been a great thrill in these last few years to be able to see him and talk with him here. And yesterday I was with Clyde Walcott and he reminded me that there's a marvellous story of my predecessor, Michael Ramsey, who was in Barbados. He was a wonderful, lovely, saintly

329

man, looking patriarchal, and he had this rather sing-song voice and he gave out his theme. He said, 'I'm going to speak to you about the three Ws.' And there was a great sigh and all the congregation looked eager. Then he said, 'Worship, witness and work,' and a great groan went up.

BRIAN We're both of us cricket nuts. Do we exaggerate the importance of cricket in character-building? Do you think it's got something that other games haven't got?

LORD RUNCIE Well, I hope it can preserve some of the sort of decencies that surround the way in which the game is conducted. And I think the need for patience and sticking with things is very important in character formation when we live in a society where short-termism and immediate satisfaction is so dominant. Partly from the communications explosion and also the huge variety of options for people about what they should believe and how they should behave, and the way in which they can change so quickly from one thing to another. I think the stabilities and the need for patience, co-operation and teamwork and, yes, something of the romance that attaches to cricket has within it the seeds of idealism without which no society will ever be well nourished.

BRIAN And it's a very good mix, because it's essentially a team game, but when it comes to the crunch, you're out there alone against Curtly Ambrose, aren't you?

LORD RUNCIE It's all up to you, but you in company with others. You can't be unaware of the other people with whom you're working. And I do think the need for decisions – I remember this as a captain, but it goes for anybody in the side, you do have to make quite a lot of decisions over quite a period of time and they're decisions that are sometimes immediate and sometimes call for reflection – I think that's character-building, too.

BRIAN You've had some great cricketing people in the Church: the present Bishop of Liverpool, a Test player, Canon Parsons, Canon Gillingham . . .

LORD RUNCIE Yes, and E. T. Killick, who died at the crease in a diocesan match. He is someone who is very well remembered in Hertfordshire even today. The influence of a cricketing parson.

36 Peter Scudamore

FOR SOME REASON MANY JOCKEYS seem to be mad about cricket, especially the jumpers, as opposed to the flat. Their season gives them a short break during the summer so that they are able to play or watch cricket and run a very useful jockeys' team, which plays for charity. At Headingley in 1989 I was able to say with some truth, 'We are very lucky to have a leg-spinner in the box with us today. He also happens to be quite a useful National Hunt jockey.' In fact, Peter, in the season just finished, had ridden 221 winners, breaking the previous record by 72.

We commentators often think that we are busy, but what about this? Peter had flown in from New York that very Saturday morning having ridden at Belmont on Friday. He had only agreed to go to America provided they guaranteed he would be able to get to Headingley by Saturday lunchtime. After watching the afternoon's play he was due to go down to Cheltenham to ride in two exhibition races against Willie Shoemaker the next day. Although he had a pale complexion, he looked pretty well on it all, and his sparse wiry figure put all of ours in the box to shame.

Headingley, 10 June 1989

PETER SCUDAMORE I wouldn't have missed this for the world. My father's a great cricketing man and that's influenced me. We used to go and watch Worcester play when I was a child and a lot of cricketers are friendly with the National Hunt jockeys. I think it's because we're on holiday when they're playing and they're on holiday when we're out riding, so they come racing, we go cricketing, and so you get to know some of the players.

BRIAN JOHNSTON So how much cricket have you managed to get this summer?

PETER I've played twice this summer. I've been lucky enough to play for the Starlight XI, raising money for terminally ill children. It's the brainchild of Eric Clapton.

BRIAN What sort of chaps do you have playing with you?

PETER Well, the last couple of times I've been out I've been bowled by Ian Bishop, the West Indies fast bowler – one of his leg-spinners, but it came very quickly to me at any rate (that's my story) – and Derek Underwood's first ball of the season absolutely clean-bowled me.

BRIAN You didn't drive it through the covers.

PETER Well, I went to.

BRIAN Where do you bat normally?

PETER Anywhere I can, basically.

BRIAN And you like a bowl; do you give it a bit of a tweak?

PETER I do, yes. Colin Cowdrey called them tweakers. I think they're definite leg-spinners.

BRIAN And how much do you manage to watch? Do you support Worcestershire still?

PETER Yes, I follow Worcestershire very closely. But I get to know a lot of the county cricketers. I know Andy Stovold very well and some of the Gloucestershire boys, so I follow them, and I know the Warwickshire boys – Andy Lloyd's a great racing man.

BRIAN Of course, you live in Gloucestershire.

PETER Yes, I've got the three counties all round me, very close.

BRIAN Do you have any particular heroes?

PETER The Scudamore family are great Botham fans. We follow Botham avidly. The editor of the *Sporting Life*, Monty Court, rings up and says, 'Botham should be dropped from the England team,' and we argue the other way for hours on end.

BRIAN Your father, Michael Scudamore, rode a Grand National winner.

PETER He won the National and the Gold Cup. He was second in the championship one year to Fred Winter, so I had a bit to follow.

BRIAN But, remarkably, I can't find that you've ridden the winner of the Grand National or the Gold Cup.

PETER No, that's all to do yet.

(Peter never did win the National or the Gold Cup, but when he retired in 1993 he was the most successful jump jockey ever. He was champion jockey a record eight times, with a total of 1,678 winners out of 7,521 mounts.)

BRIAN Did you ever think that 221 winners in the season was going to be possible? I think Jonjo O'Neill's 149 was the previous highest.

PETER I was obviously lucky I was riding for two top stables – Charlie Brooks and Martin Pipe. Martin had two hundred winners himself, which is a record. The season set off very well. It's just like making your runs at cricket: you like to get your first winner, it's like getting your first run, and then hit a few sixes, get a few trebles and four-timers, and you can say to yourself, 'If you keep up this average, you're going to ride two hundred winners.' But you don't actually believe it. Then it starts to materialise in mid-winter and people start saying, 'You'll ride two hundred winners.' You tend to get over the bigger races and then, come April time, concentrate on the two hundred.

(In the 1997/98 season Tony McCoy beat Peter's record of 221 wins with an incredible tally of 253 winners.)

BRIAN You're making it sound very easy, but that's ten months of hard work – or more. How much time do you have off between the end of one season and the start of another?

PETER We get most of June and most of July off – about

ten weeks. But it's like being a cricketer or in the theatre, it's wonderful to get paid for doing something you enjoy.

BRIAN We rather feel that up here, but we don't like to tell our bosses that. You're taller than I expected. How tall are you?

PETER I'm about five foot eight, which is about the right size, as long as I don't eat too much.

BRIAN Well, what's your average weight?

PETER I ride at ten stone, which is the minimum weight that we have to ride at. So I have to get my body weight down to about nine stone nine pounds – that's with the saddle and all the equipment.

BRIAN Well, tell us the ghastly routine that you have to get to that. It absolutely terrifies me. Give us a daily diet.

PETER I wouldn't eat breakfast, because you're either travelling or riding out at that time of the day. If I've got a light weight, I wouldn't eat lunch, so I wouldn't eat till the evening. People say, 'Oh, you're silly not eating till the evening,' but it's my immediate weight loss that I'm worried about.

BRIAN How hungry are you getting by then? I should be absolutely ravenous.

PETER By the evening you're getting hungry, but it's the matter of doing things. I couldn't diet without doing something.

BRIAN Well, Scuders, it's tremendous discipline, undoubtedly. And when you do have your evening meal, is it a good tuck-in? Yorkshire pud and roast beef?

PETER No. You concentrate, obviously, on not too many chips or white bread. I tend to eat spinach. I find it a great help to me.

BRIAN Old Popeye found it a good idea.

PETER He did. I try to eat a lot of fish and lean meat.

BRIAN It doesn't sound very attractive to me, but now you've got time off, so are you getting a better diet?

PETER Well, you get used to it, and whatever I put on I've

got to get off, so I don't like to put too much weight on during the summer. It's not too bad. It's just one of the disciplines that we have and it's just there in the back of your mind all the time. I just don't over-indulge.

BRIAN Can you give us a typical day in the winter months when you're riding out and racing?

PETER One of the great things about it is that you don't have a typical day. It's like asking Goochie what his typical day is. What your typical day would like to be is getting up late and going to Cheltenham to ride three winners.

BRIAN It doesn't happen. You get up early to ride out somewhere.

PETER Two or three times a week I'm riding out at Charlie Brooks' or Martin Pipe's. I go and school, and it usually means setting off fairly early in the morning – six o'clock-ish. Then I school up until probably breakfast time, usually arriving in the yard at about half past seven. Then I go and ride them over some jumps – usually teaching the young horses.

BRIAN You're teaching them. That's part of the thing, is it?

PETER Yes. The mutual benefit is so that I can trust the horse, I know what he's going to do and he can get used to me a little bit.

BRIAN I asked you before we came on the air what happened in New York and whether you'd ridden the horse before and you said you hadn't. How important is it to know the horse before you ride it?

PETER I got to New York yesterday and I found out all that I could about the horse. It is difficult. The horse I was riding yesterday was held up for a late run. Well, you don't know what your opposition are going to do, so you're guessing a little bit.

BRIAN Do you let it snuffle you? Do you blow up its nose?

PETER Doing a Barbara Woodhouse? (*Barbara Woodhouse presented a popular television series in the 1980s called* Training Dogs The Woodhouse Way.)

BRIAN Have you ever tried that with a horse?

PETER I always go up and give him a pat. I think if they trust you to start with you're better off. Give them a pat, try and make friends and say, 'Please – let's you and I get round safely here.'

BRIAN Well, you don't always get round safely. You've had quite a lot of body damage. What sort of things have you got that haven't been hurt? You mustn't mention them all.

PETER I've been hurt a few times. But coming back last night on the plane they showed the Centenary Test in Australia when Randall made 174 and they showed Lillee bowling, and I think I would definitely rather do what I do than face Lillee or Holding or one of those bowlers.

BRIAN That was a marvellous Test, where Randall rather baited Lillee, didn't he?

PETER It was very funny. The bouncers were coming in and he was falling over backwards and pushing his hat on to the back of his head. You forget, actually, what a great batsman he was.

BRIAN I emulated something. You remember in 1981/82 you were leading the championship and you fell off and broke your arm and John Francome drew level with your number of winners a few weeks later and threw away his saddle and said, 'I'm not riding again'?

PETER Yes, that's right.

BRIAN I did that when I was doing *Down Your Way*. I gave it up at the same total as Franklin Engelmann. I copied what John Francome did, because old Jingle up there couldn't do anything about it and you weren't able to do anything in hospital.

PETER It was a marvellous sporting gesture by John and that's what sport's about, isn't it?

BRIAN Well, it is. In cricket on the field it's a bit rough sometimes and off the field it's friendly. What about jockeys? It's a very physical game, isn't it?

PETER It's the same. Early on in a race people try to help

each other, but you come to a certain point in the race where it's really business and you don't expect help.

BRIAN But out in the country, if you're going along in the lead with someone, do you have a chat with them?

PETER Yes. It's not quite cantering along in the English country sunshine, but you'll help one another, give a little bit of room and manoeuvre not to upset one another. But at a certain point of a race then there's no mercy, and if you get done or get hurt, well, that's what you accept before you go out.

BRIAN What's the best horse you've ever ridden?

PETER Probably Celtic Shot, because I won the Champion Hurdle on him and that's the best hurdling race and the best championship race I've won, but I've been lucky to ride some very good horses.

BRIAN The difference between hurdling and the big fences – which do you prefer?

PETER I don't mind as long as I ride a winner over each. It's a great thrill to ride a good steeplechaser. I've ridden Burrough Hill Lad and Corbière – as good jumpers as I've ever sat on.

BRIAN How old were you when you first learned to ride? Were you taught in an orthodox way? Did you have fairly long stirrups as a boy?

PETER Yes, I learned the orthodox way. I never really had riding lessons. My father was always the sort of tutor in the background, but never actually gave me a lesson. I just picked it up. As long as I can remember I've ridden and played cricket. One's gone one way and one's gone downhill.

BRIAN You've just said you wouldn't have liked to have played Lillee, but would you have preferred the life of a professional cricketer?

PETER If I could dream about doing anything else, I would be a fast bowler.

BRIAN You've got slight aggression, haven't you? You've got to have to be successful.

PETER It's always appealed to me, the Lillee type, Holding type.

BRIAN What has happened to you in the Grand National? How come you haven't won it?

PETER I always blame the horse. The trainer always blames me.

BRIAN Do you do the Fred Winter thing of staying on the inside?

PETER I've done it all ways. The closest I got was third on Corbière, and then I looked like winning one year on a horse called Strands of Gold and I fell at Bechers. I was going on the inside then and everyone said that it was because I was going on the inside that I fell.

BRIAN So next year you went on the outside.

PETER And got beaten. It's one of the goals. I would love to do it.

BRIAN How different is it riding in the Grand National from riding in an ordinary steeplechase at Haydock Park or somewhere like that?

PETER You go slightly slower and horses tend to look at the fences a little bit more, because they're big and they're different, and most times horses jump better for it. People say, 'Oh, the Grand National must be frightening,' but sometimes you can have a better ride round there than you can normally. The man who valets me in the weighing-room – when we're in the weighing-room we have valets who clean all our tack and make sure we go out on time and in the right colours – is John Buckingham. He won the National on Foinavon. He's quite a good cricketer and tells some of the best cricketing stories that I know.

BRIAN Tell us one, if you can remember.

PETER The Jockeys' XI were playing in Derbyshire against a local league side which included Alan Ward, who had broken down and was having a bit of a comeback. And the local side batted first and made 250 or so and then the jockeys went in to bat and Alan Ward bowled early and knocked about three down very cheaply. So they gave the jockeys a bit of a chance. It began to look as if they were going to get the runs. They were about six wickets down and David Nicholson and John Buckingham were nine and ten, sitting there, waiting to go in. Then Alan Ward comes back on, bowling very fast, and knocks the next one out. David Nicholson, who's always captain and a very, very keen cricketer, turns to John Buckingham and says, 'Come on, you're in.' John says, 'Hang on, I'm number ten. You're number nine.' 'I'm captain,' he says. 'You're number nine.' In he goes, and Alan Ward starts walking back and, as he turns, John walks away. 'Hold on,' he says, 'I don't go that far on my holidays.' I think he lost his sense of humour with that, Alan Ward. He came roaring in and bowled one at John, who jumped out of the way. It hit him on his bottom and bounced out for four runs. He was very pleased.

And the other great story he tells is when he was umpiring and David Nicholson was bowling. John had broken his leg. David Nicholson comes roaring in and hits this player on the pad and appeals to John, and John says, 'Not out.' John, because of his broken leg, is sitting on a shooting stick and David walked back past him, kicked the shooting stick from beneath him and said, 'Rubbish.'

37 George Shearing OBE

O NE OF THE BONUSES OF MY 48 years of cricket commentary has been the way it has brought me in close touch with the blind. From our letters we know that we have thousands of blind listeners who rely on the radio cricket commentator to paint the picture of a match for them. Many of them follow the placings and movements of fielders on a Braille pattern of a cricket field. Some, like our special friend Mike Howell up at Old Trafford, actually come to the Tests, and listen in to our commentaries. They like to feel that they are part of the crowd and enjoy absorbing the excitement and atmosphere of everything happening at the ground.

Most of you will know that on every Saturday of a Test match, in addition to 'A View from the Boundary', we make an appeal on behalf of the Primary Club. The qualification to join is simple: whatever sex or age you are, or in whatever class of cricket, if you have ever been out first ball (except for a run-out) you are qualified to join. All you have to do is to send £15 to The Primary Club, P.O. Box 12121, London NW1 9WS. He will then send you a tie and membership certificate. If you are a lady there are brooches instead of ties and, if you are feeling extra generous, you can send £25 instead of £15 and you will get two ties.

The money received goes mostly to the Dorton House School for the Blind at Sevenoaks. Originally it went towards their cricket only, but as more and more members joined, the money is now used on a broader basis, especially for sport. As an example, a perfectly equipped gymnasium has been built as the result of the generosity of 'first ballers'. *(In 1996, Dorton House opened the Brian Johnston Centre, the only purpose-built nursery for blind and partially sighted children in Great Britain.)* Some of the money is also distributed to the various blind cricket clubs round the country. I happen to be president of one of these clubs called Metro, a sports and social club for the visually handicapped. They play cricket and have given exhibitions of how to play blind cricket at the Oval and Lord's. They have also been the national champions.

You can imagine, therefore, how pleased I was to receive a letter from a lady in Stow-on-the-Wold telling me that the world-famous blind pianist George Shearing came and lived there every summer, which he spent listening to *Test Match Special*. We immediately contacted him in New York and invited him to the first of the two Lord's Tests in 1990. MCC gave special permission for his wife, Elly, to accompany him up to our box in the pavilion – a privilege only those ladies who work in the pavilion enjoy.

I had met him just once, 44 years before during a broadcast from a restaurant off Bond Street. I had forgotten what a wonderful sense of humour he possessed and, from the moment he entered the box, he had us all laughing. Two years later I went at his invitation to hear him in a concert at the Festival Hall. He gave a marvellous performance and I was fascinated to watch his fingers moving swiftly across the keyboard, hitting all the right notes, none of which, of course, he could see. He is one of the happiest men I have ever met.

Lord's, 23 June 1990

BRIAN JOHNSTON Are you a jazz pianist, classical pianist or just a pianist?
GEORGE SHEARING I'm a pianist who happens to play jazz. I have said this quite frequently. I'm also a pianist who

happens to be blind, as opposed to a blind pianist. I may get blind when my work is done, but not before.

BRIAN We heard of your enthusiasm for cricket from, I think, a lady down in Stow-on-the-Wold, where you come every summer. You live in America now.

GEORGE Yes, we've lived in New York for almost twelve years and we lived in California before then. What do you think about the retention of my accent? Is there much?

BRIAN There's a little tingle of American, but mostly it's the good old basic English. And it is pretty basic – it's Battersea, isn't it?

GEORGE It is. Until I was sixteen I was very much a Cockney, and I think the thing that got me out of being a Cockney was when I was doing some broadcasts for the BBC and the announcer came on and said: (very properly) 'For the next fifteen minutes you will be hearing the music of George Shearing.' I played the first medley and said, 'Good mornin', everybody. We just played the medley of commercial popular numbers includin' "Tears on my Pillow", "Let Me Whisper I Love You", "Magyar Melody" and "Jeepers Creepers"'. And the announcer came back after the show to say, 'For the last fifteen minutes you have been hearing the music of George Shearing.' Fortunately I had some good ears and I was able to dispense with the largest part of my Cockney accent. I was in a residential school between the ages of twelve and sixteen – and I'm going to be seventy-one this August. In this school we played cricket. Now, you can imagine blind people playing cricket. First of all we played in the gymnasium. We played with a rather large balloon-type ball with a bell in it and all the bowling was underhand, of course, and this ball would bounce along the gymnasium floor. The wicket was two large blocks of wood, perhaps fifteen or sixteen inches long, bolted together with a heavy nut and bolt on each end. Sandwiched in between was a piece of plywood so that we could hear this ball when it hit the wicket. You'd know very well you were out if that happened.

BRIAN No disputing with the umpire.

GEORGE Dickie Bird would have no problems. Now, if you hit the side wall it was one run; if you hit the end wall of the gymnasium it was two runs; if you hit the end wall without a bounce it was four; if you hit the ceiling at the other end it was six; and if you hit the overmantel it was three weeks' suspension.

BRIAN Much the same rules for indoor cricket today. But, born blind, how do you picture a cricket ball or a cricket bat?

GEORGE When I was a kid I used to go out in the street and play cricket with sighted people. And my little nephew would hold the bat with me and he would indicate when he was going to swing it. We actually did make many contacts with the bat on the ball – a regular cricket bat and ball.

BRIAN What was your father? Was he a musician?

GEORGE No, Daddy was a coalman. He would deliver coal.

BRIAN With a horse and cart?

GEORGE Yes. I often wondered if he shouldn't put on his cart COAL A LA CART, or CUL DE SACK.

BRIAN Not a bad gag. Now, did he start you on music? How did you get into that?

GEORGE I'm the youngest of a family of nine. There were no musicians in the family at all, so I imagine that in a previous life I was Mozart's guide dog. I don't really know how it started.

BRIAN Can we have a look at your fingers? I'm always interested in the fingers of guitarists and pianists. Yours are fairly delicate. They're straight. They haven't been broken by a cricket ball. So when did you first feel the touch of a piano and decide that was what you wanted to do?

GEORGE Before actually trying to make music as a pianist,

I would shy bottles out of the second-storey window and hear them hit the street, and they would have quite musical sounds. I had quite good taste, because I would use milk bottles for classical music and beer bottles for jazz.

BRIAN I wouldn't talk too loud, because the police have probably got all the records. They've been looking for the chap who did that.

GEORGE I first put my hands on a piano, I think, when I was three years of age. I was listening to the old crystal set. It was stuff like the Roy Fox Band. Then I would go over to the piano and pick out the tune that I had just heard.

BRIAN Is there such a thing as Braille music?

GEORGE Very much so. In fact, I've learned a number of concertos in Braille and played them with many symphony orchestras in the United States. I have given that up because I'm a little afraid of memory lapse. I had one thirty-bar memory lapse, I remember, when I was playing with the Buffalo Symphony, and my wife noticed that I was leaning towards the orchestra. Being, of course, a musician who plays jazz, on hearing the chords of the orchestra I could immediately improvise in the style of Mozart until my mind decided to behave once again and go back to the score.

BRIAN So you can do it from Braille, but basically you're an ear pianist.

GEORGE Yes, very much. You see, if you were to do anything short of sitting on the piano, I could probably hear what you were playing. If you played a ten-note chord, I could probably hear.

BRIAN If I sat on it, it would probably be a twenty-note chord.

GEORGE Well, I didn't say that.

BRIAN George, do you remember when we first met?

GEORGE Yes, it was in Fisher's restaurant in about 1946, when we were with the Frank Weir Band.

BRIAN We did a *Saturday Night Out* when I first joined the BBC. I joined in January and this must have been about April 1946. And I was amazed then as I talked to you and I asked how you were getting home. You said, 'Oh, I've come by tube; I shall be going home by tube.'

GEORGE And I used to do it without the aid of a cane or a dog or anything else. We've had a man in the United States who used to do that. His name was Doctor Spanner and you could prove that he did it because he had all kinds of bruises all over his body where he'd got into various accidents. They used to refer to him as the 'Scar-Spangled Spanner'.

BRIAN But did you tap your way along Bond Street to the tube station?

GEORGE When I started to use a cane I did. One time during World War Two I remember somebody said to me, 'Would you see me across the road?' And I took his arm and saw him across the road. It's the only case I've heard of the blind leading the blind.

BRIAN Do you still walk around on your own if you know the district?

GEORGE Not very much. One tends to lose one's nerve a little bit when you pass sixty-five, I think.

BRIAN Oh, get away! Describe for me what you think you're looking out at here.

GEORGE Well, we are probably at one end of the cricket field, and are we looking down the length of the pitch?

BRIAN Yes.

GEORGE I have light and dark, but that's all I have. Sitting in this box, of course, it's an interesting aspect of controlled acoustics and wonderful daylight and fresh air coming in through open windows. As a matter of fact, I wouldn't mind buying a lifetime ticket here.

BRIAN Well, you'd be most welcome. When we say that the

umpire's wearing a white coat or the batsman plays a stroke, can you figure what that means?

GEORGE No. Two things that a born-blind man would have difficulty with are colour and perspective. When you think about it, you can be satisfied that you're looking at a table on a flat piece of paper, although it obviously has cubic capacity. And I suppose my education and my instruction gives me the information that perhaps you draw two legs shorter than the other two and something about the way the light gets it. I have no conception at all of colours. In fact, once when I got a cab in the mid-town area of Chicago, I was to meet the Count Basie Band on the South Side. They were all staying at a hotel mostly frequented by black people at that time, and I said to the cab driver, 'Could you take me to the South Central Hotel?' And he said, 'Do you know that's a coloured hotel?' I said, 'Really? What colour is it?' And when we got there I gave him a tip about twice the size one would normally do, to make up for his ignorance, got into the bus with the Basie band and took off and hoped that he was duly embarrassed.

BRIAN Does green grass mean anything to you?

GEORGE Oh, yes. What a lovely smell when it's freshly mowed and when it's been watered. It means a great deal to me. But I suppose if you want colour description, I would say that blue would be something peaceful; red would be something perhaps angry and green – I don't know.

BRIAN Well, it's something very pleasant to look at, if you have a nice green cricket field.

You've lived in America a long time – have you always liked cricket?

GEORGE I've always been very fond of cricket, but, as you can imagine, being in America, one has had a great many years in absentia, which always makes me sad, and I can't wait to get over here and render my wife a cricket widow.

BRIAN How much do you come over now?

GEORGE Three months a year, and my aim is to make it six months a year.

BRIAN You go to the Cotswolds, and do you sit and listen to the Test matches?

GEORGE Oh, yes, of course I do. As a matter of fact, we may catch the three-thirty this afternoon so that by five I can be in my deck chair in the garden listening to the rest of the afternoon's play. And incidentally, I think you're a very logical and wonderful follow-on from Howard Marshall.

BRIAN Did you hear him?

GEORGE Oh, many times.

BRIAN Did you hear him describe Len Hutton's famous innings at the Oval – the 364?

GEORGE Yes. I used to listen to him on the first radios I had in the 1930s.

BRIAN He was lovely to listen to. He could take his place here and show us up. In other sports, commentators of that vintage would be old-fashioned, but he would be absolutely perfect. Are you a good impersonator? Can you pick up people's voices?

GEORGE I used to do Norman Long monologues on my show.

BRIAN 'A song, a smile and a piano' – Norman Long.

GEORGE (in character)

I've saved up all the year for this
And here it is, no kid.
This here Irish Sweepstake ticket
And it cost me half a quid.
Not much of it to look at,
Bit expensive like, of course,
But if I draws a winner,
Gor, lumme, if I even draws a horse,
The quids, just think about them,
Thousands of them, lovely notes,

Not greasy – nice and new.
I'll take me wife and family
Down to Margate by the sea.
Cockles, rock and winkles,
Shrimps and strawberries for tea.
A-sitting in your deckchairs,
With your conscience clear and sound,
A-smiling at the bloke and saying,
'Can you change a pound?'
Instead of hopping out of them
Each time the bloke comes round.
Thirty thousand quid!

BRIAN That's marvellous. Did you get all that from memory or did you used to write it down?
GEORGE No, I never wrote it down. I listened to it enough until I remembered it, and I've never forgotten it since 1935 or 1936 when I first heard it, any more than I've forgotten the geographical version of the Lord's prayer.
BRIAN Which is what?
GEORGE

How far is the White Hart from Hendon?
Harrow Road be thy name.
Thy Kingston come, Thy Wimbledon
In Erith as it is in Devon.
Give us this Bray our Maidenhead
And forgive us our Westminsters,
As we forgive those who Westminster against us.
And lead us not into Thames Ditton,
But deliver us from Yeovil (or from the Oval if you
    prefer)
For Thine is the Kingston and the Purley and the
    Crawley
For Iver and Iver,
Crouch End.

BRIAN Have you ever done stand-up comedy?

GEORGE I'm far too lazy to do stand-up comedy. I sit down at the piano because I have embraced the philosophy for lo! these many years. 'Why should any man work when he has the health and strength to lie in bed?'

BRIAN You sit down at the piano. You had a quintet for many years which was famous. Did you enjoy playing with people, or do you prefer to be solo?

GEORGE Well, I enjoyed it for twenty-nine years. I've now pared down to just bass and piano, because I can address myself to being a more complete pianist with a much greater degree of freedom every night to create what comes into mind – obviously restricted by the chords of the particular tune that I happen to be playing.

BRIAN Now, in addition to playing, you are a composer. How many hits have you composed?

GEORGE Oh, I can play you a medley of my hit in two minutes. It's called 'Lullaby of Birdland'. I've composed about ninety-nine other compositions, which have gone from relative obscurity to total oblivion.

BRIAN But what do people want? When they see you, they say, 'Come on, George, play . . .' – what?

GEORGE They still want 'September in the Rain', which was one of the quintet's most famous numbers. We did ninety thousand copies of that. It was a 78 when it started.

BRIAN Now, 'Lullaby of Birdland' – I always thought that was a lovely lullaby of a little wood with the birds twittering, but Birdland wasn't actually that, was it?

GEORGE Birdland actually was a club in New York dedicated to Charlie Parker, who was nicknamed 'The Bird', and I've played Birdland many times. It was a little basement kind of dive.

BRIAN We have thousands of blind listeners. Any word for them about cricket and what it's meant to you?

GEORGE I hope they enjoy cricket as much as I do, because

I really love it. Incidentally, the Royal National Institute for the Blind put out the cricket fixtures in Braille.

BRIAN If I was to ask you to sing or hum your favourite tune to finish, what would it be?

GEORGE It would be almost anything of Cole Porter or Jerome Kern. One thing that comes to mind is:

Whenever skies look grey to me
And trouble begins to brew;
Whenever the winter wind becomes too strong,
I concentrate on you – Graham Gooch.
I concentrate on you – Richard Hadlee.

38 David Shepherd OBE

AVID IS ONE OF THOSE lucky people who leads a happy life because he enjoys his job. Not only that, he is versatile and highly successful. He is best known as an artist of African wildlife, specialising in tigers and elephants, but in fact he started as an aviation artist, and is also a portrait painter of renown. Among his portraits is one of the Queen Mother. His hobbies are driving steam engines and making money for the World Wide Fund for Nature. By selling prints of his paintings he has made hundreds of thousands of pounds for the Fund. He was justly awarded the romantic-sounding 'Order of the Golden Ark' by the Netherlands for services to wildlife conservation. An elephant from one of his prints stares down on me as I write and for some reason it only has one tusk. So it is not surprising that David is often referred to as the 'elephant man'.

Elephants and cricket don't go naturally together, though I did once see some elephants playing cricket in Bertram Mills Circus. So I had never associated David with cricket until we sat together in a box at Lord's watching the Rothman's Village Cricket Championship final. It soon became obvious that, as with everything else with which he is associated, he was an enthusiast, and he leaped at the idea of being our guest in the commentary box the following season. He brought with him a magnificent chocolate cake baked by his lovely wife Avril. On the top was the figure of an elephant holding a cricket bat in its trunk.

I started by asking David how often he was confused with David Sheppard, the Bishop of Liverpool, and David Shepherd, the umpire.

The Oval, 8 August 1992

BRIAN JOHNSTON How many times have you been asked to come and preach a sermon or umpire in a Test match?

DAVID SHEPHERD Twice, actually. There's a lovely girl from the BBC who I have yet to meet who, although I live in Godalming, keeps asking me to go on Radio Four and talk about the Bible. And I was asked to umpire, too. Terribly confusing with all these Shepherds around.

BRIAN Of course Sheppard the Bishop is with two Ps and an ARD.

DAVID He was staying with us last night, actually. He helped to make your chocolate cake.

BRIAN You told me just now that this is the first day you've ever been to a Test match.

DAVID Does that surprise you?

BRIAN Well, it does. I know you love cricket. Is it just that you haven't been able to get to it, or what?

DAVID I do love cricket and I love Test matches. I listen all the time, especially while I'm painting. But I have to say that I never have watched serious cricket.

BRIAN How does it affect your brushwork when you hear, 'He's out!'?

DAVID It's like when I'm listening to a Mahler symphony; I just can't paint at all.

BRIAN You were at school at Stowe. Did you play cricket there?

DAVID No, I was too frightened. I was a snotty-nosed, rather terror-struck little boy who fled into the art school because I was too frightened to do anything dangerous. I think it's terrifying.

BRIAN It is a hard ball, yes. So what did you do instead of playing cricket?

DAVID I painted in the art school. I was asked to captain – non-playing captain – with Denis Compton about four years ago at the Aldershot Officers' Club when we were raising money jointly for my conservation foundation and the Parachute Regiment regimental museum. It was one of those drunken afternoons where by four o'clock we were all paralytic and, instead of being a non-playing captain, I was playing. I was absolutely scared stiff. I hit the ball and I was so excited I knocked the bails off, and that's apparently not done, is it?

BRIAN Well, if you hit your wicket you more or less have to go out in most classes of cricket. Do you follow cricket in the papers? Do you have a particular hero?

DAVID Obviously I follow that lovely man David Gower because he's a trustee of my foundation and we know him terribly well, with Gary Lineker, who's also a great supporter. So that engenders an interest in cricket, when David's playing.

BRIAN So let's get down to the painting. Were you taught at school?

DAVID No, I wasn't. I always wanted to be a game warden. I was a total disaster in my early life. They told me they didn't want me as a game warden and then I decided to try and be an artist and I failed that one as well, because I was chucked out of the Slade School of Fine Art as being untrainable. I was about to drive a bus for the Aldershot and District Bus Company, because that was where we lived, when I met the man who trained me. I owe him everything. Robin Goodwin – the most amazing man.

BRIAN So what did he do? Did he take you under his wing?

DAVID Yes, he did, and he gave me three years of intensive training. It was due to the RAF, actually. I never served in the RAF, but I started painting aeroplanes. Aeroplanes were my first love, because I'd lived in London in the Blitz and an eight-year-old spotty schoolboy like me in the Battle of Britain was terribly excited by World War Two and didn't realise that people were killing each other. And that engendered my love of aviation.

BRIAN Which was the first plane you painted?

DAVID Oh, Spitfires and Hurricanes, and then a bit later Super Constellations and all those lovely old aeroplanes. I hate everything modern. I love everything old with propellers. I love steam trains, of course. But the RAF noticed my work and sort of picked me up, and it was the RAF who commissioned my very first wildlife painting in 1960 and that changed my life.

BRIAN This wasn't the famous old elephant?

DAVID No, I did that one about a year afterwards – my famous Boots the Chemist one.

BRIAN They took it on and sold it. You went in for a pill or something else . . .

DAVID . . . and you came out with an elephant. Two hundred and fifty thousand copies were sold – incredible.

BRIAN And it's achieved something on television.

DAVID It was on the wall in *Crossroads*. Fame at last!

BRIAN And in *Only Fools and Horses* – double fame. Was that one particular elephant?

DAVID No, I invented it, like the one on your chocolate cake. But that first elephant did me a lot of good, because it put my name around a lot. I'm very proud of it and very grateful, but a lot's happened since then.

BRIAN When you paint wildlife, do you actually go out there and do it? Or do you go and watch them and take photographs of them?

DAVID I take photographs. A lot of people are surprised when you say that, but Degas worked from a photograph when he was doing his ballet pictures, so I'm told. All a camera is to me is a means to an end to record the shape of something, because it's quick and convenient, but I have to take the photograph, because I'm there in Zambia or India or wherever, photographing and looking at tigers. I'm seeing them and that's what matters. Ninety per cent is seeing the scene, and I take photographs of background bits of elephants' backsides and bits of tree.

BRIAN Are you brave and sit there while they're around?

DAVID The BBC filmed my life story years ago for television, and they said, 'Let's film you walking up to two bull elephants. We'll find them in Zambia, nice and friendly bull elephants – with your easel.'

BRIAN Are there such things as friendly bull elephants?

DAVID They're all friendly. They're lovely, unless you shoot at them with an AK 47. I got within sixty paces of them and I was painting away with fourteen tubes of oil paint and linseed oil and turps and there was a team of fourteen of us, the whole camera crew. It was absolutely dreadful.

BRIAN Did they decide to charge you?

DAVID The cow the next day did charge us. It was so funny.

BRIAN Are they more lethal than the males? It depends if they've got a little one, I suppose.

DAVID You can't fool around if they've got young. The tragedy is you can't fool around with any animal, because you don't know if it's been shot at with an AK 47 or had its foot blown off by a land mine. All these things have happened and I've seen the results of this ghastly business.

BRIAN To horrify us, an AK 47 is what?

DAVID It's one of those ghastly automatic rifles which you can buy for £30 in Zambia. Now that human beings have stopped shooting each other, you can buy them off the shelf. And the dear old elephant's on the way out, like the tiger is and the rhino, and that's why I'm such a passionate conservationist. Because I owe all my success to the animals and it's so easy to raise money through my paintings.

BRIAN How serious is it for elephants or tigers?

DAVID Well, I'm glad you asked me about the tiger, because only last week I got a press cutting from India about one poacher who's just slaughtered twenty-one tigers single-handed. And the tiger is now on the way out faster than we can possibly believe. It's frightening. They're probably down to about eighteen hundred.

BRIAN They do that for the skins?

DAVID Yes. There are sick people in the world. They poach mountain gorillas. My wife and I had this wonderful experience with mountain gorillas in Rwanda last year and since then one of the silverbacks has been killed by poachers. They kill the gorilla, cut the hand off; it then goes solidified and strange people buy that for an ashtray. This will shock your listeners, but it's true. Can you imagine stubbing your cigarette out in a gorilla's hand? There are some incredibly sick people in this world, there really are.

BRIAN You did a famous tiger painting – you've done a lot of tigers.

DAVID Yes, I'm very lucky. I raised a lot of money with a painting called *Tiger Fire* which went towards saving the tiger. We raised £127,000 in six weeks with the painting. I don't say that because I want thanks. It's so exciting, because I owe so much to the wildlife.

BRIAN I was wondering how you earn a living, because you give all your money to charity, very nearly, when you paint these things. Do you do the odd one for yourself?

DAVID Well, I'm sometimes in my studio, but this foundation that I've started has taken over our lives. The beauty of it is that it's tiny. There are only five of us and it's based in my own house.

BRIAN Who are you?

DAVID My daughter, Melanie, is the co-ordinator, and we have a couple of other girls and Claire – she runs the trading company. We've given away about a million and a half pounds already in the first couple of years. The point is it's small, so if people support us they know where the money goes.

BRIAN And do you do new paintings or do you sell the old ones?

DAVID I'm painting all the time, anyway, as hard as I can. But it's so exciting trying to raise money. I did a little painting last year in two hours and it went for £11,000 that evening. I feel humble when I say that, because there are people who'd take two years to raise £11,000 with a flag tin in the high street, getting frostbite at the end of the day and five quid in the tin. That's the hard way to raise money for charity, and I'm so lucky, because I'm painting anyway. I'm a compulsive painter; I'm miserable if I'm not painting.

BRIAN What about the rhino? There's the odd white rhino still.

DAVID In Zambia there are seventeen rhino left; when I first went there, there were two and a half thousand. Again, because of sick people wanting rhino horn. Man is the sickest, most dangerous animal on earth. Man is the only animal that destroys through greed and ignorance, and the poor old rhino is on the way out like the tiger is. We can't go on doing this. We've only got one world and we share it with all these other lovely animals. But I don't give up, because there are some wonderful children I'm meeting all the time in my foundation. It's the children that matter. They are so worried now about what we do. So's the good old British public.

BRIAN How can they help you with your foundation? What do you want from them?

DAVID They join us, the kids. Gary Lineker is our captain and you can't have a better man than that. He's a lovely man. And they get a newsletter, and we believe that if they support us they can get the incentive of feeling that they can help in retrieving the damage that my generation has done.

BRIAN Didn't you hire a helicopter to try and find the poachers?

DAVID I gave a helicopter. I raised money with a lot of other artists. We raised enough money in about twenty minutes to buy a Bell Jet Ranger helicopter.

BRIAN Did you catch any poachers?

DAVID Yes, it did.

BRIAN Is it illegal now for them to shoot tigers and elephants in these countries?

DAVID It's all strictly illegal, but while there's a financial motive to go and kill a tiger and escape capture they'll go on doing it. There are people who will do anything to make money.

BRIAN In all of this the king of the animals seems to have got away free. There are plenty of lions aren't there?

DAVID They breed like rabbits.

BRIAN Do tigers not breed like rabbits?

DAVID No, they're a different animal altogether. Lions are not endangered in any way, and I don't think he's the king of the beasts, anyway. He's a scraggy old hearthrug compared to an elephant. When you see them lolling with their legs in the air – OK, he's an impressive animal when he's angry, but you cannot possibly improve on an elephant. In my new book there's a lovely photograph on the cover of me four feet away from an enormous bull elephant. He's drinking from a waterhole. I went right up to him and my wife took the photograph. They're not dangerous.

BRIAN Have you got an affinity with elephants? Are you good with them? I mean, if I went up to him he mightn't like me.

DAVID They'd love you, Brian.

BRIAN Don't look at my nose like that.

DAVID As long as they haven't been shot at by poachers, they'll leave you alone. Actually, in my case, I think they do know me. They say, 'Oh, God, Shepherd's coming again. Another picture in Boots the Chemist.'

BRIAN What's all the mystery of an elephant when it dies? They go to secret places.

DAVID It's all a lot of nonsense. I get worked up about this. There are a lot of scientists who are trying to find out a lot of answers to these mystical things about elephants. An elephant's been known to carry a tusk out of a dead elephant for twenty-seven miles before it dropped it. Why pick up a tusk? Why didn't it pick up a leg bone or a rib? They've got brains bigger than ours, and I hope we'll never find out, because it's lovely to leave them alone and just wonder. Same with the whale. That's got a bigger brain than we have. Wonderful things. They migrate from Alaska right down to California and back again and they don't use computers and navigational instruments.

BRIAN We've been talking about animals, but what about the railways? When did you get attracted to engines?

DAVID I think every small boy wanted to drive a train. But why Avril my wife's still married to me after thirty-two years, I don't know, because I bought two enormous 140-ton steam engines off British Rail and I've got a railway in Somerset and I promised faithfully last year I would not collect any more big toys. Well, about a year ago we were in Johannesburg when South African Railways presented me with 220 tons of steam engine as a gift. Why? Because I asked them if they could give me one and they did, and I'm bringing it home next year.

BRIAN And where will it go?

DAVID To the Somerset Railway.

BRIAN How is that going?

DAVID It's going very well, considering the recession. The lovely thing about it is it's a registered charity, and when I go down there we talk about elephants. All the lovely public comes to ride on steam trains and they talk to me about elephants. The two are inseparable.

BRIAN And everybody's an amateur on it, aren't they?

DAVID Never use the word 'amateur', because we are more professional than professionals. They are volunteers, yes.

BRIAN You mustn't deride the word 'amateur', because in cricket it was a great word.

DAVID I don't deride it, but in the railway context, in the worst sense an amateur can kill people on a steam engine, because they're heavy things. But we can't do anything stupid because we're run by all the regulations that BR are run by. You're hauling fare-paying passengers, so you've got to run it as a serious business.

BRIAN What sort of mileage is yours? Where do you go?

DAVID We go from the bottom of the hill to the top of the hill – two and a half miles.

BRIAN I did a *Down Your Way* from there and you can have a meal on it. It must be a very quick meal.

DAVID Well, we can stop. We've saved a bit of Britain's heritage. I'm sounding pompous now, but I think our heritage is important and in this age we're too damn keen to sweep aside everything in the name of progress. We live in a sixteenth-century farmhouse and that lovely old farmhouse will stand up long after all these tower blocks round the Oval have fallen down in a cloud of dust.

BRIAN Are you inspired, like Jack Russell, looking round the ground to do a painting of the Oval?

DAVID He drew my portrait, dear old Jack. He's a jolly good artist, actually. But no, I couldn't paint this, to be honest. It's just not my scene.

BRIAN You've actually done some portraits, haven't you?

DAVID I've done portraits, but nobody knows about them. The most exciting thing I've ever painted was a twenty-foot-long painting of Christ for an Army church. And nobody knows I do that sort of thing, you see.

BRIAN Who else have you done?

DAVID The Queen Mum. I had a fantastic time painting the Queen Mother.

BRIAN Does she come to you or do you go to her?

DAVID I'm not that important. I went to Clarence House and had six one-hour sessions with her altogether. It was an absolute riot, because we talked about Africa all the time and never did any work.

BRIAN She would have talked about cricket if you'd asked her, because she's mad on cricket.

DAVID I know, but we talked about HMS *Ark Royal* and

other things I've painted, like Lancaster bombers. Then I painted President Kaunda of Zambia.

BRIAN He helped you quite a bit, didn't he?

DAVID He did, tremendously, and I love Zambia. He's no longer president but he's a dear friend of mine. A great conservationist.

BRIAN Has his influence helped?

DAVID I like to think so. There are a lot of people in England who think that immediately a black country becomes independent they eat all their animals. In Zambia's case there was one national park when it was a British colony. There are now nineteen. They really are concerned and they're trying jolly hard with no resources, because they're very poor, these little countries. I'm very touched, particularly by the children. The children in these black countries are absolutely marvellous. They're fully aware of what we're doing and they're damn well going to do something about it.

BRIAN What has been your impression of coming here to the Oval?

DAVID First of all the lovely atmosphere, because I love atmosphere, whether it's in Africa to see elephants or here at the Oval. You can feel it. One of the stewards said, 'You're David Shepherd, aren't you? Have you got a cake for Johnners?' I said, 'Of course I've got a cake.' I daren't come near you without a cake.

BRIAN It is a friendly game and I wish you'd come more often to it.

DAVID I could catch the bug, but conservation's taking up so much of my time.

39 Graham Taylor

I HAVE BEEN LUCKY FOR the most part of my life in having a job which I have enjoyed. I expect there are others, too, which I would also have liked to do, such as acting. But there are two jobs which I would definitely not want to do: cricket selector and manager of the England football team. I am all for a quiet life without pressures and undue criticism. Both of these jobs get plenty of both, the football manager having the worst of it. The cricket selector does at least have his fellow selectors to share the criticism and abuse (at least he should have, but nowadays the selection of the England team does seem to be largely in the hands of the captain). In football, however, the England manager is the supremo with sole responsibility for selection of the side.

It must be a tremendous burden, but you would not have guessed it had you seen Graham Taylor in our box at Edgbaston *(Graham Taylor was the England football manager from July 1990 to November 1993)*. It was admittedly his brief 'off season', but he appeared completely relaxed, and we enjoyed a lot of laughs.

Edgbaston, 27 July 1991

GRAHAM TAYLOR Because I was in a minor county, my cricketing heroes were national ones – May and Barrington. When I heard that Ken Barrington had passed away, it's one of the moments that will always remain with me. The fact that he'd died was very upsetting to a relatively young man, as I was at that time. I'd never met the man, but he was a throwback to my boyhood, when these people meant a lot to me.

BRIAN JOHNSTON He was a very intense character who took things tremendously to heart. I took him back to London after a Test here when he'd played a very slow innings. I think he was about an hour between 89 and 100, and then, when he got to 100, he hit five fours running or something like that and he got tremendously criticised for that. And I took him back and he was so depressed then, it meant so much to him, and he was actually dropped for one Test match. He came back and made a couple more hundreds. And on the West Indies tour when he died, he'd taken all the problems very badly. He fought for England. It was like seeing the Union Jack walk out when Barrington went out to bat. He'd be the sort of character you'd love to have in any football team.

GRAHAM Well, I think in anything, when you're up against it, you want the fighters. You've got to have the fighters; you've got to have the people who show some stickability.

BRIAN Are you a batsman or a bowler?

GRAHAM I'm not really a bowler. I like the batting. My father has always said to me that one of the worst things he ever did was to send me for coaching. He said that before, when I saw the ball, I used to try to hit it, and when I came back from coaching I used to try to play everything technically correctly. I think he would have very much liked me to develop not only my footballing, which, fortunately, I got a career in, but my cricketing ability as well. I always remember as a young lad anything down my leg side as a left-hander, I loved. But then, after coaching, I seemed to have to play every ball 'correctly'.

BRIAN I think your coaches weren't right. You get someone like Denis Compton, who was a natural. He went to a chap called Archie Fowler at Lord's in the 1930s. He said, 'Right, I won't tell you anything.' But he did just teach him the basic forward defensive stroke, because Denis, in the end, was one of the best defensive batsmen if necessary. But they let him do all the unorthodox strokes.

GRAHAM I'm sure that's right. I think that no coaching in many respects is better than bad coaching. I've always believed that. One thing I remember about my coaching is this business that you must play yourself in. Prior to that, if the first ball had been bowled to me and it was there for hitting, I always used to think that you should hit that one. And I tended, when I played cricket, to be quite boring. But the worst thing about trying to play yourself in is if you get out. Because then you've lost it anyway.

BRIAN Basically, a bad ball is a bad ball, whenever it comes.

GRAHAM Not that I would ever have made any real level as a cricketer, but I enjoyed it.

BRIAN I know you were manager at Lincoln, Watford and Aston Villa. How much coaching have you done yourself?

GRAHAM I've done a reasonable amount of coaching, but I'm a great believer in playing to people's strengths. In other words, I don't believe in taking people out and coaching on a real weakness that they have. I believe in coaching people to their strengths, because I think that something that a person is good at he's interested in getting better at, and I think it gives him a tremendous amount of confidence and consequently any weaknesses – and we all have weaknesses – improve through having a greater confidence. The strengths come through and they override the weaknesses. So I like to think both collectively and individually that my coaching's based on getting people to believe in themselves.

BRIAN You've got to be a tremendous psychologist, though, haven't you? You've got to treat every single person differently, because everyone is different.

GRAHAM Well, everyone is different. I don't like it when people say, 'Treat everybody the same.' I'll treat you the same if you are the same, but you're not, so you treat everybody differently.

BRIAN How do you get to know people? Do you wait till an individual comes to join the team?

GRAHAM Well, I was twenty years a manager, because I had to finish the game at a relatively young age.

BRIAN You had hip trouble.

GRAHAM I had a hip injury, yes, so I finished when I was twenty-eight and I became manager of Lincoln, basically because there was a boardroom difference, as there tends to be in football, and somebody supported me. And my first nine games as a manager we drew seven and lost two, and I remember people at Sincil Bank at Lincoln shouting, 'Taylor out! Taylor out!' Now, when you're twenty-eight years of age and you're married and you've two girls under four and you've got a mortgage, that's pressure. Pressure's not the top of the First Division, and pressure, in many respects, is not being the manager of the England side. Pressure, really, is if you get out of a job and you don't know where your next job is going to come from.

BRIAN I tell you what I would have done, if I'd been a manager. Before I signed a contract I'd have said, 'I cannot be sacked in the middle of a season. I'm prepared to be sacked at the end of a season.'

GRAHAM It's give and take. I think if you can't be sacked, then neither should you walk out.

BRIAN No, you abide by your contract.

GRAHAM Contracts now seem to be just a word, and when it suits either party they're very easily terminated, and that doesn't help the status or standing of any of the professional games.

BRIAN How are you influenced by the press? You get a bad press; poor Micky Stewart gets a bad press. When things go right, it's OK. Do you read it a lot? Do you try to meet the people and talk to them about it?

GRAHAM What I try to do is to be very open in terms of answering questions. You know that you're going to be abused. The disappointing aspect is that so many things that you say are abused and misused to create headlines. But I don't think I'm going to alter that. So one of the things that I've decided – and I don't mean to be offensive to anyone – is that basically I read as little as I can. Far more people know about the things that have been written about me than I do. And it's the best way to go.

BRIAN Now, another thing. We are slightly critical nowadays about the training methods used by cricket. We think they overdo it, and if you play enough cricket you don't need to do all these extraordinary exercises. We look back at the past when they didn't have all these pulled hamstrings and Achilles tendons, and now they tend to and yet they run round the ground for forty minutes. What is your view of the training?

GRAHAM Well, I don't know too much about the cricket training. But what I do know is, you have to be fit to play it. You have to be fit in this day and age to play any sport at the top level. There are specific fitnesses. As a professional footballer, before I became a manager, I was fit to play football and I'm perfectly certain I wouldn't have been fit to play cricket. There's a complete difference between getting fit to play football and being fit sometimes to stand and field for a day and a half and also bat with concentration. So I think there are specific ways of being fit.

BRIAN No doubt football these days is so much faster because they're so much fitter. I used to go and watch Alex James, and he had all the time in the world to sell four dummies and pass the ball three times. He wouldn't get away with it today.

GRAHAM I think cricket must be the same, Brian. I see the pace these fellows are bowling at! So many people talk about the England football side, and the interesting thing

367

is that I consider myself an expert in that field. I don't consider myself an expert in either cricket or athletics, which are my next loves. So I can spectate at cricket and I can spectate at athletics far better than I can at football. I have been listening to Freddie Trueman when he sits here. There's a top-class professional cricketer and he's watching cricket with a very critical eye. Now, I watch football like that. When I'm watching cricket, I'm spectating.

BRIAN There is this difference with cricket. The captain on the field is in charge, and it's very difficult to see what your relationship is in soccer with the captain, as the manager. You're sitting there on the bench. How much does the captain have to say out on the field?

GRAHAM Well, one of the biggest things that you find is that there tend to be fewer and fewer leaders. We all tend to want to follow a little bit. I think it's the way of society more than anything else, but we don't have so many characters in terms of leadership. But the role of captain on a cricket side has always seemed to me almost like a player-manager. He's in charge and a lot more decisions have got to be made in a cricket match by the captain than the decisions made in ninety minutes by the captain in football. Interestingly, one of the last few people to combine the two sports was Phil Neale, and I signed Phil Neale as a footballer at Lincoln City. He's done so well. As a young boy I couldn't see captaincy material basically in Phil – certainly not in football. But how well he's done in cricket.

(Phil Neale was captain of Worcestershire for nine years and was appointed cricket manager of Northamptonshire for 1993.)

40 Leslie Thomas

LESLIE IS AS HILARIOUS IN real life as are his characters in his many novels. I suppose he does sometimes stop talking, but I have never experienced it! He is a very funny man with a tremendous knowledge of so many things: his time in the Army, his travels round the world, his spell as a writer on the *Evening News*, his collection of antiques and, of course, after a late start, his love of cricket.

He worships cricketers and enjoys nothing better than playing cricket alongside old England players for the Lord's Taverners. He may not be a great cricketer, but he takes it very seriously and tries like mad. In September 1992 I was umpiring in a Taverners' charity match on a lovely little school ground in the Close at Salisbury, where Leslie now lives. He caught a sizzling catch at deep mid-wicket, made it look very easy and tossed the ball up in the air like a true professional. I'm glad to say, though perhaps he was disappointed, that the Taverners did not rush up and kiss him!

He is a permanently busy man. When he joined us at the Oval in 1981 he had come up especially from Somerset and was off the next day to play cricket at Arundel. He had just returned from travels abroad, was preparing to launch his fiftieth novel, *The Magic Army*, in October and had already begun yet another book, *A World of Islands*. I started by asking him how much he enjoyed his travelling all round the world.

The Oval, 29 August 1981

LESLIE THOMAS The trouble is, going to these places abroad you miss the cricket and I have to try and find you on the overseas service and all I get is the Top Forty – whatever that may be.

BRIAN JOHNSTON Were all those novels on the Army based on your actual experiences when you were in the Army?

LESLIE Yes. My entry in *Who's Who* says 'rose to the rank of lance corporal', which is all I ever did.

BRIAN Were you stationed abroad?

LESLIE Yes, in Singapore, where we played cricket. I remember getting off a plane in Singapore once and asking the taxi driver to take me to the Padang, where they played cricket, and I sat under the same tree where I sat as a soldier when I was eighteen years old and watched cricket – and I swear it was the same two batsmen still in.

BRIAN When did cricket start in your life, then?

LESLIE Well, I never told anyone this, Brian, but very late. I was telling my son last night that at the age of twelve I didn't know how many men were in a cricket team.

BRIAN Oooh – sacrilege!

LESLIE I know, it's a terrible thing to say, but I was brought up in wartime in Newport, Mon., which was not a centre of cricket, despite what Wilfred Wooller told me recently, that they did play matches there. I honestly didn't know anything about the game until I went to live in Devon, and it was March and I was batting in the nets and another batsman got behind me because I was missing so many of the balls.

BRIAN Where was this in Devon?

LESLIE In Kingsbridge.

BRIAN Very nice – on the river down there.

LESLIE Yes, in fact my novel, *The Magic Army*, is set at that period during the war in Devon. It's about the huge invasion army waiting to invade Europe.

BRIAN And did you develop into a batsman in the end?

LESLIE No, I never did. Actually, this is a fraud. I've played cricket all my life and frankly I've never been much good, except I've always been very enthusiastic. I love the game. I love playing it, watching it, reading about it – everything about it. When I was in my teens, if I made a duck on a Sunday I couldn't sleep the whole week and it made me miserable, but now, you see, I go out for the fun and strangely enough I do get some runs. I've had a couple of fifties, and I made 10 not out for Prince Charles' XI.

BRIAN Not on a horse.

LESLIE Well, almost. It was on the polo ground at Windsor – the first time cricket had ever been played there. I was playing golf yesterday with a great friend called Ben, and he's very tough and he thinks cricket's a poof's game and he told me so. So I said I'd send Lillee round to see him, and he said, 'There, I told you – Lily.'

BRIAN Are you any good at golf?

LESLIE So-so. I played with Peter Alliss on television a couple of years ago and I did reasonably well. I think that some days I play like Arnold Palmer and some days like Lilli Palmer.

BRIAN You did that *A Round With Alliss.* How many holes did you get through?

LESLIE Oh, about five. I had a two on one hole; it was terrific. But I think he's a tremendous man.

BRIAN What about cricket, though. Have you supported Glamorgan?

LESLIE Do you know, I've just been asked to write a chapter for a book that's coming out next year in which each chapter is about a different county, and I'm writing about Glamorgan – about the daffodil summer, the summer they won the championship. I went to see Wilfred Wooller the other day, had lunch with him, and he was terrific. I'd never met him before. I love cricketers, you know. Sir Leonard Hutton is a great friend of mine, because I used to write a column for him when I was on a newspaper. I saw him at Lord's the other day and I'm always so pleased to see him, and I think it's mutual; we really like each other.

BRIAN You wrote his cricket column for him?

LESLIE Years ago, yes. I was on the *Evening News* and it was headed SIR LEONARD HUTTON SAYS, and underneath, in very small type, 'as told to Leslie Thomas'. But I didn't mind, it was a great privilege.

BRIAN Did you learn a lot from him?

LESLIE Tremendous, yes. Terrific sense of humour. He's a singular man. Some people think he's a very hard man, but he isn't. He's one of the most interesting men I've ever met. We were at Worcester, and on the first day I bought lunch. On the second day he bought lunch – he was getting about fifty thousand quid more than me – and on the third day he brought sandwiches. I'd got a little packet of crisps, and he said, 'Those crisps look OK.' So I said, 'Well, help yourself.' And he delved into the crisps, ate a handful and then said, 'They're better with salt.' So I said, 'There's some salt there somewhere.' He had some more, and by the time he'd finished there were three crisps in the bottom of the packet. So I said, 'Well, you might as well eat them all now.' And he said, 'No, lad, you eat them. They're your crisps.'

(Sir Leonard Hutton died in September 1990 at the age of 74.)

BRIAN You say you didn't know about cricket till you were twelve. Who did you watch? Who were your heroes?

LESLIE Oh, R. S. Ellis of Australia in the Australian Services team in 1945. Spin bowler. I modelled my bowling on R. S. Ellis. A blank look's come on your face. R. S. Ellis – same team as Cristofani and Miller. The first cricketer I ever saw, in fact, was Keith Miller – at the Leyland Ground at Kingston-on-Thames. He was reading a sporting paper and I asked for his autograph, and he said, 'Have you got anything good for the four-thirty?'

BRIAN That's typical Miller.

LESLIE You know, to sit up here today is absolutely wonderful for me. It's so cosy, isn't it? And you get drinks and eats.

BRIAN But you kept so quiet there.

LESLIE Well, I did for once in my life, because I was fascinated. You can actually see the ball moving and I know that all this stuff you do on the radio is absolutely true. I live in Somerset now, where they're all cricket barmy – men, women and children – and when Botham was making his runs at Headingley we had a house full of workmen and one got so excited he fell down the ladder.

(This conversation took place six weeks after the famous Headingley Test of 1981, when Ian Botham's innings of 149 not out enabled England to beat Australia by 18 runs.)

BRIAN Why have you gone to Somerset?

LESLIE My son's going to Millfield. That's the sum total of it. And we want him to go as a day boy. I want him to be able to spell. I think he'll have a wonderful time there.

BRIAN Can you spell?

LESLIE I'm not bad. I always think spelling is something you can get from a book. People say to me, 'Who actually writes your books? Do they put the full stops in?' Because they think I couldn't possibly do it.

BRIAN Can you listen to Test match commentary going on as you write, or do you have to shut yourself away?

LESLIE I sneak off every now and then and turn the television or the radio on. Something happened to me last year which I just couldn't believe. I went to the Centenary Test Match Dinner and I was sitting next to Bobby Simpson, and I went out for something or other and when I came back he said, 'There's a young man over there would like your autograph.' So I said, 'Why didn't he ask?' He said, 'Oh, he's very shy.' So I signed the autograph and asked, 'Who is it for?' He said, 'That chap over there, Kim Hughes.' I thought, my God, I should ask for his autograph.

(At this time Kim Hughes was the Australian captain.)

BRIAN Have you ever thought of writing a book with cricket as a background to it?

LESLIE No. Cricket does tend to creep into a lot of my books. *The Magic Army*, which I've just finished – it's a very long novel, about a quarter of a million words – as the armies go off to invade Europe, there's a village cricket match taking place. I checked the local papers down there and on 6 June there was a cricket match. There's the story of a titled lady who was absolutely shocked as she was coming back from Dover at the time of Dunkirk with troops and wounded and everything on her train and as they went past Wimbledon there were fields full of cricketers in white.

BRIAN It all goes back to Sir Francis Drake. 'The Armada can wait; my bowels can't.' Isn't that what he said?

LESLIE Is that what he said?

BRIAN They said he was playing bowls, but he had to rush off when he saw the Armada coming. But your book – a quarter of a million words!

LESLIE It took three years.

BRIAN Do you do a wodge and then sort of correct?

LESLIE I do about a thousand words a day. In fact, the BBC have done a television documentary about the writing of this book. It's in three parts. They followed me around and they filmed the writing and the research and all that sort of thing.

BRIAN Do you keep yourself to a thousand words a day or do you do as many as you feel you can that day?

LESLIE The worst mornings I sit there, just as you have to come here when there's no play and it's raining, and I put my hands on that typewriter and I write a thousand words whatever. That's being professional, I think.

BRIAN Yes, it is, but supposing you don't get that inspiration?

LESLIE Oddly enough, the morning you don't get the inspiration, if you just press on and press on, it's frequently the best morning that you have.

BRIAN You get these marvellous comic scenes. If they're not taken from life, how do you conjure them up?

LESLIE Well, a lot of them are taken from life, because life's very funny, I think. If you look at it from a certain angle and see the amusing things – even in the most dreadful tragedy. I saw the most grotesque thing in Spain. We were having dinner in an open-air restaurant by a road that was just like a killer track. There were accidents all the time along this stretch of road and there was the most frightful crash just below us. There was a man in the restaurant playing one of these little organs, and he switched to the *Dead March*. There were people lying about everywhere, but that's the sort of grotesque humour that does happen in life.

BRIAN What about your time in Fleet Street?

LESLIE I worked on the *Evening News* when it sold a million and a half copies a night – no thanks to me – but it was a great newspaper then and I had a wonderful life. I went to about eighty countries. I travelled with the Queen and the Duke of Edinburgh, and I went all over the world. In fact, when I wrote my first novel, *The Virgin Soldiers*, and it became a best-seller, it was a double-edged thing because it meant I had to leave Fleet Street, and in fact I went back and got an office in Fleet Street, because it was home. Now I only miss Fleet Street at lunchtime.

BRIAN One of the things they say you're interested in is antiques. Is that so?

LESLIE Yes. My wife had an antique business for some years and we have a sort of collection of bits and pieces. We had a stall in Portobello Road at one time. It was great fun. People used to come down and see me standing there in the morning and think, Oh he's down on his luck, poor fellow. I used to go and buy bits of china and if we made ten pounds at the end of the day or twenty pounds – this is some years ago – we were so happy. More than all the royalties. I suppose it's ready money.

BRIAN Now what about the winter? You wouldn't be tempted to follow a team round on tour?

LESLIE No, I've seen relatively little cricket abroad, strangely enough. I saw a Test match once in Trinidad. I came straight off the boat, went to the day's play in the Test match and got straight on the boat again and went away. It was when Cowdrey made a big score.

BRIAN Well, you're going to watch the rest of the day with us, I hope.

LESLIE You bet. This is where I'd like to come every time I come to the Oval.

Index